THE ROUGH GUIDE TO
WALKS IN AND AROUND LONDON

This fourth edition written and researched by
Helena Smith

ROUGH
GUIDES

Contents

A NOTE TO READERS

At Rough Guides, we always strive to bring you the most up-to-date information. This book was produced during a period of continuing uncertainty caused by the Covid-19 pandemic, so please note that content is more subject to change than usual. We recommend checking the latest restrictions and official guidance.

Introduction to
Walks in and around London

London's green heart, village-like districts and salty maritime past provide an inspiring backdrop for a leisurely stroll. Or take a short train ride from the city to explore the charms of the bucolic southeast, with its rolling chalk hills, medieval country churches, prehistoric remains and ancient timbered inns. In all seasons, and whatever the weather, the footpaths of the capital and the tracks and hedgerow-lined lanes of the southeast of England reward those in search of the great outdoors.

London itself is unique in the way it mixes up the urban and the pastoral. This is the largest city in Western Europe, with a population of 9.3 million, but sizeable and often idyllic stretches of green space have been conserved, some at the very centre of the capital. These green spaces were widely used in the Covid-19 lockdowns.

In fact, over a third of London is made up of greenery, not only in the famous parks and gardens, but also in less obvious places – canal paths, disused railway tracks and reclaimed industrial land – as well as along the banks of the Thames, winding sinuously through the city. These hidden footpaths give a fantastic insight into the social, architectural and industrial history which is woven into this vibrant, modern city. Despite the sprawl of suburbs that girdles the metropolis, many parts of **southeast England** remain miraculously unspoilt. Fast train services make it very easy to reach open countryside from just about anywhere in London – indeed, it's surprising just how far from the capital you can get in a single day and still have time for a rewarding walk and a great pub lunch.

To the south and west of the capital there's sweeping **downland**: the lush North Downs and the barer and more open North Wessex and South downs. You'll find

BLENHEIM PALACE

spectacular stretches of **coast** – from towering sandstone cliffs at Hastings to wavy chalk formations further west – as well as areas of precious ancient **woodland**, at their most extensive in the New Forest. The **Thames** cuts a green swathe west of the capital, linking a chain of attractive towns and villages, while to the north are the pristine wooded **hills** of the Chilterns and the flatlands of the **Fens** around Ely. The striking variety of landscapes around the city is part of the attraction – from the prettily manicured landscapes of the Kent Weald to the hauntingly bleak chalk uplands of the Wessex Downs.

CATCHING THE TRAIN

For information on train times, journey durations and costs, call 08457 484950 or see http://nationalrail.co.uk. For travel in the capital, go to http://tfl.gov.uk.

As with London itself, the southeast has always been a densely inhabited area, and the impact of human activity on the land is no less profound, visible in Iron Age forts, medieval field terraces and grand country-house estates. All the landscapes described in this Guide, whether the bogs of the New Forest or the windswept crests of the South Downs, bear the marks of cultivation: a testament to the people who cleared, drained, shaped and even – in the case of the prehistoric chalk figures that dot the region – drew upon the land for millennia. However, in a time of accelerating climate change, the wisdom of human intervention in the landscape is being challenged. Rewilding projects such as the visionary scheme at Knepp in Sussex are demonstrating

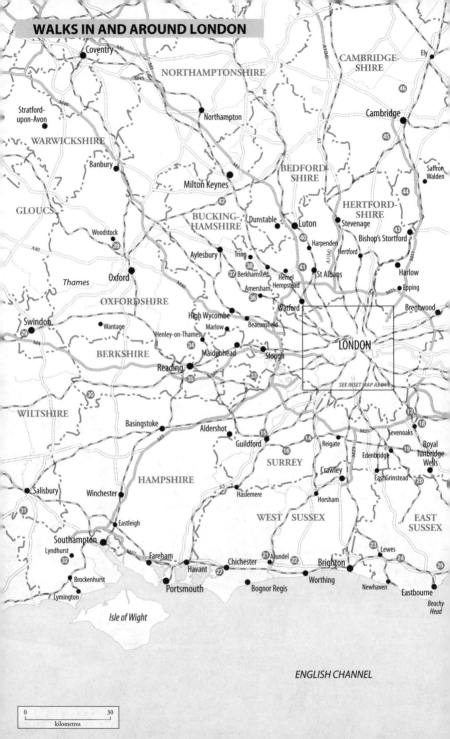

WALKS IN AND AROUND LONDON

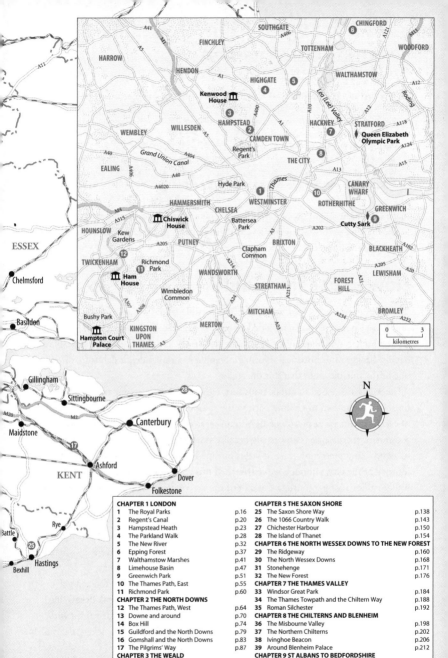

SOUTHGATE
CHINGFORD **6**
FINCHLEY
TOTTENHAM
WOODFORD
HARROW
HENDON
WALTHAMSTOW
HIGHGATE
4
HIGHGATE **5**
Kenwood House
WILLESDEN
HAMPSTEAD **2** **3**
CAMDEN TOWN
HACKNEY
STRATFORD
7
Queen Elizabeth Olympic Park
WEMBLEY
Regent's Park
8
EALING
Grand Union Canal
THE CITY
Hyde Park
CANARY WHARF
1 WESTMINSTER
10
HAMMERSMITH
CHELSEA
ROTHERHITHE
GREENWICH
Chiswick House
Battersea Park
Cutty Sark **9**
HOUNSLOW
Kew Gardens
PUTNEY
Clapham Common
BRIXTON
BLACKHEATH
TWICKENHAM
Richmond Park
WANDSWORTH
LEWISHAM
12
Ham House **11**
STREATHAM
FOREST HILL
Wimbledon Common
MITCHAM
BROMLEY
Bushy Park
KINGSTON UPON THAMES
MERTON
Hampton Court Palace

ESSEX
Chelmsford
Basildon

0   3
kilometres

Gillingham
Sittingbourne
28
Canterbury
Maidstone
Ashford
Dover
KENT
17
Folkestone
Rye
Battle
25
Bexhill
Hastings

N

TIME FOR TEA: FIVE TOP TEAROOMS

Fir Tree House Tearooms Home-made cakes and a lovely Kent garden – what more could you ask for? See page 99

The Orchard Tea Garden Make like Rupert Brooke and enjoy tea and scones on a deckchair in this paradisal Cambridgeshire orchard. See page 249

Peacocks Tearoom Ely boasts this deliciously inviting and homely tearoom, voted the best in the country by the Tea Guild. See page 254

Petersham Nurseries Café An elegant option for a secluded afternoon cuppa, with abundant greenery, exotic antiques scattered about and excellent food. See page 61

Watts Gallery Tea Shop Tea in vintage china plus scones, jam and cream, served at a former pottery at the Watts Gallery near Guildford. See page 81

that more natural landscapes have immense benefits for wildlife and carbon storage. In the lifetime of this Guide, it's hoped that our concept of a manicured and tamed countryside will receive a profound shake up.

How to use this Guide

The walks in this book are designed to be accessible from the capital as **day-trips** using public transport; we've also included some two-day **weekend walks** (although these can also be broken down and done as separate day-trips). Each walk includes a map, route details, background historical information and a recommended lunch stop, often in one of the fine old pubs that dot the region.

The walks are geared to **public transport**, either starting from one train station and finishing at another, or circling back to the station where you started. At the beginning of each account we've given details of train services and network providers; we haven't recommended specific trains, partly because timetables are subject to change, and also to avoid being prescriptive. Most walks outside London are within an hour's train journey of the city, although we've stretched this criterion where we think a really great walk justifies a longer journey. For all but the very longest routes, starting your train journey at around 10am will ensure that you can get to the specified pub for lunch and do the walk in good time.

There's at least one circular walk in each chapter, convenient if you're **driving**, although virtually all the non-circular walks can also be done by drivers: just make a short train trip back to the beginning of the walk to pick up your car.

Ticket prices can be surprisingly high, even for shortish journeys. You can get discounts by booking specific services in advance, but flexible **off-peak tickets** are handy when you don't know what train to aim for. You get savings of a third with **GroupSave** (3–9 people travelling together) or "kids for £2" – these tickets are available across train companies as a walk-up or online purchase.

If you're eligible, it's worth buying a **railcard** giving discounts of a third on the standard fare. National Rail has a range of such cards aimed at **young people** (aged 16–25 and 26–30), **senior travellers** (60 years and over) and **people with disabilities**; other options include its **Two Together** and **Family & Friends** railcards. All are accepted

FIVE TOP SPOTS FOR WILDLIFE

The Arun The Arun River near Arundel sees a multitude of geese and ducks, as well as rare migratory birds. See page 116

The Fens The watery fens provide a home for many wetland birds, including wigeons and redshanks. See page 251

The New Forest Timid otters, dainty sika deer, small shaggy ponies and, in autumn, free-roaming pigs let loose to eat the acorns. See page 176

The Pett Level Crisscrossed by water channels, the level attracts a mass of birdlife, especially herons and swans. See page 140

Woburn Huge herds of deer plus a safari park full of elephants, zebras and other African wildlife. See page 232

on all train lines, and cost £30 per year (£20 for the disabled card); details on http://railcard.co.uk. If you don't qualify for any of these and you're only going to travel in the southeast of England, try the **Network Railcard** (http://network-railcard.co.uk; £30), which gives the holder and three other adults savings of a third on off-peak journeys in the area. Other types of travelcard, from one-day two-zone cards to annual all-zone ones, should get you some discount on the price of your train ticket – it's always worth asking about this, as you're unlikely to be told. It's best to **buy your train ticket** before getting on board; on many lines, you aren't permitted to buy a cheap-day return from the conductor and you can get stung for a ticket that costs almost twice as much.

COW ETIQUETTE

On several walks in this book, you'll find yourself sharing a field with **cows**, which, more often than not, will carry on grazing as you pass them. But they are curious and playful. The worst thing you can do is run if they approach, as they will run after you, thinking it's a game. If they come too close, just startle them with a "boo" and wave your arms and they should back off. They may come back, but just repeat. Never go into a field with calves, as the mothers may be aggressive. Cows can perceive dogs as a threat: if you're pursued when dog-walking then let go of the lead, and the cows will chase the dog rather than both of you.

PICK UP A PLOUGHMAN'S: THE REGION'S BEST PUBS

The Crown Inn Back-to-basics traditional boozer on the village green at Groombridge. See page 109

Fleur de Lys Whitewashed, thatched and a thousand years old, serving posh pub grub. See page 178

George & Dragon A low-beamed and friendly pub in Darwin's village – some of the food is cooked from his wife Emma's recipes. See page 72

The King William IV This eighteenth-century hillside boozer features an open fire and Surrey Hills ales on handpump. See page 76

The Mayflower They've been serving beer in this cosy pub since the *Mayflower* set sail from here in 1620. See page 58

The Stag & Huntsman Popular country inn tucked away in the brick-and-flint village of Hambleden. See page 190

The Two Brewers Cramped, cluttered and full of atmosphere, with an excellent wine list. See page 187

Ye Olde Fighting Cocks Arguably Britain's oldest pub, with an octagonal timber frame which once had a cock-fighting pit at its core. See page 230

In the interest of making every walk a great day out, we've recommended the very best **pubs** and **cafés** along the way. These are often housed in exceptional old buildings, and we've also tried to uncover places that dish up especially good but reasonably priced food – mains average £9–12. Phone numbers are given for all the pubs listed – most stop serving **lunch** at 2pm, but if you think you're going to arrive later it's worth phoning ahead to say you're on your way. They will generally put aside cold food – a ploughman's or a sandwich – for you.

The **distance** of each walk is flagged at the top of each account, and the level of **difficulty** is indicated alongside. The grading system we've used – "easy", "moderate" and "strenuous" – assumes average fitness. At the start of each walk we calculate how long it will take, but bear in mind that this is the minimum duration: it doesn't factor in any stops and is based on a fairly steady 4km per hour. Metres and kilometres are used throughout the Guide – to figure out the distances in miles, multiply the number of kilometres by 0.62.

The **maps** in this book are sourced from Ordnance Survey originals, with the route and the places you pass along the way picked out in colour. Our maps also show contours and the surrounding roads and paths, so, combined with the route details in the text, they should keep you on the right track. To view the walks in a fuller context, you may want to take the relevant **Ordnance Survey Landranger** (1:50,000) or **Explorer** (1:25,000) maps – we've listed these at the start of each account. Or purchase the OS Maps app (£23.99), which gives you access to unlimited OS Explorer and Landranger maps. For sights, EH denotes English Heritage and NT National Trust: take the relevant membership card with you.

The first chapter of this Guide covers **London** itself: we describe canal, river and woodland walks. Subsequent chapters move clockwise round the capital, starting with the green ridges of the **North Downs** and the bountiful **Weald**, followed by the undulating **South Downs**. The **Saxon Shore** chapter explores a stretch of Sussex and Kent coast, much of it reclaimed from the sea over the last thousand years; next comes the chalky **North Wessex Downs**, dotted with prehistoric remains, and then the **New Forest**, which comprises great tracts of ancient forest and heathland. **The Thames Valley**

ROMAN WALLS AND WHITE HORSES: THE BEST OF ANCIENT BRITAIN

Anderida A still formidable ring of Roman walls, built to keep Saxon pirates at bay. See page 143

Calleva This major Roman settlement escaped subsequent development, and the town walls and amphitheatre remain remarkably intact. See page 193

Cissbury Ring A huge hillfort on the Sussex downs, dating back to around 300 BC and later used as an Armada Beacon site. See page 117

Devil's Dyke Constructed by the Catuvellauni tribe, pre-Roman invaders from what is now Belgium, this dramatic deep ditch runs through dense woodland. See page 222

Fishbourne Palace Features the finest *in-situ* Roman mosaic floors in the country. See page 152

Ivinghoe Beacon At the eastern end of the Ridgeway, this gentle hill is the site of one of the country's earliest forts, dating back to the eighth or seventh century BC. See page 206

Stonehenge This stone circle is one of the most photographed sights in the world, but nothing can prepare you for seeing it across a field as you approach. See page 171

Verulamium Dotted around a spacious park in St Albans, these are the remains of a major Roman trading post. See page 230

Wayland's Smithy Fronted by sarsen stones and more than 5000 years old, this still intact tomb on the ancient Ridgeway is named after a Norse god. See page 163

The White Horse Near to Waylands' Smithy, the chalk White Horse at Uffington has been running across the hillside for 3000 years. See page 163

chapter describes a prosperous, attractive corner of the southeast, while to the north lies the chalky escarpment of **the Chilterns**. **Hertfordshire** and **Bedfordshire** are home to a string of attractive market towns surrounded by plentiful Roman and Celtic remains. To the north of London, gentle riverside walks in **Essex** give way to the flat, watery farmlands and wide-open skies of the **Fenlands**.

There are three **two-day walks** in this Guide which cover sections of established routes: the Pilgrims' Way leads through hop gardens, orchards and forests to Canterbury (see page 87); the South Downs Way provides a stretching hike along the downs and the white cliffs (see page 127); and the Ridgeway, the oldest road in the country, takes you to Neolithic tombs, Iron Age forts and the famous White Horse (see page 161). For these routes we give suggestions for **accommodation** as well as

WRITERS AND ARTISTS IN THE SOUTHEAST

Charleston Farmhouse The country home of the Bloomsbury Group, with wall paintings, portraits and pottery by Duncan Grant and Vanessa Bell. See page 124

Down House Immerse yourself in Darwin's Kent idyll, where he wrote *On The Origin of Species*. See page 72

Monk's House Virginia and Leonard Woolf's Sussex home, with a wooden lodge in the garden where she wrote *Mrs Dalloway*, *To the Lighthouse*, *Orlando* and other works. See page 129

Watts Gallery and Chapel A gallery designed by Victorian portraitist G.F. Watts to house his work, plus a Byzantine-style chapel built by the painter and his wife. See page 81

William Morris tiles The country church of St Mary the Virgin in Clapham features gorgeous decorative tiles by William Morris. See page 119

WHAT TO TAKE

To avoid forgetting something crucial for your walk, here's a **checklist**. Some of the items on this list are optional, some are seasonal and most are obvious. It goes without saying that you should wear a decent pair of waterproof walking shoes or boots; muddiness can be a feature of these walks even in summer, and trudging along with wet feet is a real misery.

- **Money**
- **Railcard**
- **Mobile phone with OS Maps app**
- **Water bottle**
- **Waterproof jacket/cagoule and trousers**
- **Spare layer – jumper or fleece**
- **Snacks**
- **Sun hat/woolly hat**
- **Sun cream**
- **Sunglasses**
- **Camera**
- **Antihistamines (hay fever/allergy tablets)**
- **Plasters**
- **National Trust/English Heritage card**
- **Compass**
- **OS map**

eating and, as with the recommended pubs, we've tried to suggest places that are out of the ordinary, from B&Bs in historic houses to a stunningly located youth hostel.

Where appropriate, we've suggested when might be a good **time of year** for a particular walk: Windsor Great Park, for example, is at its best in late spring with the rhododendrons and azaleas in full bloom, while the orchards of Kent dazzle with blossom in spring and have a more mellow appeal in autumn, when the trees are heavy with fruit. But, in general, any time of year is a good time to do these walks and, in the temperate climate of southern England, you're unlikely to encounter truly wild weather. There are, of course, fewer hours of daylight for winter walks, but the austere beauty of wintry landscapes can hold as much appeal as more verdant summer ones.

London

REGENT'S CANAL

1 London

Greater London doesn't immediately spring to mind as a place for a quiet, off-road walk, though even the most urban of the capital's landscapes can conceal surprisingly sylvan patches. In the centre of the city, the royal parks, some of them former hunting grounds, provide a continuous stretch of greenery, with mature trees, wide lakes and abundant flowerbeds. But paradoxically it's the remnants of the capital's Victorian industrial age – the nineteenth-century canals and railways which did so much to shape London – that now provide some of its best walks. There are also surviving pockets of ancient woodland, notably at Highgate and Epping, and some gorgeous stretches of towpath along the Thames. All the walks in this chapter are within the girdle of the M25, and within travel zones 1–6.

The Royal Parks

Trafalgar Square to Lancaster Gate

Distance and difficulty 4.5km; easy
Minimum duration 1hr 15min
Trains Northern/Bakerloo Line to Charing Cross (zone 1); return on the Central Line from Lancaster Gate (zone 1)
Maps OS Landranger 176: *West London*; OS Explorer 173: *London North*

Many visitors and even residents of London are unaware how far the parks at the heart of the city extend. This route takes you from the centre of London – **Trafalgar Square** – to Green Park, St James's Park, Hyde Park and Kensington Gardens, ending up at the tube station at Lancaster Gate. You'll cross a couple of roads, but otherwise can enjoy uninterrupted greenery all the way. These parks are designated "royal", along with four other London green spaces, because they are hereditary possessions of the monarchy, whose city hangout – **Buckingham Palace** – you pass en route. Most of the eight parks, including spacious **Hyde Park** and neighbouring **Kensington Gardens**, are former royal hunting grounds, though the origin of **Green Park** was a swampy burial place for lepers in the Middle Ages, and **St James's Park** was a zoo under James I in the early 1600s.

You won't go hungry on this route – there are plenty of kiosks and cafés along the way. But we suggest a stop towards the end, at the waterside **Lido Café** in Hyde Park. The **Serpentine Gallery**, also in Hyde Park, has changing exhibitions of contemporary art. Take swimming gear if you fancy a dip in the (summer-only) lido.

Getting started

0.5km From the southwest side of **Trafalgar Square**, enter the wide avenue of **the Mall** via **Admiralty Arch**. You pass a statue of Captain Cook on the left, telescope in hand and coil of rope at his feet. The vine-covered bunker to your left is the **Admiralty Citadel**, constructed in 1940–41 as a bomb-proof centre of operations and still used by the Ministry of Defence. Cross **Horseguards Road**, and turn into St James's Park – not the immediate left turn, but the next one.

St James's Park

1km Follow the sign for the *Inn the Park* going straight ahead into **St James's Park**, with its bright herbaceous borders, palm trees, plane trees and deckchairs. Curve to the right

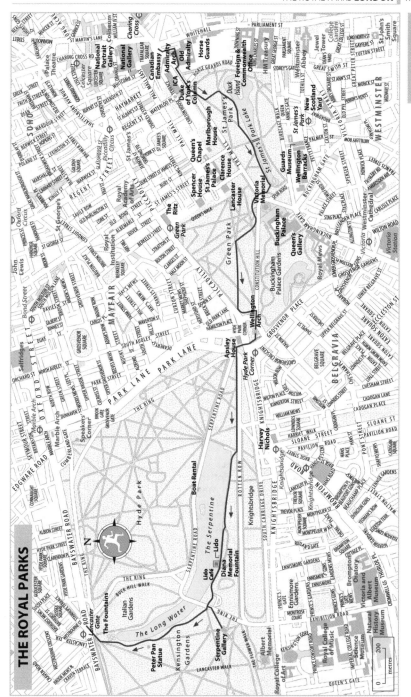

1

in front of the timber *Inn the Park* café and follow the path along the **lake**, staying on the north side rather than crossing the bridge.

The park is most famous for its exotic white pelicans, and you might also see grey herons, coots, tufted ducks, cormorants and even kestrels and woodpeckers. Iridescent azure damselflies and brightly coloured emperor dragonflies skim the water in summer, and at night pipistrelle bats flit among the trees. The curving contours of the borders and of the lake itself (which was once an angular canal) were the creation of Regency architect **John Nash**, who laid out the park in 1826–27. His planting scheme – mixing trees wreathed with climbers with shrubs, bulbs and herbaceous plants – is still followed.

You approach **Buckingham Palace**, which is fronted by a startlingly shiny angel statue and has been the official residence of the royals since 1837. Curve round to the right in front of the low wall. You're now back at the Mall, in front of the monumental 25m fountain/statue of **Queen Victoria**, carved from 2300 tonnes of white marble. Cross the Mall and walk behind the curved balustrade into Green Park.

Green Park

1km A long avenue of plane trees marches up **Green Park**, and to the left are the ornate black and gold Canada Gates. Opposite the last column of the gate (inscribed with the word Canada), go straight ahead up **Broad Walk**, between the trees and the gas lamps; this is one of the last areas of London lit by gas, and it's worth returning at night to see the soft glow of the lamps. After 100m, turn left on the path that leads diagonally up to the top left-hand corner of the park. You'll soon see the Wellington Arch – you're heading for this rather than for busy Piccadilly which runs along the top end of the park.

Exit the park at the stone **Memorial Gates**, constructed in 2001 to remember the dead of the Indian subcontinent, Nepal, Africa and the Caribbean in both world wars. Cross the road and go under the huge **Wellington Arch** (daily: April–Sept 10am–6pm; Oct 10am–5pm, Nov–March 10am–4pm; £5.70; EH), built to celebrate Wellington's victory over Napoleon at Waterloo; there's an entrance fee to see the exhibits inside the arch, and to climb to the top.

Beyond the arch, walk towards the **Royal Artillery memorial**. At the crossing, head towards the Hyde Park Corner **Underground sign** – in the middle of the crossing turn right, and cross into Hyde Park. A double pedestrian crossing takes you into the park.

Hyde Park and Kensington Gardens

2km Once in **Hyde Park**, go left along **Rotten Row**, a wide dirt avenue where you might see horses being exercised – the ride was constructed in 1690 as part of King William III's carriage route from Whitehall to Kensington Palace. Go straight ahead along Rotten Row, or detour into the formal **rose gardens** to the right. You then pass the secluded **Dell**, with its overhanging maple and plane trees. Beyond the Dell, walk up the sloping path to the right to the edge of the **Serpentine Lake**. Follow the path that runs along the southern bank of the lake, a wonderfully wide expanse of water, busy with pedaloes and rowing boats in summer. This was the scenic setting for triathlon and marathon swimming contests in the 2012 Olympics.

In summer, you can bear right through a low wooden gate to a **bathing area** (June to mid-Sept & May bank hols 10am–6pm; £4.80); otherwise, stay as close as possible to the lake.

EATING AND DRINKING

Lido Café The Serpentine, Hyde Park W2 2UH, 020 7706 7098. Beyond the bathing area is the attractive *Lido Café*, a pavilion-like structure with pillars, a clock tower and weather vane and outdoor seating. You can get big breakfasts and hearty lunches (eggs Benedict £9.50, superfood salad £10, flatbreads from £10.50) as well as tea, coffee and cakes. Daily 8am–9pm, closes earlier in winter.

Beyond the café you come to the **Diana Memorial Fountain**, built from Cornish granite; there's a gigantic bronze ibis statue ahead. Head left at the ibis, curving round to the road. Cross over and go through the gates by the horse chestnut trees – turn left and then right to reach the **Serpentine Gallery** (Tues–Sun 10am–6pm; free; http://serpentinegalleries.org), which has changing exhibitions of contemporary art. A key date in the park's calendar is the annual opening of the **Serpentine Pavilion** in June. Each year the gallery invites an international architect – someone who hasn't had a commission in England before – to design the summer pavilion, and the structure is then used as a café and learning centre. Past pavilions include a steel-framed marquee structure by Zaha Hadid, Daniel Libeskind's origami-inspired aluminium folds, Herzog & de Meuron and Ai Weiwei's collaboration which explored the archeology of earlier pavilions, and Olafur Eliasson and Kjetil Thorsen's "spinning top".

Come out of the gallery and go back the way you came, and then carry on along the bank of the lake, known beyond the bridge as the Long Water rather than the Serpentine; look out for bright green parakeets in the trees on this stretch. The far side of the bridge marks the entrance to **Kensington Gardens**, only separated from Hyde Park in 1728; the gardens have a more formal and structured feel than their neighbour. The path meanders away from the lake for a short while, but you come back out at the water at the statue of **Peter Pan** playing the panpipes with fairies, mice, rabbits and squirrels at its base. Peter's creator J.M. Barrie himself commissioned the statue in 1912, and it is located at the spot where Peter, having flown out of the nursery window, landed by the Long Water. Beyond the statue are some formal Italianate gardens, with stone urns, fountains and benches. Exit the park here at Marlborough Gate; across the road is **Lancaster Gate tube station**.

1 Regent's Canal

Camden Lock to Little Venice

Distance and difficulty 5km; easy

Minimum duration 1hr 15min

Trains Northern Line to Camden Town (zone 2); return on the Bakerloo Line from Warwick Avenue (zone 2)

Maps OS Landranger 176: *West London*; OS Explorer 173: *London North*

The **Regent's Canal**, completed in 1820, was constructed as part of a direct link from Birmingham to the newly built London docks. This enticing and secluded stretch along the canal's **towpath** starts off at **Camden Market**, but soon leaves the city streets behind to follow the canal through leafy **Primrose Hill** and around the northern edge of **Regent's Park** and **London Zoo**, passing right by Lord Snowdon's colossal tetrahedral aviary. The walk ends at the canal basin of **Little Venice**, with its narrow boats cheerfully decorated with flowers and painted pots. From here, you can head back to Camden Market by canal boat or home from Warwick Avenue **tube**, just a few hundred metres north of Little Venice.

With a **café** and a **pub** at the end of this route, you won't go hungry or thirsty.

Getting started

0.5km Take the right-hand exit out of **Camden tube**, turn right and head up Camden High Street for 200m towards **Camden Lock**. Turn left just before the bridge over the canal, joining the canal-side path on its south side right by the lock. A few metres ahead, a high-arched bridge crosses the canal at the boundary wall of the market courtyard. Cross this bridge and turn left along the northern bank of the canal.

The arrival of the canal in Camden led to a period of rapid development as the city sprawled north, and by the end of the Victorian era Camden Town had become one of

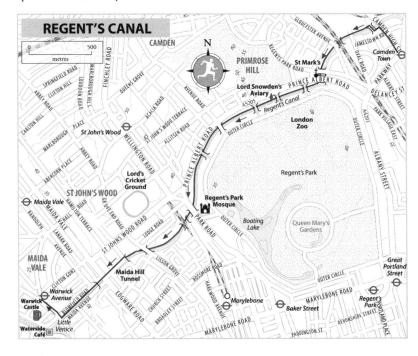

1

BUILDING THE REGENT'S CANAL

The **Regent's Canal** was designed to link the Grand Union Canal, which terminated at Paddington, with the docks on the Thames at Limehouse. A company to oversee the construction and running of the canal was established in 1812; one of its directors was the celebrated architect **John Nash** – it was Nash who secured the patronage of the Prince Regent (later George IV), after whom the canal is named. Despite royal approval, the project suffered from a couple of significant early reverses. In 1815, one of the canal company's directors, Thomas Homer, was convicted of embezzling canal funds and sentenced to transportation, while in 1818 an experimental new lock at Hampstead had to be scrapped at great cost in favour of a conventional system. In all, the project came in at twice its original budget and four years behind schedule. The canal was finally opened in 1820, though its problems didn't end there. By 1835, it was running short of water and the River Brent had to be dammed and diverted to fill it – and the resultant reservoir needed extending in 1837, and again in 1854. The most dramatic event in the canal's history, however, occurred in 1874, when a barge carrying gunpowder exploded at Macclesfield Bridge – or "Blow Up Bridge", as it subsequently became known. Despite such mishaps, it was continuously used as a commercial route until the mid-twentieth century; it's now used exclusively for recreational purposes.

the capital's most notorious slums. Camden is now best known for its **market**, centred on a cobbled courtyard amid disused timber wharves and warehouses.

Primrose Hill to Regent's Park

4km The towpath continues past slick new apartment buildings and under Victorian bridges as you walk through affluent **Primrose Hill**. The attractive gardens of Georgian townhouses tumble down the opposite bank, while the spire of Victorian **St Mark's Church** pokes up above the willows ahead.

At St Mark's the canal turns west, passing under two more Victorian wrought-iron footbridges and running on through the northern edges of **London Zoo**. Most of the zoo lies to the south of the canal, but the northern reaches – most notably the tent-like, aluminium-framed **Aviary** designed by Lord Snowdon in the 1960s, which looms right above the towpath to your right – run beyond the canal and right up to Prince Albert Road, at the perimeter of Regent's Park. There are good views into the enclosures from the canal, but if you'd like to see more of the zoo consider getting the combined **boat and zoo ticket** from the Waterbus Company at Little Venice (see page 22).

Beyond the zoo, the canal continues around the northern edge of **Regent's Park**, passing under Macclesfield Bridge and past several grandiose Victorian mansions, built in bombastic Palladian style, while behind rises the minaret of **Regent's Park Mosque**. A few metres beyond the last of the mansions, the canal reaches the western boundary of the park.

To continue the route beyond the park, take the signposted crossing point and follow the route for a kilometre; this bypasses into **Maida Hill Tunnel**, a 250m-long tunnel under Edgware Road, too narrow and low for a towpath (it's so small, in fact, that traffic lights have to be used to control the movements of barges through it).

Blomfield Road Moorings and Little Venice

0.5km Head on down Blomfield Road. The wrought-iron railings between the road and the canal mark the boundary of the private **Blomfield Road Moorings**, home to dozens of colourful houseboats festooned with potted flower tubs, painted metal jugs, quirky furniture, topiary figures and other unusual bric-a-brac. The towpath forms part of the moorings, so you'll have to follow Blomfield Road for the first few hundred metres before rejoining the towpath just before Warwick Avenue.

1

A few metres ahead the path leads under a road bridge and comes out at the canal basin of **Little Venice**. A pool formed by the junction of the Paddington Branch and the Regent's Canal, this spot was formerly known as **Browning's Pool**, after the poet Robert Browning, who once lived in a house overlooking it and is credited with giving the basin its Italianate name. Today, the canal is still home to an artistic community, and you'll find a puppet theatre and a couple of floating cafés.

EATING AND DRINKING

Waterside Café Warwick Crescent W2 6NE, 020 7266 1066. Moored on the far side of the canal, the *Waterside Café* barge serves simple drinks, sandwiches, cakes and biscuits on board and at canal-side tables. From £6.50 for snacks. Daily 9am–5pm.

Head over the wrought-iron bridge to the left bank of the canal for a boat back to Camden: the **Waterbus Company** (April–Sept; 020 7482 2660, http://londonwaterbus.co.uk; £9,) runs between Little Venice and Camden Lock, making a couple of stops along the way. Alternatively, double back along the right bank of the canal for **Warwick Avenue tube station** (zone 2), 200m north along Warwick Avenue itself. Before you reach the tube, a left turn down Warwick Place brings you to the flower-smothered *Warwick Castle* **pub**, a snug place with wood panelling and Victorian stained glass.

Hampstead Heath

Across the heath to Kenwood

Distance and difficulty 5.25km; easy

Minimum duration 1hr 20min

Trains Overground train to Hampstead Heath station (zone 2) from stations between Richmond and Stratford

Maps OS Landranger 176: *West London*; OS Explorer 173: *London North*

Eight-hundred-acre **Hampstead Heath** is London's most beautiful open space, with its rolling grassland, sweeping urban vistas, ancient woodland and artfully designed eighteenth-century parkland. To its north is **Kenwood House**, which boasts a wonderful collection of paintings and an enticing café. This circular walk takes you from Hampstead Heath station to the house via the bathing ponds (take your swimming things in case the natural waters appeal), and back to the station via Keats's House. Back at the station, *The Garden Gate* **pub** is well worth a visit.

Getting started

0.5km Coming out of **Hampstead Heath station**, turn right to head up South Hill. After a few metres, bear right onto Parliament Hill road, passing tall, red-brick gabled houses on either side. After 250m, Parliament Hill ends quite abruptly and you're on the heath. Go straight ahead on the path.

Parliament Hill to the bathing ponds

0.75km At the first crossroads in the path, after 50m, make the short detour up **Parliament Hill**, much loved by kite-flyers. From an elevation of 97m you get a panoramic view of the city, from Canary Wharf in the east via St Paul's to the BT Tower, Regent's Park and the Shard. Crystal Palace is sometimes visible in the far distance. The hill is supposed to have earned its name because Guy Fawkes's co-conspirators gathered here to watch parliament in flames – if their plans had come off they would certainly have had a spectacular view.

DIDO BELLE AT KENWOOD

One of the most celebrated and unusual portraits to emanate from Kenwood, though it now hangs in Scone Palace in Scotland, is that of **Dido Belle** and her cousin Lady Elizabeth Murray. The two young women are dressed in sumptuous clothes with a fashionably sylvan scene behind them: the picture, attributed to Zoffany, resonates with their charm and affection for each other, expressed by the hand that Elizabeth tucks under Dido's elbow. What makes the painting unusual is that Dido is black, and that she is not presented in a subservient role, but as a genteel, lively and marriageable woman.

Dido's father is thought to have been John Lindsay, a naval captain, and her mother Maria Bell, a slave in the West Indies. Dido was brought up by Lindsay's uncle, **Lord Mansfield**, the owner of Kenwood House and a high-powered judge; in 1772 he made a significant ruling on the legality of slavery that was a stepping stone on the way to abolition. Lord and Lady Mansfield had no children of their own, but also raised another great-niece, Lady Elizabeth. Dido was well educated: she could play music and read and write, and oversaw the dairy and poultry at Kenwood, a task that was well within the remit of a refined young woman. Mansfield's social prominence and the elegance of the house meant that she would have moved in the most fashionable society.

The year Lord Mansfield died, 1793, Dido married John Davinier, a gentleman's steward. They had three sons and lived in Pimlico, in comfortable circumstances, though not in the splendour provided by Kenwood. Her life was celebrated in the 2013 film *Belle*.

1

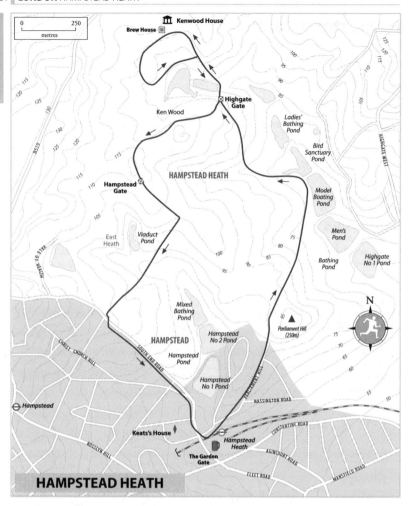

HAMPSTEAD HEATH

To rejoin the walk, go back down to the path you were on before and turn right. The path leads through the gently undulating park, with its tall grasses and clumps of mature beech and oak trees; it's a playground for north Londoners on a sunny day, with people picnicking and playing football. Smaller paths lead off to either side, but stay on the major tarred route. Some 300m beyond Parliament Hill you'll see a line of trees ahead of you and a wooden fence, behind which are the **bathing ponds**. The ponds are natural – the heath is the source of several of London's "lost rivers", including the Fleet.

The path slopes down towards the line of trees, with a fence and a path running alongside it; when the path you're on joins the one along the bathing ponds, go straight ahead. To your right, sheltered by trees, is the men's pond, a well-known spot for London's LGBTQ community, and vividly described in Alan Hollinghurst's *The Line of Beauty*; beyond this is the more open Model Boat Pond ringed by park benches, where you'll often see model boats and toy yachts being put through their paces. At the far end of this pond, turn left up the hill, away from the water.

1

Towards Kenwood House

1km Around 150m further on the path splits into three – take the right-hand fork which, after just 100m, crosses a tiny plank bridge. Go straight up the path ahead. After 200m you join a tarred path – go straight ahead here for around 10m until you come to a crossroads with a mature oak to your right. Go straight ahead, through **Highgate Gate** into **Ken Wood**.

Bear right on the dirt path into secluded woodland, through holly bushes, rhododendrons and azaleas. You'll soon see a lake through the trees to your left. The path, now tarred, emerges into open picturesque parkland. As you ascend the hill in front of you, **Kenwood House** is revealed in all its wedding-cake Neoclassical magnificence.

EATING AND DRINKING

Brew House Kenwood House NW3 7JR, 020 8341 5384. Located in the "service wing" of Kenwood House, the *Brew House* is a perfect place to stop for lunch or afternoon tea. The interior features *trompe l'oeil* decoration, while outside there's a terraced cottage-style garden. Food, including their hot breakfasts, is free-range and locally sourced, with scones and jam and cakes at teatime; they also serve Sunday roasts plus veggie and vegan options and kids' meals. Daily April–Sept 9am–6pm; Oct–March 9am–dusk.

Kenwood House and grounds

0.75km The **house** (April–Oct daily 11am–5pm; Nov–March daily 11am–4pm; free; EH; http://english-heritage.org) dates from the seventeenth century, but owes its current appearance to Robert Adam, who remodelled it for Lord Mansfield in the 1760s and 70s. The graceful proportions, gilded friezes, glittering library and stucco ceilings are stunning, but what really distinguishes it is the Iveagh Bequest made in 1927, the then owner gifting the house with a superb collection of paintings by Vermeer, Hals, Romney, Gainsborough, Reynolds and Turner. For many the highlight is a sombre late self-portrait by Rembrandt, craggy and impressionistic.

To continue, walk past the house, on the side facing the lake. Continue along the wide, gravelled, tree-lined avenue just beyond – look out for the Barbara Hepworth figurative sculpture on the lawn to your right.

Just beyond here the path forks – take the left-hand fork with the **Henry Moore sculpture** on the left. The path curves down the hill, with trees on the right and open parkland to the left. Continue on the gravel path towards the lake.

The path splits at the bottom of the hill; bear left instead of crossing the little wooden bridge to the right. Skirt the **lake**, keeping it on your right-hand side, and then head uphill to rejoin the tarred path on which you approached the house.

Through Ken Wood and back to the heath

1.5km Return to **Highgate Gate**, on the edge of **Ken Wood**, but instead of exiting the wood, turn right and stay within the boundary, delineated by iron railings. Carry on for a meandering 500m along the edge of Ken Wood, with picket fences on either side. Eventually you come to **Hampstead Gate**, where you exit the wood.

Follow the path that curves round to the left for a few metres, ignoring the two tracks to the right. At the crossroads, go straight ahead. The wide dirt path leads through woods, soon following a gentle descent. After 250m at the wood's edge you come to another junction in the path in more open parkland. Turn right here, to descend the hill.

Go straight ahead and you eventually come to a wide avenue of limes, planted to replace trees lost in the great storm of 1987. After 300m you come to the edge of the park at **East Heath Road**, which is lined by red-brick mansions.

1

Back to the station

0.75km Turn left down East Heath Road and continue downhill for 600m. **Keats Grove**, to the right just before the parade of shops, is a quintessential leafy Hampstead street, with graceful Regency villas and Victorian mansions with lush gardens. On the left of the road is the house where the poet **John Keats** lived from 1818 until he departed for Rome, where he died in 1821 at the age of 25. It was in the garden here that Keats wrote the *Ode to a Nightingale*, and in the four-poster bed that he first coughed blood; as a medic he was in no doubt that consumption was the cause, describing the blood as his "death warrant". Although the house is now in one of the most desirable and wealthy parts of London, at that time the handsome villa was divided in two and made quite a humble dwelling; next door lived Fanny Brawne, with whom Keats fell deeply in love.

Back on East Heath Road, now called **South End Road**, cross the road to reach the station. If you want a pint before you go back, *The Garden Gate* **pub** is a great nearby option. Just continue on South End Road, past the turn-off to the station; you'll see the looming monolith of the Royal Free Hospital ahead of you and the pub on the left-hand side behind a long brick wall.

EATING AND DRINKING

The Garden Gate 14 South End Rd NW3 2QE, 020 7435 4938, http://thegardengatehampstead.co.uk. This welcoming boozer serves up strong organic farm cider on tap and has a good wine list. The spacious paved garden is circled by a sheltered terrace, while inside there's wood panelling and colourful Victorian glass. Food is nothing special, but it's a great stop for a drink. Mon–Thurs noon–11pm, Fri noon–midnight, Sat 10am–midnight, Sun noon–10.30pm.

1 The Parkland Walk

Finsbury Park to Alexandra Palace

Distance and difficulty 9.5km; easy

Minimum duration 2hr

Trains Victoria Line tube or Overground train from King's Cross to Finsbury Park (zone 2); return by Overground train from Alexandra Palace (zone 3) to Moorgate

Maps OS Landranger 176: *West London*; OS Explorer 173: *London North*

The **Parkland Walk** follows the course of the former **Great Northern Railway**, which was dismantled and transformed into a footpath in the mid-1980s. Starting in Finsbury Park, the walk follows the leafy corridor of the former railway through cuttings and across embankments to **Highgate**, then continues through **Queen's Wood** and **Highgate Wood**, two remnants of the Forest of Middlesex, the once-great tract of woodland that covered the whole of the north London area. Beyond the woods, the walk resumes along the course of a former branch line of the railway to the sprawling Victorian **Alexandra Palace**. For **lunch**, secluded *Queen's Wood Café* is a great option.

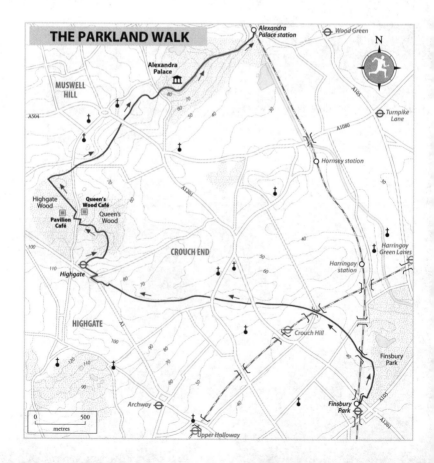

1

THE GREEN MAN

The precise origins of the **Green Man** remain obscure. Images of a human head surrounded by a mass of leaves have been found on memorials across Europe, some dating from as early as the second century AD. Within a few generations, similar images had begun to appear on Christian tombstones, and figures growing out of – or even made from – leaves became a common decorative feature of many European churches and cathedrals right through to the nineteenth century.

It's usually thought that the Green Man was a pagan symbol embodying the natural cycle of birth, death, decay and regeneration, being subsequently incorporated (like so many other such symbols) into Christian mythology. The Green Man is also linked with **Spriggan**, a mischievous but essentially benevolent creature who is fond of stealing children from cruel parents or money from greedy men and keeping both safe in the woods.

It was for the Green Man's association with renewal that Victorian romantics adopted him as **Jack in the Green**, who heralded in the spring in their May Day celebrations, part of the nostalgic search for a "Merrie England" that included the revival of morris dancing. Spriggan has also entered the popular consciousness through such quintessentially English figures as the **Green Knight**, from the Arthurian legend of Sir Gawain, and **Robin Hood**, who acquired many Spriggan-like features during his evolution into the character we think of today.

Getting started
0.5km Head out of the main exit at **Finsbury Park tube station** (follow signs for Station Place) and turn left across Stroud Green Road. Just to the left of Rowan's tenpin bowling alley, go through the Stroud Green gate by the cycle park and turn onto the first gravel path to the left. You'll soon see a "**Capital Ring**" sign; this is part of a 126km walking route round the capital. Beyond the tennis courts you come to a T-junction; turn left here, following the sign to Highgate. You cross a small footbridge over the railway, then turn right to join the course of the former Great Northern railway.

Finsbury Park to Crouch End station
2.5km The disused railway soon climbs to higher ground, widening out and cutting a broad swathe through the city sprawl. It starts to feel positively rural, with the wooded hilltops of Highgate and Hampstead ahead of you, and the suburban development on either side obscured by trees and bushes.

After about 1.5km, the path dips under **Crouch Hill** road by way of a Victorian arched bridge. A few hundred metres beyond is a little adventure playground. Just beyond this you come to the ghostly ruins of **Crouch End station**, whose weed-strewn platforms and arches constitute the most intact railway remains along the entire route. Don't miss the sculpted **Green Man** (see above), climbing out of the fifth arch on the right. Crowned with oak leaves, this impish figure – the work of local artist Marilyn Collins – represents the pagan spirit of renewal, his hands grasping the arch as he pulls himself out from the undergrowth. Incorporated in the modern bridge at the far end of the station platform is all that is left of the old station building; overgrown steps to the right lead down from the old ticket office.

Highgate terminus
1.5km Beyond the old station, the route continues for another 1.5km through a dell-like cutting up to **Highgate**. The first part of the Parkland Walk ends here, a couple of hundred metres before the cavernous tunnels just south of Highgate station. The old rail line continued through these tunnels, calling at Highgate station before reaching Alexandra Palace, but the tunnels have long since become overgrown and the path that leads up to them is now fenced off. Instead, follow the side path that forks left and up onto **Holmesdale Road**. Turn right here and then right again at the T-junction with

1

busy Archway Road and head up to the traffic lights for a few metres, opposite the entrance to **Highgate tube station**.

Queen's Wood

1.25km At the traffic lights, turn right onto **Shepherd's Hill** and then left down the track just before the library on the far side of the road. This leads down to **Priory Gardens** road. Turn right here and head uphill; just before the road bends and makes its final steep ascent back to Shepherd's Hill, turn left, following the signed path as it descends steeply between the houses into **Queen's Wood**.

Along with adjacent Highgate Wood, Queen's Wood is a pocket of undisturbed and ancient woodland that comprises an atmospheric tangle of hornbeams and oaks – though it's less well known, less visited and less landscaped than its neighbour.

Follow the Capital Ring signs, taking the broad stepped path ahead of you. The route crosses **Queen's Wood Road**; continue to follow the Capital Ring signs through the wood. The path emerges, 250m after crossing the road, at fairytale *Queen's Wood Café*, a timbered chalet-style building surrounded by trees and backed by an organic garden.

EATING AND DRINKING

Queen's Wood Café 42 Muswell Hill Rd N10 3JP, 020 8444 2604, http://queenswoodcafe.co.uk. Hippy-ish vegetarian *Queen's Wood Café* is open daily, serving good salads, Jamaican curry and falafel for around £8.50, as well as all-day breakfast and home-made cakes. May–Oct Mon–Fri 10am–5pm, Sat & Sun 10am–6pm; Nov–April Mon–Fri 10am–4pm, Sat & Sun 10am–5pm.

Into Highgate Wood

1km Past the café, head up the tarred path and cross the road at the pedestrian crossing, heading into the hornbeam and oak trees of **Highgate Wood**, through the New Gate entrance. Turn right into the wood, again following the Capital Ring signs. Continue for 300m to a T-junction marked by a tall wooden fingerpost. To find out more about wildlife in the woods, turn left and head down towards the playing fields, on the edge of which you'll find the wisteria-covered *Pavilion Café*. Just beyond the café there's a small **information hut** with leaflets and displays about local conservation work and guided tours, such as the popular night-time bat walk.

To continue the walk from the fingerpost, turn right at the T-junction and carry straight on to reach a marble **water fountain**, carved with an excerpt from Samuel Taylor Coleridge's *Inscription for a Fountain on a Heath*: "Drink, pilgrim, here; Here rest!" (though the fountain's sorry trickle of water doesn't provide much sustenance today). From the fountain, take the main fork left to the edge of the wood and turn right in front of Bridge Gate. Carry on for 250m to leave the woods by the Cranley Gate exit.

Towards Alexandra Palace

1.25km Passing through Cranley Gate, turn left onto **Muswell Hill Road** and take the path under the road a few metres ahead to regain the Parkland Walk, which here runs on higher ground than before, with the land dropping away sharply to the right and affording sweeping views across London. Even on a cloudy day you can pick out the City and the towers at Canary Wharf, while on a clear day the views stretch south to the Crystal Palace radio transmitter and beyond. The panoramic views are short-lived, however. After around 750m you reach an underpass beneath **Muswell Hill Park Road**, on the far side of which the path leads round to the right, up a ramp with a plastic awning, and deposits you in a sheltered park beyond. Either loop around the park will take you to the exit on the east side onto **Alexandra Palace Way**, with the western facade of the palace itself standing proud on the hill above.

Alexandra Palace

1.5km Alexandra Palace, or "Ally Pally" as it's affectionately known, was built in 1873 as a People's Palace to rival Crystal Palace in south London and remains an enduring monument to the self-assurance of the Victorian era, stretching for over 300m along the brow of the hill and dominating the local skyline. As a commercial enterprise, however, it never really took off, largely thanks to a fire that devastated the palace just days after it opened. In 1936, the BBC leased part of it to make the world's first public television transmission, and it continued to be used for television broadcasts until after World War II (during which time it was used to house German POWs) – a massive radio transmitter stands at the east end of the building, a legacy of the BBC years. Left empty and semi-derelict for many years, however, the palace fell victim to another disastrous fire in 1980, after which it was again rebuilt. It's now used as a conference and exhibition space, and is a lively weekend venue for antiques and craft fairs. Around the palace, **Alexandra Park** tumbles down to the northern reaches of Hornsey, giving fine views across the city – from Telecom Tower in the west, through the high-rises of the City over to the towers of Canary Wharf in the east.

You can take the regular **W3 bus** back to Finsbury Park from any one of several stops along wide Alexandra Palace Way, or continue 750m east along this road to **Alexandra Palace station**, from where there are frequent services (every 10–30min) to Moorgate. Just beyond the theme-park-style boundary – a hefty wooden banner supported by totem-pole-style posts that marks the eastern edge of the Alexandra Palace estate – a footbridge (slightly hidden in the trees) leads off to the right across the rail tracks to Alexandra Palace station.

1

1

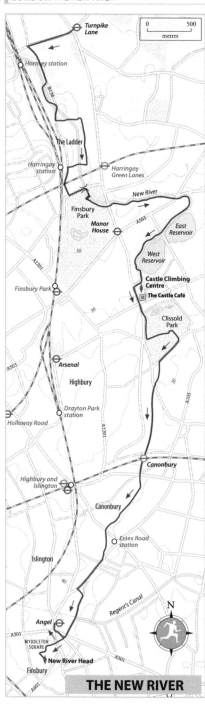

0 500
metres

THE NEW RIVER

The New River

Turnpike Lane to Sadler's Wells

Distance and difficulty 10.5km; easy
Minimum duration 2hr 30min
Trains Piccadilly Line to Turnpike Lane (zone 3); return on the Northern Line from Angel (zone 1)
Maps OS Landranger 177: *East London*; OS Explorer 173: *London North*

This excellent walk was devised by Thames Water – as their blurb states, it's not new and it's not a river. The **New River** is actually a canal, completed in 1613 to carry fresh drinking water from a Hertfordshire spring to the capital. The intention was to deliver Londoners from contaminated water; this gently flowing channel must have saved thousands of lives. The whole route runs for 62km, from Chadwell to Islington, but the section described here takes you from **Turnpike Lane** to **Sadler's Wells**, the former "New River Head". The first stretch is secluded and can be dicey, so be aware – or start the walk at Finsbury Park. It's intriguing though to follow the thread of the canal through some diverse areas, from **Haringey** to **Stoke Newington** through **Canonbury** to **Islington**. The character of the water itself changes: in parts it's a wide waterway with a gentle current, in Canonbury it takes on a country stream quality, and for stretches it disappears altogether. Part of the charm is spotting the water – and imagining how it would have looked cutting a bolder swathe through early seventeenth-century London.

Note that it's not a good route for cyclists, as there are lots of kissing gates which are awkward with a bike. Of all the **eating places** along the way, *The Castle Café* is the most appealing and unusual.

Getting started

1.5km Take the **Turnpike Lane** and Wood Green High Road exit to leave the tube station. Then turn left at the end of the subway, following the Turnpike Lane South Side sign. Exiting

1

LONDON'S WATER

Before 1600, London's water needs were supplied by the none-too-clean **Thames**, plus streams, springs and wells, with water being sold door to door in wooden buckets by water carriers, known as cobs. This arrangement was unsanitary and dangerous – many poorer Londoners were drowned attempting to collect their own water – and it was challenged in 1600 by **Captain Edmund Colthurst**. Together with **Sir Hugh Myddleton** (whose impressive portfolio career included goldsmithing, clothmaking, adventuring, mine-owning, banking and engineering), Colthurst hatched a plan to cut a channel through the Lea Valley, bringing water for 62km, from springs at Chadwell and Amwell in **Hertfordshire** to the spectacular **New River Head reservoir** at Sadler's Wells. From here the water was distributed to the city via 640km of elm pipes.

King James I stepped in to help fund the project, which required two hundred labourers to cut and reinforce the channel, as well as mathematician Edward Wright to plot the course and ensure a steady flow of water. In 1613 the New River was opened, and a celebration play was staged at the Round Pond in Islington.

It's a tribute to this piece of engineering genius that, supplemented by bore holes and wells, the New River continues to carry eight percent of London's water for treatment.

---

the tube, head down Turnpike Lane, a scruffy, lively, multicultural mix with corner stores, a Turkish hairdresser's, a Mauritian restaurant, shisha garden and Indian fabric shop. At the end of the street turn left on Wightman Road towards the mosque. When you reach the mosque, cross the road and head right onto Hampden Road. Cross the road and you'll see a metal kissing gate, leading you onto the signed New River Path.

The Ladder and Finsbury Park
3km The wide and flowing canal has a grassy path on its right-bank side. At the end of this 500m stretch, cross left over the little wooden bridge, at a point where the grill in the river collects floating rubbish. Walk up the slope to join the road; the New River disappears under the road here. You come out at a green metal kissing gate. Turn right up the road.

Turn left onto Seymour Road – a little more than halfway down the road, turn right onto the narrow alley called Haringey Passage (next to no. 82 Seymour Rd). You're now cutting across a network of streets, known as **The Ladder** for their grid-like orderliness. Pass the Haringey Children's Centre. Keep going up Haringey Passage to Umfreville Road, and turn right up the hill – you cross the canal as it flows between the terraced houses. Turn left onto Woollaston Road, right onto Atterbury Road and then left onto Wightman Road. Wightman Road becomes Alroy Road on the other side of the railway bridge. At the end of the road turn left along the wooden fence towards Harringay Green Lanes station.

Go along the wooden fence along the edge of **Finsbury Park**. Through the fence you'll see the New River, flowing into the park. Just beyond the river, turn right into Finsbury Park – you'll see a baseball pitch down to the left. Coming through the park, cross over a little bridge – the metal sign on the fence opposite signals the New River. Turn left and follow the course of the canal – don't take the path up to the right – just follow the right bank of the canal. You come out onto **Green Lanes**. Cross over at the crossing and go through the green kissing gate just down to the left – continue along the canal.

You're now on a raised section of the New River – which can get very muddy – with grassy banks and tall grasses to either side and swans floating along. You start to get some views, of a tall industrial chimney and the distant spire of St Mary's Church in Stoke Newington. At the end of this stretch, you come to a red-brick bridge – go through the kissing gate and cross the busy Seven Sisters Road – you'll see the next

1

stretch of the walk on the other side, just to the left. Go through another green kissing gate, back on the right-hand bank of the canal. Walk under the chestnut tree, and carry on straight ahead. At the end of this stretch go through the kissing gate at a low wooden bridge and up the steps. Carry on, through another kissing gate, heading down into **Stoke Newington**; at this point the New River resembles a stream rather than a canal.

Through Stoke Newington

3.5km A small brick building sits over the canal – you emerge here at the watery expanse of the east reservoir. It's an intriguing mix of urban and rural: you'll see St Mary's and, beyond, the glassy peak of the Shard. You now approach the recent development of Woodbury Down, joining the landscaped parkland that winds along the edge of the new estate and borders the **Woodbury Wetlands**, a new nature reserve on the east reservoir. Birds to look out for include the reed bunting, great crested grebe and Canada goose. Cross over the road and continue through the development, past a silver ball sculpture with water flowing over it.

Carry on along the canal, curving towards the Art Deco **watersports centre** on the west reservoir, with the reservoir beyond: you pass right by the centre's stacked canoes. Cross the low wooden bridge towards the crenellated **Castle Climbing Centre** with its tall brick towers. This eccentric castle-like folly was a Victorian pumping station, redesigned in the 1990s by Nicholas Grimshaw, architect of Cornwall's Eden Project.

EATING AND DRINKING

The Castle Café Green Lanes N4 2HA, 020 8211 7000, http://castle-climbing.co.uk. *The Castle Café* sits at the top of the centre, and you eat surrounded by climbers. Much of the food comes from the kitchen garden out back and it's all delicious and affordable: courgette and apple cake for £2.50 for example, salads at £2 a scoop and tea for £1.50. Mon–Fri noon–9.30pm, Sat & Sun 9am–6.30pm.

Coming out of the climbing centre, turn left onto Green Lanes. Cross Lordship Park and go straight ahead towards **Clissold Park**; take the first left turning into Clissold Park, at the Capital Ring sign. Turn right up the paved path that leads along the edge of the park. You come to a small brick pump house on the right-hand side; turn left here through Clissold Park. After around 200m, you'll see a low fence where the canal reappears, and starts to flow through and around the park.

Facing the deer enclosure, turn left over the little metal bridge, then right to follow the left bank of the canal. You're now facing eighteenth-century mansion Clissold House, and the canal is thick with bulrushes. Follow the curve of the canal round past Clissold House. Coming out of the park, turn right onto Church Street. At the *New River Café and Restaurant*, turn left onto Clissold Crescent, then almost immediately right onto an **alley**. This takes you along Aden Terrace past 150m of allotments, backed by a mini tower block.

Come out of the alley, cross Green Lanes at the zebra crossing, then go down the street ahead of you – **Petherton Road** – with a grassy strip down the middle signalling the canal running underneath. The path winds through the avenue of chestnut trees between the houses. At the end of the green strip, go straight ahead at the roundabout, following the New River sign. At the second roundabout at the *Snooty Fox* pub, carry on straight ahead. Go past Canonbury station, up Wallace Road. At the end of Wallace Road, cross over into the garden ahead.

Canonbury to Sadler's Wells

2.5km The elongated **parks** you now walk through are wonderful examples of mid-twentieth-century landscaping, converting the canal into something resembling a

natural stream, and throwing in fountains, willow trees, pines and boulders in an artful Japanese style.

Come out onto Willow Bridge Road, turn left for a couple of metres facing the *Marquess Tavern*, then carry on through the next stretch of garden. You'll see a circular brick building with a tiled conical roof. This was a **watch hut** for the eighteenth-century linesman, whose job was to prevent bathing and fishing which would dirty the water supply. The wooden bank round the hut – known as a revetment – is the only part of the original channel that survives.

Come out at Canonbury Grove, and cross Canonbury Road to continue. Pass the playground up Astey's Row and into scenic **Astey's Row Rock Garden**, walking under the large willow tree.

At the end of the garden, turn left down the steps and right onto **Essex Road**, past Get Stuffed, the taxidermy shop. The canal is submerged at this point – to follow its original route head left onto Colebrooke Row. But as you can't see the water here anyway, it's worth carrying on down Essex Road to see a **statue** of the ruffed and cloaked Sir Hugh Myddleton (see page 33), just beyond the tip of Islington Green. Backtrack a few metres to go down Camden Walk, then turn right onto Camden Passage. Just beyond Annie's vintage dress shop, turn left down Charlton Place, a long Georgian terrace. Then go right onto Colebrook Row. Walk along Colebrook Row Gardens, which run down the middle of the street, then straight ahead through **Duncan Terrace Gardens**. Writer and essayist Charles Lamb lived here from 1823–27, with a view onto the open channel of the New River. Look up at the end of the garden to see three hundred wooden birdboxes, beautifully sculpted around the tree trunks.

Coming out of the gardens, cross City Road and then Goswell Road, heading straight up Owen Street. Cross over at the lights and go up Chadwell Street into wide and grand **Myddleton Square**. Walk up the left-hand side of the square, and turn left up Myddleton Passage. Go through the gates straight ahead for a display about the walk. This is the site of the **New River Head** (daily 8am–4pm, 7pm in summer), the water distribution point. An old engraving shows the head in 1752 with St Paul's dominating the skyline beyond. Traces of a windmill, engine room, pump house and nineteenth-century workshops survive but are inaccessible, having been incorporated into a gated development.

You might want to detour here onto Rosebery Avenue to visit the glassy modern **Sadler's Wells** dance theatre. Otherwise, retrace your steps, heading left up Goswell Road instead of going straight ahead. At the junction soon after turn right up Islington High Street to reach **Angel tube station**.

Epping Forest

Queen Elizabeth's Lodge to Connaught Water

Distance and difficulty 11km; shorter walk 5.5km; easy–moderate

Minimum duration 2hr 45min; shorter walk 1hr 20min

Trains Liverpool Street to Chingford (zone 5; every 20–30min; 30min); return from Chingford to Liverpool Street (every 20–30min; 30min). You can use an Oyster card/contactless payment for this journey. Bikes can be carried on the train outside peak hours

Maps OS Landranger 177: *East London*; OS Explorer 174: *Epping Forest & Lee Valley*

Starting in the northeast fringes of London, the ancient deciduous woodland of **Epping Forest** stretches along a high gravel ridge for almost 20km into the Essex countryside. Originally a royal hunting ground, Epping Forest was opened to the public in 1878, since then it has been managed by the Corporation of London. Covering some six thousand acres, the forest is London's largest public open space, and its sheer scale comes as a surprise to the first-time visitor, not least because of its proximity to urban sprawl. It remains a popular spot, and at any time of year you can expect to share the forest with plenty of horseriders and cyclists, as well as many fellow walkers. This is a good option for mountain biking – the tracks can get muddy, but there are few gates and no stiles to cross.

This circular walk heads from **Chingford station** up to **Queen Elizabeth's Hunting Lodge** before heading north into the heart of the forest. The midway point is the woodland village of **High Beach** – the *Kings Oak* here makes a good **lunch** stop. The second half of the walk takes you further east, past the Iron Age earthworks of **Loughton Camp** and on to **Connaught Water**, the largest of the 150 ponds that dot the forest. You can **shorten the walk** from 11km to 5.5km by deviating off the main route at the top of Long Hills and rejoining it at Fairmead Road.

Getting started

0.4km From **Chingford station**, turn right onto Station Road (the A1069). Almost immediately, **Chingford Plain** – the grassy expanse on the forest's edge where royalty once hunted – opens up before you, with the forest beyond. Follow the main road as it heads uphill, keeping the plain on your left and the large houses of Forest Avenue to your right.

Queen Elizabeth's Lodge and Butler's Retreat

0.1km At the brow of the hill, just beyond the mock-Tudor *Royal Forest* pub and The View forest visitor centre, **Queen Elizabeth's Hunting Lodge** comes into view. Built for Henry VIII in 1543, and renovated for Elizabeth I in 1589, the lodge served as a grandstand from which hunts on the plain below could be watched – as such, it would originally have

---

THE FOREST RETREATS

On May 6, 1882, Queen Victoria officially opened Epping Forest as "an open space for the recreation and enjoyment of the public" as outlined in the Epping Forest Act of 1878 – an act that made the London Corporation responsible for the forest's conservation and effectively prevented landowners from enclosing land or selling it off for development.

Dubbed the "**Cockney Paradise**", Epping Forest soon began to attract visitors in their tens of thousands. Both Chingford Plain and High Beach became crowded with day-trippers, who were entertained with donkey rides and other fairground attractions, while giant refreshment rooms – or "**forest retreats**", as they were popularly known – were also set up to cater to the crowds. The larger retreats could seat up to two thousand people at a time, though only one of these survives: **Butler's Retreat** (see page 38), which opened in 1891 and is still going strong today, although its capacity has fallen from six hundred people to just forty.

1

been open to the elements, though its timber frame was later enclosed with plaster. There's no evidence that either monarch ever actually used the building, but the association with Elizabeth stuck, and by the seventeenth century the lodge had acquired its present name. Used variously as a law court, tearooms and a family home, it now houses a small **museum** (March–Sept Wed–Sun 12.30–5.30pm, Oct–Feb Sat & Sun 11am–4pm; free), with low-key exhibits on the history of the building; as you'd expect, there are great views from the gallery across the plain, where hunts would have taken place.

Next door to the lodge is **Butler's Retreat**, a traditional whitewashed and red-tiled Essex barn which was subsequently converted into a "forest retreat" (see page 37) to cater for the crowds of urban pleasure-seekers who frequented the forest during the late nineteenth century.

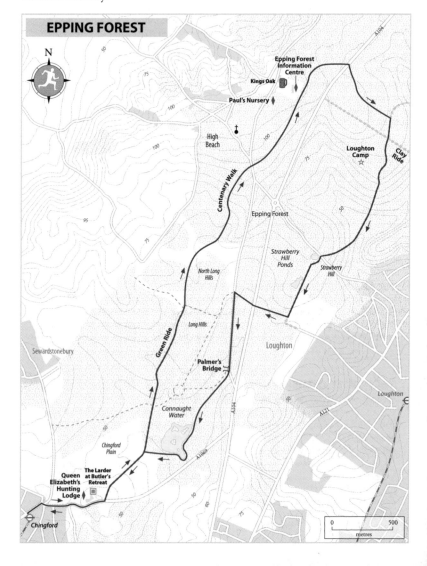

EATING AND DRINKING

The Larder at Butler's Retreat 12 Ranger's Rd E4 7QH, 020 7998 7858, http://larder.london.co.uk. At this historic building they serve up snacks, meals and hot drinks, such as the all-day Forest Fry breakfast (£10.50), Buddha Bowl (£8.50) and soup of the day (£6.20). Daily 9am–4pm, until 6/7pm in summer.

Into the forest

3km At the water fountain behind *The Larder at Butler's Retreat*, follow the path with the black arrow and cattle sign straight ahead towards the **forest**. After 500m you reach the edge of the forest. Follow the path straight ahead into the trees, which form an impressive avenue known as **Green Ride**. Head straight on for around 1.5km, passing straight over a crossroads after 500m.

Around 1km from the crossroads, the main path bears sharply to the right; follow this for the **shorter loop** described below. To continue on the main route, take the track to the left here, which carries straight ahead along the right-hand side of a small clearing studded with oaks, up **North Long Hills** and out of the trees to the edge of **Whitehouse Plain** – cows are often let out to graze here, reflecting the forest's status as common land. The path snakes its way north for 750m, up along the left-hand edge of the plain and then back into the trees to climb steeply uphill to a minor road. Down to the right, the **green shack** in the car park is a popular stop for cheap tea, bacon sarnies and sweets.

If you want to **cut the walk short** here, continue along Green Ride as it bears around to the right before the clearing described in the main route. In a few minutes you'll reach a north–south trail; turn left (north) onto this to head round to Fairmead Road (see page 40).

Up and Down Ride to High Beach

1km Cross the road and pick up the trail on its far side, which runs parallel to the busy A104, whose traffic can dent the forest's tranquillity here, especially during the summer. The roar of cars is compensated for though by the dramatic landscape here, as the trail – the aptly named **Up and Down Ride** – begins to rollercoaster through ancient coppiced and pollarded woodland.

A few metres beyond the final rise out of Up and Down Ride you pass the site of a former forest nursery, **Paul's Nursery**, over to your left. The nursery was reincorporated into the forest in 1920, though it's still home to exotic plant life found nowhere else in the forest, including foreign maples – spectacular in autumn – lilies of the valley, azaleas and rhododendrons.

Some 750m beyond Paul's Nursery, the track comes out on the road into **High Beach** village. Before you reach the road, take the track to your left (signed with a scored-through horse and bike) on the near side of Oak Plain Pond, to reach the **Epping Forest Information Centre** (Easter–Oct Mon–Sat 10am–5pm; Nov–Easter Mon–Fri 11am–3pm, Sat & Sun 11am–5pm; 020 8508 0028). The centre has good displays on the forest's history, flora and fauna, and past and present management techniques. Behind the information centre lies the village of **High Beach**, little more than a clutch of houses, a green area and a **pub**.

EATING AND DRINKING

Kings Oak Paul's Nursery Rd IG10 4AE, 020 8508 5000, http://kingsoakhotel.com. The pub itself offers filling bar meals, while the attached kiosk serves takeaway tea, soup (£3) and coffee and great home-made cakes, including slabs of superb bread and butter pudding for £2. Pub daily 11am–11.30pm.

Towards Loughton Camp

1.5km From High Beach, go back the way you came along the trail towards Up and Down Ride; after a few hundred metres, turn left at the first proper fork, signed with a blue arrow. This track takes you in around 400m to the busy **A104**, the main road through the forest.

1

Cross the road to the small car park opposite, then take the main track leading out of it, following the blue arrow southeast into the forest. About 750m further on, this trail joins another heading south. Turn right onto this, passing the wide, grassy avenue of **Clay Ride** a few metres further on to your left.

A hundred metres or so south of Clay Ride, to the right of the trail, take a 200m detour (signed with the blue arrow) to the earthworks of the Iron Age settlement of **Loughton Camp**, a twelve-acre site that is now somewhat obscured by beech trees inside and around it. Dating from around 500 BC, this is one of two earthworks in the forest (the other is Ambresbury Banks, in the northern reaches of the forest): it's thought that these sites were bolt holes for local people and their livestock during periods of tribal warfare, rather than permanently settled places. Eighteenth-century highwayman Dick Turpin is also said to have used the camp as a hideout.

Loughton Brook and Fairmead Road

2km Go back to the main track to resume the walk. Past the camp's southern reaches the trail descends sharply to tiny **Loughton Brook**, then rises steeply again towards the road into nearby Loughton. To the left of the trail you can see the brook twisting and turning as it meanders along the valley floor, carving out a surreal landscape of exposed tree roots and muddy flats.

Cross the Loughton Road and continue along the trail to the left of the man-made **Strawberry Hill Ponds**, created as fishponds in the nineteenth century and still used for fishing today. Follow the track as it leads downhill, past fields and the greenhouses of Loughton nurseries on your left, to reach a trail where you turn to the right, 750m or so from the road. Continue for another 750m to arrive back at the A104.

Cross the road, go through the gate, then take the trail to the right, which leads across heathland, skirting the northern side of the nearest trees before joining the paved **Fairmead Road** (now closed to through traffic) a few hundred metres further on. Where you meet the road, a path leads off into the woods; this is where you'll come out if you took the short cut described earlier (see page 39).

Turn left onto Fairmead Road and head south for just under 1km. Ignore the first turning to the right, and take the second turning soon after it, with a "no horseriding" sign.

On to Connaught Water

3km Continue along the path, which follows the left bank of a tiny stream to **Connaught Water**, 750m beyond the turning, an attractive man-made lake which was created in 1893 by damming tiny Ching Brook and digging out the adjacent marshy area. The lake is very popular with day-trippers, even on the bleakest of winter days, and is also home to a rich variety of **wildfowl**, including the striking multicoloured mandarin ducks that breed here over winter and are easily spotted from early October through to spring.

Follow the circular path around the lake to the opposite side of the water, where a sluice marks the exit point of the tiny brook that feeds Connaught Water. Take the path down to the left to follow the brook for a few metres. Go straight ahead, then cross the gravelled path and head back uphill to *The Larder at Butler's Retreat* (see page 38). From here, retrace your steps back up to the main road, turn right and head downhill, past Queen Elizabeth's Hunting Lodge and Chingford Plain, to reach **Chingford station**.

Walthamstow Marshes

Hackney to Walthamstow

Distance and difficulty 13.75km; easy–moderate
Minimum duration 3hr 15min
Trains and buses Overground train to Hackney Central (zone 2) from stations between Richmond and Stratford, or buses #38, #55, #106, #242 from central London; return Victoria Line from Walthamstow or Overground Walthamstow (zone 2) to Liverpool Street
Maps OS Landranger 177: *East London*; OS Explorer 173: *London North*

Hackney and **Walthamstow** are both vibrant and densely populated boroughs. But if you think these two areas are all grit and no green spaces, you're in for a big surprise. This route cuts a green slice from Hackney Central to the heart of Walthamstow, linking three **waterways** – the Regent's Canal, Hertford Union Canal and River Lee Navigation – and taking you to the site of the Queen Elizabeth Olympic Park and through the sweeping open spaces of the Hackney and Walthamstow **marshes**. The walk is bookended by two hugely contrasting **markets**: genteel "farmers' style" Broadway Market, on Saturdays (see page 43), where you can grab a coffee and put together an excellent picnic for the walk, and the sensory overload that is Walthamstow Market (Tues–Sat), Europe's longest, with a continuous colourful kilometre of stalls piled high with cheap clothes and homeware. Walthamstow village even provides a secluded **pub** for a post-walk pint: the inviting *Nags Head*.

With flat terrain and no stiles, this is a good option for bikes and prams.

Getting started

0.25km From the eastbound platform of Hackney Central, exit the station down the long sloping path. At the bottom of the slope you come out onto Amhurst Road – bear right under the railway bridge to emerge onto wide Mare Street. Go straight down Mare Street, past the **Hackney Empire**, a flamboyant Victorian variety theatre. Cross Wilton Way and the piazza in front of the imposing Art Deco Town Hall. Ahead of you is the library and Hackney Museum. Cross the road in front of the library and head down Hackney Grove, the narrow **cycle and walking route** to the right of the museum.

London Fields and Broadway Market

1km The cycle route leads you alongside the museum for 200m; at the end, cross the road to head down narrow Martello Street, underneath the wide railway bridge. You pass the *Pub On the Park* with its outdoor terrace – carry on down the road for 100m with the metal railings of **London Fields** to your right. The entrance to London Fields is flagged by two metal poles with balls on top – turn into the entrance then bear left, down the long straight cycle route.

The cycle route leads through the park for 250m; at the end, cross the road at the pedestrian crossing and head straight on into **Broadway Market**. For centuries Broadway Market was used by drovers from Epping Forest, who took their cattle along here, via the grazing at London Fields, for slaughter at Smithfield.

SUNDAY LEAGUE FOOTBALL

There are a staggering 82 **football pitches** – as well as facilities for rugby and cricket – on Hackney Marsh. This haven of Sunday league football was once a training ground for the young David Beckham; Bobby Moore and Terry Venables also played here in their youth. Most Sundays, around a hundred games will be played on the Marsh, which makes for a great spectacle.

1

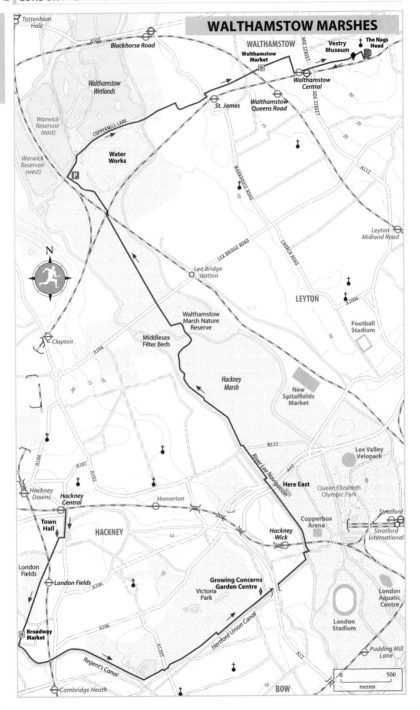

WALTHAMSTOW MARSHES

After 300m you come to the end of Broadway Market – cross the road and go through the metal gate onto the Regent's Canal: turn left and head along the canal towards the giant gas tower.

EATING AND DRINKING

Broadway Market http://broadwaymarket.co.uk. On Saturdays Broadway Market comes to life for the weekly market, a foodie's paradise: try the Sporeboys stall near *Climpson & Sons* for freshly fried mushroom sandwiches. You can also pick up great picnic goods: quality cheeses, quiches and pies, cakes and tarts and fresh fruit. F. Cooke at no. 9 is an atmospheric old pie-and-mash shop. Sat 9am–5pm.

Regent's Canal and Victoria Park

2.5km This section of the **Regent's Canal** has a different feel to that described in the second walk of this chapter (see page 20): it's semi-industrial with red-brick wharf buildings, but on a sunny day, with birds bobbing along, it has a definite charm of its own. Part of a network of London waterways, the canal is an important migratory route for cormorants, coots, moorhens and mallards.

After 400m you pass under a rail bridge and then a bridge labelled Mare Street – bikes often shoot through these bridges at high speed, so take care. Pass the entrance to Victoria Park and keep going along the canal. Underneath another bridge, decorated with a VR and a crown sculpted in stone, you come to a section of the water that's overhung with trees and lined with canal boats.

Just before the canal lock, turn left into **Victoria Park**, bearing right onto the wide pavement that borders the lake. Head towards the domed lakeside *Pavilion Café* and the loos; keep these to your left and exit the path via the grand wrought-iron blue gate. Take a left out of the gates with the roundabout in front of you. A zebra crossing takes you across Grove Road; go through the second set of blue gates, which leads you to the next section of the park.

Turn right, up a wide avenue of plane trees. After 500m you'll see to your right a wrought-iron **pedestrian bridge** over the Hertford Union Canal at Gunmaker's Gate. Don't cross the bridge but go through the ornate gate and head down the brick path to your right. At the bottom, turn left along the canal, passing under the pedestrian footbridge.

The Hertford Union Canal and the River Lee Navigation

2.25km The **Hertford Union Canal** initially runs along the eastern edge of Victoria Park, where it is lined with tall grasses and overhung with weeping willows and tall plane trees. You soon pass a lock and a brick lock-keeper's cottage; at the second lock you come to the prettily landscaped **Growing Concerns Garden Centre**, where they sell ice cream and coffee.

Some 250m beyond the garden centre you go under a wide road bridge, towards another lock. The canal is wider and feels more industrial at this point, without the seclusion of the earlier section. The path dips under a thin metal pedestrian bridge, with a tall glass and wood development on the opposite bank. From here you can see the giant oval of the London stadium on the dramatically revitalised site of the 2012 London Olympics; the area has been reinvented as the spacious Queen Elizabeth Olympic Park, which contains the London Aquatic Centre and other attractions. Just beyond the apartments you bear round to the left and the Hertford Union Canal meets the **River Lee Navigation**. Just 50m beyond this bend, at the metal road bridge, you need to cross to the opposite bank of the canal (staying on the same side of the road) and continue along the canal in the same direction, following the wooden sign to Hackney Marsh. After 400m you come to the huge box-like Here East development, which styles itself an 'innovation and technology campus' and contains an array of cafés and restaurants. Soon after you pass under two adjoining road bridges.

1

Hackney Marsh

2km Just beyond another road bridge, you come to the edge of the **Hackney Marsh**. Instead of following the canal-side path here, take the tarred path, signed with a blue **National Cycle Network** marker. After 50m follow the path through the grass to the right to emerge at the wide spaces of the playing fields (see page 41) on the Hackney Marshes.

Curve around the edge of the playing fields for 500m until you reach a red metal **footbridge**. Cross the footbridge, following the sign towards the Walthamstow Marsh Nature Reserve. On the other side, go straight ahead through the metal gate. Take the tarred path that curves around the **Middlesex Filter Beds** – the path dips under a road bridge and heads uphill. You'll soon see the Lee Valley Riding Centre.

Walthamstow Marsh

2km Coming up the slope from the road bridge, the views open out and you are on the edge of **Walthamstow Marsh**. This, one of the last of London's marshlands, was managed under the system known as **lammas** from Anglo Saxon times to the early twentieth century. The land was enclosed in spring so that grass could grow, and opened for grazing in August on Lammas Day. In an echo of this ancient tradition, cattle are still brought onto the marsh in the summer for grazing.

Go straight ahead, following the long path ahead of you. This is the most open part of the walk, with meadows to the left, a line of pylons ahead and, to the right, horses grazing in their paddocks and a line of low industrial buildings beyond.

Follow the path for 750m, approaching the twin-arched railway bridge. Don't go under the bridge; just before you reach it, bear right onto the concrete path that dips down under a metal bridge. Go under this bridge then head up the path; for this stretch the banks of the path are bordered by elderflower and wild rose bushes.

Around 750m beyond the railway bridge you come to a little car park. Go through it and turn right, following the sign towards Walthamstow.

Towards Walthamstow

3km From here you follow a leafy lane, lined with cow parsley, wild roses, elderflower and willows, towards **Walthamstow**. After 500m you come to the extensive Thames Water treatment works and after another 750m to a pair of metal gates with leaf shapes imprinted in them.

You are now on Coppermill Road, to the left of which is the extensive Walthamstow Wetlands, a newly designated area that's a haven for birds such as overwintering pochard and gadwall, as well as kingfishers and peregrine falcons. Go straight ahead up the road, passing *The Coppermill* pub on your right. After 300m, turn right on to Leucha Road, following the cycle-route sign towards Walthamstow. To either side you'll see the distinctive **Warner Houses**, built by the Warner family at the beginning of the twentieth century to provide quality affordable accommodation. They are in fact purpose-built flats or "half houses", their arched recessed porches sheltering two doors – one leads to the upper flat and one to the ground floor. Other features to look out for are terracotta heads and other ornaments, and the swirly "W" device denoting Warner.

Tranquil Leucha Road leads, after 300m, to a T-junction, where you'll suddenly be greeted by a very urban racket and a line of kebab shops, Turkish bakeries and pizza joints. Turn left here, then almost immediately right up the High Street, the site of **Walthamstow Market** (see page 46).

After 750m, you'll see a wide square to the right – cut through this to get to the **train and bus stations**. The bus station is to the left, the train and tube lie across busy Selborne Road.

1

EATING AND DRINKING

Walthamstow Market High St. Walthamstow Market is proud to advertise itself as Europe's longest, its stalls piled with pound-a-bowl fruit and veg, synthetic lingerie, peacock feathers, lurid kids' toys, cut-price electrical goods, harness-style pitbull collars, Ghanaian fabrics and football memorabilia. Carts sell jellied eels and Jamaican patties, while to either side of the street are pound shops and discount clothes stores. Look out for L. Manze at no. 76, a beautifully tiled pie-and-mash shop that's an intriguing survivor of the old East End. Tues–Fri 8am–5pm, Sat 8am–5.30pm.

Walthamstow Village

0.75km This worthwhile detour allows you to explore the surprisingly verdant **village** heart of Walthamstow, taking you to *The Nags Head* pub. Pass the bus station to your left and head up Selborne Road. At the junction at the top of Selborne Road, go straight ahead at the pedestrian crossing onto St Mary Road. Follow St Mary Road for 250m; at the end of the road head up Church Path, with a row of terraced cottages to the left and the Vestry House Museum to your right.

Continue straight ahead, passing the eighteenth-century Squire's Almshouses and St Mary's Church to your left. To your right is the wattle-and-daub **Ancient House**, a restored fifteenth-century hall house. Cross the road here and turn right onto Orford Road. On the left you'll see *The Nags Head* pub.

EATING AND DRINKING

The Nags Head 9 Orford Rd E17 9LP, 020 8520 9709. This place serves Belgian fruit beers and real ales and has an extensive wine list; head for the pretty terraced garden at the back or curl up on one of the battered sofas inside. There's live jazz on Sundays, and menu choices include tarts, salads and Turkish *lahmacun* (mains from £9). Mon–Thurs 4–11pm, Fri 2–11pm, Sat & Sun noon–11pm.

Retrace your steps towards the bus station: opposite it is the tube station and Overground.

Limehouse Basin

Bethnal Green to Wapping

Distance and difficulty 5.5km; easy
Minimum duration 1hr 20min
Trains Central Line to Bethnal Green (zone 2); return on the Docklands Light Railway from Limehouse (zone 2)
Maps OS Landranger 177: *East London*; OS Explorer 173: *London North*

This straightforward route runs down the **Regent's Canal** to the watery landscape and gleaming developments at **Limehouse Basin**, a once mighty dock that degenerated in the late Victorian period into one of London's most notorious slums. Here the canal joins the Thames, and you can go west on the **Thames Path** to **Wapping** and enjoy a drink at the characterful *Prospect of Whitby* pub, established in the reign of Henry VIII.

For an insight into the social history of the area, it's worth timing your visit to coincide with the limited opening hours of the canalside **Ragged School Museum**, a moving memorial to the charity and energy of Dr Thomas Barnardo.

The route makes for a good Sunday stroll – foodies could punctuate it with **Sunday lunch** at Gordon Ramsay's gastropub *The Narrow*, on the edge of Limehouse Basin. It's also a great option for cyclists, who can continue up the Thames Path to the Tower of London and beyond, unhampered by gates or stiles.

Getting started

0.75km Exiting **Bethnal Green** station, head north up busy Cambridge Heath Road – keeping the Museum of Childhood to your right – and carry on for 750m. Just beyond Vyner Street, to your right, is a bridge over the **Regent's Canal**; cross the bridge and descend the steps on the right to join the towpath. Go left here, heading east along the canal.

Victoria Park to the Ragged School Museum

2.5km Pass the entrance to **Victoria Park** and keep going along the canal. Underneath a bridge, distinguished by a VR and a crown sculpted in stone, you come to a section of the water that's overhung with trees and lined with canal boats, with a picturesque lock keeper's cottage to the left, at Old Ford Lock.

Passing under Roman Road Bridge, you come to the edge of **Mile End Park**. This is one of London's newest parks, in what was once a heavily industrialized area, crammed with wharves, warehouses, shirtmakers and factories, and it features play areas, an eco park and an indoor climbing wall.

Head straight along the towpath, with warehouses to the right and Canary Wharf rearing up ahead of you. At **Mile End Lock** the path dips and goes under Mile End Road Bridge; some 500m further on is the Ragged School Museum, which you can access from the canalside by taking Ben Jonson Road.

The Ragged School Museum

The **Ragged School Museum** (Wed & Thurs 10am–5pm, first Sun of the month 2–5pm; free; http://raggedschoolmuseum.org.uk), housed in Dr Barnardo's second ragged school (the first was in Stepney), is a gem of a place, offering both an insight into enlightened education for the Victorian poor and into the social history of Tower Hamlets, from the matchworkers' rebellion at the Bryant & May factory to the dark days of the Blitz. The first floor has a classroom done out in the colours Barnardo specified, while the top floor is dedicated to domestic life in the East End, with a re-creation of a tiny kitchen.

At the canalside entrance of the museum you'll find a small **café**.

1

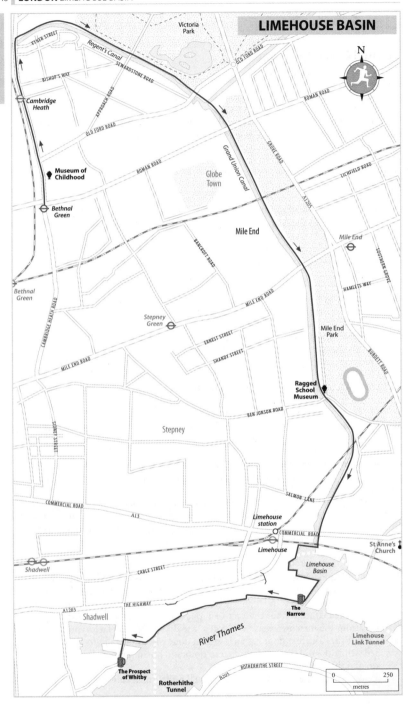

LIMEHOUSE BASIN

N

Victoria Park

VYNER STREET

Regent's Canal

BISHOP'S WAY

SEWARDSTONE ROAD

APPROACH ROAD

OLD FORD ROAD

ROMAN ROAD

Cambridge Heath

OLD FORD ROAD

ROMAN ROAD

Globe Town

Grand Union Canal

GROVE ROAD

LICHFIELD ROAD

A1205

Museum of Childhood

Bethnal Green

Mile End

Mile End

SOUTHERN GROVE

Bethnal Green

CAMBRIDGE HEATH ROAD

BANCROFT ROAD

MILE END ROAD

HAMLETS WAY

Stepney Green

ERNEST STREET

Mile End Park

SHANDY STREET

MILE END ROAD

BURDETT ROAD

Ragged School Museum

SIDNEY STREET

Stepney

BEN JONSON ROAD

COMMERCIAL ROAD

A13

SALMON LANE

Shadwell

CABLE STREET

Limehouse station

COMMERCIAL ROAD

St Anne's Church

Limehouse

A1203

THE HIGHWAY

Shadwell

Limehouse Basin

Limehouse Link Tunnel

The Narrow

River Thames

The Prospect of Whitby

Rotherhithe Tunnel

ROTHERHITHE STREET

B205

0   250
metres

DR BARNARDO

Dr Thomas Barnardo was born in 1845 to an Irish father and a Jewish mother, and came to London from Dublin at the age of 20 to train as a missionary at the Bow headquarters of the China Inland Mission. Profoundly affected by the sight of children begging and sleeping outdoors, he began preaching in the streets and teaching at a ragged school. Increasingly absorbed by this new mission, he gave up his plans for China. In 1876, he converted some nearby warehouses and began schooling the children of the poor people in the local area, alongside helping them gain employment.

What marked Barnardo among other benefactors was that he helped all children, regardless of race or disability. The Ragged School Museum traces the stories of young West Indians who worked on ships and, becoming destitute, were taken under Barnado's wing. He is thought to have saved more than sixty thousand kids, including those whose parents worked at the nearby gasworks, from extreme poverty.

Towards Limehouse Basin

0.75km Back on the towpath beyond the Ragged School, go along the stretch of scrappy parkland with a tall brick chimney at the far end. Head under the railway bridge, onwards up the towpath to **Salmon Lane Lock**, where you go under a little metal bridge and past a lockhouse. Around 300m further on, you emerge at the shimmering marina of **Limehouse Basin**, where the Regent's Canal meets the Thames.

Here you pass under a long brick railway viaduct built in 1840 – the second oldest in the world and now traversed by DLR trains; bear right for Limehouse station.

The Thames Path

1.5km Continuing to the Thames Path, go down the right-hand side of the basin, following the path round the water's edge. Looming over the basin on the opposite side is Hawksmoor's church of **St Anne's**. The highest church clock in London, it was an important landmark for shipping.

Continuing along the path, you pass the freestanding Limehouse Lock office with its octagonal roof. Just beyond, cross the thin metal bridge over the lock, turning right after to come to the **Thames Path**. Turn right again and cross the road bridge over the basin, where you can absorb the magnificent view west along the Thames. At the edge of the basin you'll find *The Narrow* **gastropub.**

EATING AND DRINKING

The Narrow 44 Narrow St E14 8DP, 020 7592 7950. A Gordon Ramsay-owned gastropub with a great riverside setting. The food is fairly pricey but hearty and good, with mains such as steak and chips and Cumberland bangers for £17–22. Mon–Fri 11.30am–11pm, Sat noon–11pm, Sun noon–10pm.

For more of a traditional boozer experience, keep going along the Thames Path towards Prospect Wharf. This stretch of the path initially follows Narrow Street, an atmospheric run of looming converted warehouse buildings. After 250m at the end of the street the Thames Path continues, becoming an actual path. The path joins the river, which is spectacularly wide at this point, with fine views back to Canary Wharf. Another 500m further on, you reach King Edward Memorial Park (dawn–dusk). Carry on through the park, past its little bandstand – at the edge of the park the path detours from the river's edge for a 100m stretch. You pass a playground and some tennis courts, and at the end of the path turn left onto the road, and over a red metal bridge to *The Prospect of Whitby* pub at **Wapping Wall.**

1

THE RISE AND FALL (AND RISE) OF LIMEHOUSE BASIN

The glossy developments of the marina and its rather sanitized air convey little of the fact that **Limehouse Basin** was once a powerhouse of London's economy. The area was named for the fourteenth-century lime kilns that once sat by the river, and it was a significant port from Tudor times. It was in 1820, though, with its inauguration as the Regent's Canal Dock, that Limehouse Basin became truly significant. The basin was a crucial conduit between central London, the River Lee Navigation, the Thames and the world's oceans – it was a busy, vital place where coal from Northumberland and ice and timber from Scandinavia were loaded onto barges and carried up the canal. Much larger than today's marina, the dock was once so busy with ships from all over the world that you could walk right across it, from one vessel to the next.

With crews often discharged at the end of a voyage, it became an area where **immigrants**, including African and Chinese sailors, settled. The Chinese people at Limehouse gained notoriety for supposed vice and the association with the opium trade, though in reality theirs was a generally law-abiding, if closed, community. In fact, the image of the debauched, iniquitous Chinaman owes much to the fiction of the period: Sherlock Holmes visited the fog-swathed streets of Limehouse to gather information on suspects; Sax Rohmer invented master criminal Fu Manchu; and Wilde's Dorian Gray visited the area's opium dens to "buy oblivion".

Eventually, as maritime activity declined and canals were superseded by the railway, the area declined too and became an overcrowded slum. When it was shattered by bombing during World War II, the Chinese community relocated to Soho. In 1969, the basin closed to commercial traffic, to be reborn and redeveloped in its current incarnation in the 1980s.

EATING AND DRINKING

The Prospect of Whitby 57 Wapping Wall E1W 3SH, 020 7481 1095. Built in 1520, this is the oldest riverside inn in London. It's an atmospheric old place, with a higgledy-piggledy dark interior, flagstone floors, a long pewter bar, varnished wood, river views and a small terraced garden. They serve reasonable food: burgers, fish and chips and so on for £12–16. Mon–Wed & Sun noon–11pm, Thurs–Sat noon–midnight.

From here you can retrace your steps to the basin and **Limehouse DLR**. Another option is to carry on along the Thames Path to Tower Bridge (2km). Otherwise, take the D3 bus, which stops just in front of the pub, and runs between Crossharbour and Bethnal Green.

Greenwich Park

1

Blackheath to Canary Wharf

Distance and difficulty 5km; easy
Minimum duration 1hr 15min
Trains Overland Charing Cross to Blackheath (zone 3), Southeastern; return on Jubilee Line from Canary Wharf (zone 2)
Maps OS Landranger 177: *East London*; OS Explorer 161: *London South*

This short urban walk takes you through two of London's most distinctive green spaces – open **Blackheath** and gracious **Greenwich Park**, whose hilltop vantage point takes in one of London's great visual spectacles: the curving Thames and the City framed by the magnificent Old Royal Naval College. From Greenwich town, a **foot tunnel** leads beneath the river and deposits you on the **Isle of Dogs**, where a built-up route along the Thames brings you to glitzy Canary Wharf. There are lots of sights along the way – **Greenwich Market**, the **Royal Observatory**, the **National Maritime Museum**, **Queen's House** and the **Cutty Sark**, so you may want to take a few hours to savour this route in full.

Getting started

0.3km Come out of Blackheath station and turn left onto Tranquil Vale. After 100m take the right-hand fork heading up towards the heath. Bear left on Montpelier Vale towards **All Saints' Church**.

Blackheath

0.6km You are now on **Blackheath**, an open expanse of grass surrounded by tall Georgian and Victorian houses. The grim legend is that the heath was a mass burial ground during the **plague** in the middle of the fourteenth century – hence the name. The heath's other claim to fame is that it was the point where Wat Tyler rallied the **Peasants' Revolt** in June 1381. One of the causes of the rebellion was the political instability that followed the plague, as well as high taxes. Tyler's Kentish rebels entered London via Blackheath, setting fire to buildings, attacking government officials and seizing the Tower of London. The rebellion spread to other parts of England; it was soon extinguished, but carries resonance to this day for left-wing protesters.

Past Victorian All Saints' Church, bear straight ahead and then right on the path, following the sign to Greenwich. You're heading towards the pyramid-topped tower of Canary Wharf. You come out at the Talbot Place sign – follow the path along the line of gas lamps, traversing the heath.

Cross busy Shooters Hill Road at the lights, and head down **Duke Humphrey Road**. You come to Blackheath Gate, which has been an entrance to Greenwich Park since the fifteenth century.

Greenwich

1.6km Once inside **Greenwich Park**, go straight ahead, down wide tree-lined Blackheath Avenue. The red-brick building off to your left is the **Ranger's House** (March–Oct tours only Mon, Tues, Wed & Sun 11am & 2pm; £9.50; EH; 020 8294 2548), a Georgian mansion with a collection of Dutch Old Masters, Renaissance bronzes and portraits by Joshua Reynolds and George Romney.

You come to a roundabout after 400m: to the right is *The Pavilion Café*. And ahead lies a gorgeous panorama with the river curling below – the Dome is to the right, the Gherkin and St Paul's Cathedral to the left, and in the middle sits the magnificently symmetrical Old Royal Naval College, the National Maritime Museum and the high masts of the *Cutty Sark*. Surveying the view of Greenwich is a statue of James Wolfe, a British military leader who defeated the French at Quebec in 1759.

EATING AND DRINKING

The Pavilion Café Charlton Way SE10 8QY, 020 8853 4777. The two-tiered octagonal pavilion houses a small café serving mains such as grilled haloumi burger for £10, plus a big array of generously sliced cakes. Daily 9am–6pm.

To the left of the viewpoint a cluster of buildings comprises the **Royal Greenwich Observatory** (daily 10am–5pm; £14.40; http://rmg.co.uk/royal-observatory), now

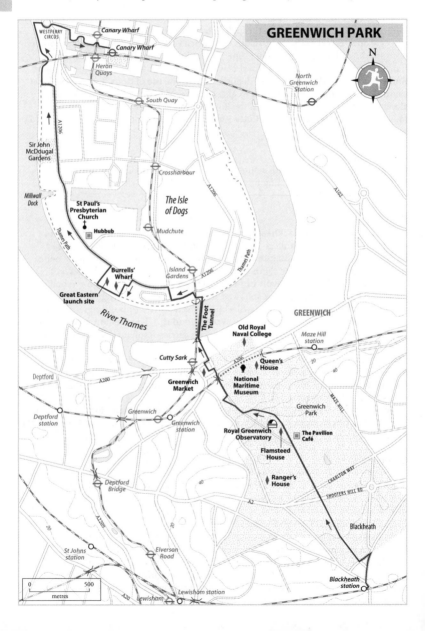

1

a museum. As well as being beautiful, these late seventeenth-century buildings have played a significant part in the history of navigation and the study of the universe; this is the location of the prime meridian, the point at which the world sets its clocks. A noticeable part of the complex is Sir Christopher Wren's **Flamsteed House**, surmounted by a large red ball which drops at 1pm each day, and which was designed to allow navigators on the Thames to check their chronometers. Another treasure within the museum is the collection of John Harrison's **marine clocks**, used to calculate longitude at sea, and there's also a **planetarium**.

From the observatory, take the steps downhill and head to the left-hand corner of the park, towards the masts of the *Cutty Sark*. At the black and gold swirling wrought-iron gates go straight ahead down toward the river – it's worth detouring left on Turnpin Lane into early eighteenth-century **Greenwich Market** (Tues–Sun 10am–5pm; http://greenwichmarketlondon.com) to browse the stalls and shops. Walk down through the market, emerging at a cluster of columns. Turn right then left to get back to the street you were on to reach the *Cutty Sark*. En route you can detour to visit the **Old Royal Naval College** with its spectacular painted hall, the **National Maritime Museum** and the stately seventeenth-century **Queen's House**, designed by Inigo Jones.

The most famous sight of all, though, is the mighty 1869 tea clipper **Cutty Sark** (daily 10am–5pm; £13.50; http://rmg.co.uk/cutty-sark), which has been sitting here in a dry dock since 1954. Swept by fire in 2007, it has since emerged from a huge restoration, and is well worth a visit. A basement gallery allows you to view and even touch the shining copper hull of the ship.

The Foot Tunnel

0.3km The circular red-brick building with a domed roof beyond the ship is the **Foot Tunnel**, opened in 1902. Descend the steps or take the lift to walk through the tunnel, which is lined with ceramic white tiles. Steps and a lift at the other end bring you up to the Isle of Dogs.

The Isle of Dogs

2.2km Contained on three sides by water, the **Isle of Dogs** is home to one of London's two financial centres. In parts characterized by gleaming towers of startling blandness, it also has a down-at-heel side: this, combined with a few last remnants of ancient naval history, makes for a jumbled urban landscape and an intriguing atmosphere.

From the tunnel exit there is a great river view back to Greenwich, taking in the *Trafalgar Tavern* and the park. Turn left from the tunnel onto Ferry Street. At the 1722 *Ferry House* pub – which claims to be the oldest on the Isle – turn left, following the sign for the *Great Eastern* launch site.

Turn right at the river and another dramatic view opens up, with the Shard straight ahead. After 500m you come to **Burrells' Wharf** – once an ironworks (Brunel's *Great Eastern* was built here), it became a paint, varnish and colour factory, before being converted into apartments in the 1980s. Beyond on the right is the launching point of the **SS *Great Eastern***. This is where Isambard Kingdom Brunel attempted to launch his huge ship – the largest of its day – built by 2000 men and boys and with capacity for 10,000 troops. After many failed attempts, the ship set sail, but its working life was relatively short – it served for just sixteen years as an Atlantic passenger liner. The giant rectangular timbers of the launch site are the last remnants of the ship's story, and make for an epic sight in themselves.

Follow the Thames Path sign to the right through a modern estate. This brings you back onto Westferry Road, where you turn left to continue the walk. After 600m you'll see the ornate red-brick **St Paul's Presbyterian Church** on the left, converted into an arts centre called The Space (http://space.org.uk) – the *Hubbub* bar and restaurant upstairs is a nice place to pause the walk.

EATING AND DRINKING

Hubbub 269 Westferry Rd E14 3RS, 020 7515 5577. Upstairs in a converted church under the wooden eaves, this endearingly ramshackle bar and restaurant dishes up steaks, burgers, salads and wraps (£9–12). In summer you can eat on its brick terrace, surrounded by plants. Mon–Wed 11am–11pm, Thurs–Sat Mon 11am–midnight, Sat 10am–midnight, Sun 10am–10.30pm.

Some 200m beyond is the Millwall Slipway; turn left on Arnhem Place to rejoin the Thames Path parallel to Westferry Road, as it passes through riverside public gardens. After another 500m you pass a building called Cascades, one of the area's first such residential developments. Bold if rather ugly, its sail shape and portholes pay homage to the maritime surroundings.

Keep going along the Thames Path towards Canary Wharf. The last of the docks here closed in the 1980s, from which point a government scheme to promote regeneration resulted in a proliferation of glass towers housing international banks, presenting a major challenge to the City as London's financial heartland. More than 100,000 people are employed here, and the space-age architecture and scale is impressive if alienating. You'll find street-food stalls here at weekday lunchtimes, on West India Quay and CrossRail Place.

At Canary Wharf pier, turn right and head up the stairs to **Westferry Circus**, ringed by handy bus stops. Or go straight ahead to reach **Canary Wharf Underground station**.

The Thames path, East

London Bridge to Rotherhithe

Distance and difficulty 3km; easy

Minimum duration 45min

Trains Northern/Jubilee Line to London Bridge (zone 1); return on the Overground from Rotherhithe station (zone 2)

Maps OS Landranger 177: *East London*; OS Explorer 173: *London North*

This short stretch of the **River Thames** takes you on a walk through London's maritime and social history. It is crammed with sights, and for this reason we've kept it short, as you'll probably want to take time out for at least one of the attractions, which include **HMS** *Belfast*, **City Hall**, **Tower Bridge** and the **Brunel Museum**. The walk ends at an ancient **pub**, *The Mayflower*, at the site where the eponymous ship set sail for America in 1620. If you're planning to visit on a Saturday, book in advance for campfire cocktails at the little **outdoor bar** by the Brunel Museum.

The start point is London Bridge station, served by buses, trains and the Underground. And the end point, Rotherhithe, has an Overground station, one stop north of Canada Water which is on the Jubilee Line. There are, of course, plenty of options for **continuing the walk** in either direction – west to the South Bank (1.5km), or east to the parkland and historic buildings of Greenwich (4.5km).

Getting started

200m Come out of London Bridge station, and head onto Borough High Street. To the right you'll see the **Southwark Needle**, a tall pointed sculpture made of Portland stone which marks the point where traitors' heads were impaled at a gate to the city: William Wallace, Wat Tyler, Thomas Cromwell and Guy Fawkes all met this gruesome end here. Turn right at the sculpture towards London Bridge. Just before you get to the bridge, turn right and head down the steps to join the **Thames Path** along the river.

London Bridge to Shad Thames

1.3km You soon pass under the metal pillars of **St Olaf's House**, whose name recalls an eleventh-century church which survived until 1734, built in honour of a Norwegian

---

THE MAYFLOWER

As you're sipping your pint at *The Mayflower* pub, take a look out of the front window to contemplate the embarkation point of the square-rigged ship that took the first Pilgrims on a tough two-month trip to the New World – more specifically Cape Cod – in 1620. These **Pilgrim Fathers** were Puritan Protestants, dissatisfied with the Church of England and its remnants of Roman Catholic practice, and seeking to establish a "purer" church.

One hundred Puritans made the trip, from Rotherhithe to Southampton and from there across the Atlantic. The journey was – in every sense – a rough one. Food was short, the cabins were too cramped to stand up in and the ship was lashed by huge waves. One passenger, Elizabeth Hoskins, gave birth to a son, the wonderfully named Oceanus, on board, and two passengers died en route. On arrival in Cape Cod, half the passengers died in the first winter, which they spent on the ship, wracked by scurvy, tuberculosis and pneumonia. The survivors, assisted by **Captain Christopher Jones**, established a fortress settlement – New Plymouth – in the spring of 1621. In early April, ballasted by stones from New Plymouth, the *Mayflower* set sail for home, with a much-diminished crew. Jones returned but died within a year, his health broken by the voyage. And the battered *Mayflower* came back to her berth in Rotherhithe, hard by the captain's grave in the churchyard of St Mary's.

Despite this rocky start, the departure of the *Mayflower* marked the beginning of a large-scale Puritan emigration, with 21,000 people joining the New England colonies in the 1630s and 40s.

1

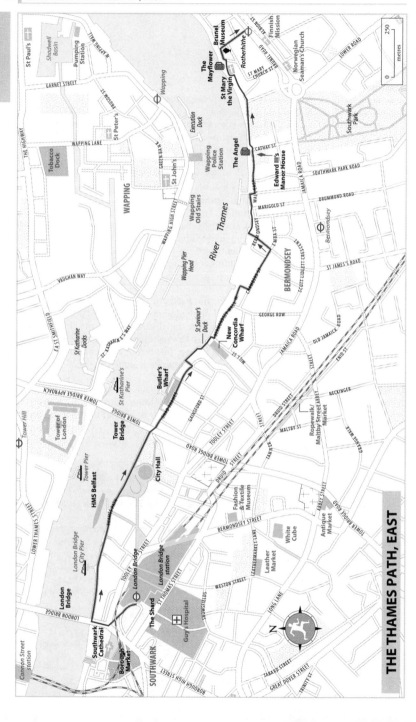

THE THAMES PATH, EAST

king who helped King Ethelred protect London from the Danes in 1014. The current elegant Art Deco building was built for the Hay's Wharf Company and now houses the consulting rooms of London Bridge Private Hospital.

Across the river is a dense jumble of new and ancient buildings: you'll see 20 Fenchurch Street, better known as the **Walkie Talkie building** for its swollen, rounded shape. The next landmark is **HMS** *Belfast* (daily 10am–5pm; £17.10; 020 7940 6300, http://iwm.org.uk), a Royal Navy light cruiser which saw action at the Normandy landings and in the Korean War and gives a vivid sense of twentieth-century life at sea. You come almost immediately to **Hay's Galleria**, an impressive enclosed wharf which was a nineteenth-century docking point for tea clippers from India and China, but which now houses a lacklustre collection of chain shops.

Some 200m beyond and sitting on a wide piazza is **City Hall** (Mon–Thurs 8.30am–6pm & Fri 8.30am–5.30pm), the rounded glassy home of the Mayor of London and the London Assembly; the building hosts regular exhibitions about the city. Across the water sits the Tower of London, a thousand-year-old castle turned prison turned museum, and, ahead, turreted **Tower Bridge** (April–Sept 10am–5.30pm, Oct–March 9.30am–5pm; £9; http://towerbridge.org.uk). This Victorian engineering marvel features twin roadways which open to allow shipping to pass; check the website for bridge-lift times. As well as tours of the engine rooms and structure, a new glass floor allows for dizzy views of the river below.

Beyond Tower Bridge, the path leads through a ceramic tiled arched bridge along a paved and atmospheric backstreet, known as **Shad Thames**. Above you the warehouse buildings are connected by latticed wrought-iron bridges, once used as conduits; for barrows filled with imported goods. Vast quantities of tea, coffee and spices were stored here in the nineteenth century before being transported upriver.

At the end of the street is the former Design Museum, now owned by Zaha Hadid Architects. Turn left to rejoin the Thames Path, where you'll see a monumental **sculpture** by Eduardo Paolozzi; the geometric bronze *Head of Invention* lies on its side, decorated with a quotation about the supremacy of nature by Leonardo da Vinci. Another unmissable spectacle is one of the construction sites of the Thames Tideway, a vast project to build a 25km 'super sewer' under the Thames.

Bermondsey wharves

1km Past the sculpture, fantastic views of the surrounding **Bermondsey wharves** open up – some warehouses are still fronted by painted metal cranes. At New Concordia Wharf you cross a pedestrian bridge over the River Neckinger, an enclosed waterway which rises in Southwark – its weird name is thought to derive from "devil's neckcloth", slang for the hangman's noose, as pirates were hanged here in the seventeenth century. An intricate walkway leads round the wharf buildings; down to the left you'll see some houseboats, often marooned on the mud. Beyond in the distance is the pointed glass tower of Canary Wharf. You come out at two Thames Path signs – take the one closest to the river that goes straight ahead past Reid's Wharf on Bermondsey Wall West. From here, a narrow road takes you through private gardens and converted warehouses. Follow the towpath sign round down the lane and then left on Chambers Street.

The sign for Bevington Street is ahead; 20m before you reach it follow the left-hand Thames Path sign leading you back towards the river. You pass a mock Tudor former pub, faced by a little Georgian house and a modern development. From here you reach a tree-lined stretch of the river, which starts to widen at this point.

An open paved area features a group of bronze statues entitled **Dr Salter's Daydream**, which pay touching homage to a married Quaker couple whose social work in Bermondsey in the first half of the twentieth century made them local heroes. You soon pass the *Angel* pub, rebuilt in 1837 but with a history going back to the 1600s. There's a grassy bank to your right; the path curves around it. At the

1

far side of the bank, head to the left following the National Cycle Network sign. Across the river you'll see King Henry's Wharves, which still feature an impressive crane mechanism.

Rotherhithe

0.5km You come out onto Rotherhithe Street, lined with brick warehouses, where street signs such as "East India Court" and "Bombay Court" are a testament to the area's trading past. The path emerges at the 1716 **Church of St Mary the Virgin**, where a memorial featuring a figure with a staff carrying a child pays tribute to Captain Christopher Jones of Rotherhithe (see page 55). Just beyond the church is an 1821 **Watch House**, established to house constables whose duties included protecting the churchyard from grave robbers. Inside the tiny building, the *Watch House Café* (Wed–Sun 7.30am–3pm,) serves excellent coffee plus pastries and sandwiches, and has some outside seating in the park.

Back on the Thames Path past the church you come to the sixteenth-century *Mayflower* **pub**, which once overlooked the berth of the *Mayflower* ship. Beyond the pub, you go under a metal bridge, covered in wisteria.

EATING AND DRINKING

The Mayflower 117 Rotherhithe St SE16 4NF, 020 7237 4088, http://mayflowerpub.co.uk. The sixteenth-century *Mayflower* is one of London's oldest pubs. There's a slightly kitsch but enjoyable feel to the cluttered decor, and snug wooden booths and latticed windows add to the old-world atmosphere. The pub grub is excellent: mains (from £12) include ale-battered haddock and seasonal sausages. Mon–Sat 11am–11pm, Sun noon–10.30pm.

The Brunel Museum

Past the pub, a tall brick chimney on the right signals the unique and fascinating **Brunel Museum** (Sat & Sun 10am–4pm/5pm; £6; http://thebrunelmuseum.org.uk). Designed by Sir Marc Isambard Brunel (father of the more famous nineteenth-century engineer), the engine house here held steam-powered pumps which extracted water from a tunnel under the Thames, which in itself is the oldest part of the Underground system. To the left of the museum, metal steps lead up to a little garden enclosed by a metal fence. There's a pop-up **outdoor bar** here hung with lanterns – the *Midnight Apothecary* (Sat 5.30–10.30pm; £12; tickets from http://midnightapothecary.designmynight.com) – where you can enjoy campfire cocktails made with home-grown ingredients, as well as a bonfire and toasted marshmallows. In front of the museum and café is a tree – a false acacia – introduced from the US in the seventeenth century and planted widely for shipbuilding, until Brunel began to build in iron.

Turn right onto Railway Avenue to reach **Rotherhithe station**, on the Overground network.

1 Richmond Park

Petersham and the park

Distance and difficulty 10km; easy

Minimum duration 2hr 15min

Trains District Line tube or Overground train from Waterloo to Richmond (zone 4)

Maps OS Landranger 176: *West London*; OS Explorer 161: *London South*

This circular walk explores **Richmond Park**, London's largest green space, with its great herds of deer, sweeping grassland and venerable oak trees. This is no manicured city park, but a real chunk of pristine green within easy reach of the centre of town. While it's hugely popular with dog-walkers, cyclists, horseriders and walkers, its vast 2500-acre extent means that you can get a real sense of open space

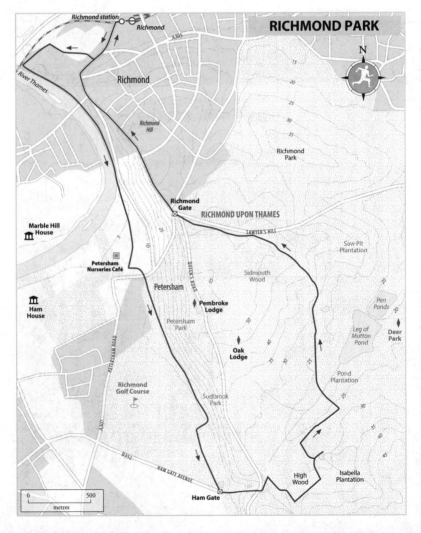

1

RICHMOND'S PARAKEETS

Keep an eye out in this section of the park for the colony of ring-necked **parakeets** that are breeding here with great success – there may be up to a hundred pairs. One urban myth suggests that they escaped from a container at Heathrow, another that they were let loose by Jimi Hendrix, though it's more likely that they are descended from pets who fled the cage and that recent mild winters have allowed their numbers to flourish. The parakeets' startling lime-green feathers, rosy-red beaks and harsh squawk make them pretty easy to pick out.

and solitude; lack of signage adds to the wilderness feel, and the complex tracery of tracks and horse rides can make finding your bearings a bit tricky. This route takes you from Richmond station across **Richmond Green**, a jousting ground in the Tudor period, and along the **Thames** for a stretch. From the riverside you cut across meadows to Petersham, where the *Petersham Nurseries Café* serves up award-winning lunches and cakes in irresistibly pretty surroundings. The route then runs into the park, and loops via the **Isabella Plantation** through grassland and woodland to land you at **Pembroke Lodge**. From here you descend spectacular **Richmond Hill** to return to the station.

May and June are the best months to see the azaleas and rhododendrons of Isabella Plantation, and you may also see baby deer at this time. Alternatively, there's stag-rutting action in the autumn – three hundred red and three hundred and fifty fallow deer roam free in the park.

Getting started

2km From **Richmond station**, turn left onto Richmond's main street, The Quadrant. Follow the road (which subsequently changes its name to George Street) for roughly 400m. Turn right down tiny Brewer's Lane onto Richmond Green and cross the green on the path ahead of you, to the top left-hand corner. At the crenellated villa ahead of you, turn right and head down Old Palace Lane, which curves left and takes you down to the river. At **Richmond Riverside** turn left onto the towpath, passing under picturesque Richmond Bridge. Follow the path for 1km till you reach a porticoed brick building on the left. Go through the metal kissing gate, and turn left, following signs for Petersham.

Petersham

0.5km The tarred path leads across the meadow for 300m, till you reach another metal kissing gate – carry on up the tarred path between the hedgerows. You come out onto a lane with the church ahead of you; turn right to reach **Petersham Nurseries**, home to an award-winning café and the more casual teahouse. On the left after 200m, a gap in the fence leads to the nursery buildings.

EATING AND DRINKING

Petersham Nurseries Café Church Lane TW10 7AB, 020 8605 3627, http://petershamnurseries.com. Tucked among the bedding plants at Petersham Nurseries is a leafy teahouse, which sells cafetières of excellent coffee, loose-leaf teas, salads, quiches, soup and home-made cakes, from Chelsea buns to sticky beetroot cake. The "café" here is actually a justly-celebrated restaurant. Tues–Sat 9am–5pm & Sun 11am–5pm.

Coming out of Petersham Nurseries, turn right to go back towards the lane to the church. Turn right on this lane, and just before you reach the church follow the **Capital Ring** sign to the left, down the narrow path along the graveyard. You come out onto Petersham Road – cross over it and go straight ahead, into the park.

1

Across the park to Ham Gate

1.5km Follow the wide track straight ahead of you, with the playground to your right. Up to the left are the icing-white Georgian buildings at the top of Richmond Hill, while down to your right after 400m, behind a fence, is Sudbrook Park and Richmond Golf Course. Beyond the golf course, the park opens out again, with some fine solitary oaks up to the left, and a swathe of grassland to the right. You emerge onto the road that runs through the park – down to the right is **Ham Gate**.

The park was a **royal hunting ground** from the thirteenth century, but was enclosed by Charles I in 1637 – he raised a 16km brick wall around the purloined land, causing immense controversy. It wasn't until 1758 that public access to the park was secured by local brewer John Lewis, who fought a fierce battle that resulted in his own bankruptcy.

Isabella Plantation

1km Cross the road and turn left after 10m, taking the path that initially runs parallel to the road and then veers to the right, up the hill. Go up the steepish hill for 200m through the bracken, and at the tarred road cross over and turn left, following the road. At the signed road junction for Ham Gate take the path immediately opposite, heading right, away from the road. Just 50m beyond this you reach a wide **horse ride**, where you turn right, heading gently uphill towards High Wood. After 250m, at the edge of the wood, take the narrow path that leads left, along the outer edge of the tree line. The path runs straight ahead for 250m along the trees, until you come to a gate that leads into **Isabella Plantation**.

Go through the gate, taking the path that leads left into the plantation, soon coming to a heather garden. From here you can detour to explore the plantation: enclosed in 1831, it is a showcase for acid-loving plants such as rhododendrons, camellias and azaleas, and is also thick with bluebells in May. Otherwise, bear left at the heather garden, keeping the little stream to your right. You come out at **Peg's Pond**; circle the pond, keeping it to your right, and exit the plantation, via the wrought-iron gate at the eco loo, into the car park.

To Richmond Gate

3km From the car park, take the paved road which curves to the right. Turn right at the road at the blue cycle route signs, and continue for 400m. To the left you come to **Pond Plantation**, a dense cluster of rhododendrons and woodland. Just before you reach this, turn left off the road, up the horse ride. After 100m you cross a little stream; at the junction soon after go straight ahead. Down to your right is expansive Pen Pond. The path makes a gentle climb up the hill – close at hand to the right is little Leg of Mutton Pond, while to the left is the birch and beech woodland of Queen Elizabeth's Plantation. The path leaves the edge of the plantation, and comes to a junction with a much broader dirt track, marked with the **Capital Ring** sign.

The path curves round a fenced **wildlife sanctuary** and runs slightly uphill, with views to the right of London's skyline landmarks, spectacular on a clear day. Follow the path as it meanders towards a bulky red-brick building, the former Star and Garter home.

Richmond Gate to the station

2km The path emerges at **Richmond Gate**. Go straight ahead down **Richmond Hill**, past the former Star and Garter home (built for sailors, soldiers and airmen with disabilities in 1924 but now repurposed as luxury homes) on the left, and a 1720s terrace, with its tall porticoes and wrought-iron verandas, to the right.

Head straight down, past Richmond Hill's shops and cafés, to reach Richmond Bridge. Go straight ahead on **Hill Street**, and follow the curve to the right on its continuation, George Street, to get back to **Richmond station**.

1

The Thames path, West

Richmond to Hampton Court Palace

Distance and difficulty 15–18km; easy–moderate

Minimum duration 3hr 45min–4hr 30min

Trains District Line tube or Overground train from Waterloo to Richmond (zone 4); return by Overground train from Hampton Court or Teddington (both zone 6) to Waterloo

Maps OS Landranger 176: *West London*; OS Explorer 161: *London South*

This riverside walk begins in urbane **Richmond** and then heads upriver along the **Thames Path**, through some of Greater London's most bucolic landscapes. Passing meadows and woodland, you come to two fine country estates: creamy-white **Marble Hill**, on the far bank of the river, and red-brick **Ham House**, on the river's near side. Beyond the house, there's a cross-river detour for a pub lunch and a visit to **Eel Pie Island**. Back on the left bank, you pass through more meadows before reaching **Kingston upon Thames**, where you cross the river to reach the northern boundary of **Hampton Court Park**. There are great views into the park from the towpath, which flanks the eastern boundary of the estate. The walk ends in the attractive village of **Molesey**, at the main entrance to **Hampton Court Palace**.

Getting started

1km From **Richmond station**, turn left onto Richmond's main street, The Quadrant. Follow the road (which subsequently changes its name to George Street) for roughly 400m. Turn right down tiny Brewer's Lane, crammed with small shops, onto Richmond Green. Cross the green on the path ahead of you, to the top left-hand corner. Joining the road at the crenellated villa ahead of you, turn right and go straight ahead down Old Palace Lane, which curves left and takes you down to the river. Turn left onto the towpath to reach **Richmond Riverside**. The riverside was pedestrianized and terraced in the late 1980s, which, along with the Georgian buildings that flank it, makes the whole place feel a bit like a stage set. It's a busy spot, especially on sunny summer days.

To Ham House

2km Head under **Richmond Bridge** – built in 1777, this elegant five-arch span of Purbeck stone is London's oldest extant bridge – and follow the path as it hugs the river bend. Beyond, to the left of the towpath, cows graze placidly in Petersham Meadows.

Peeking through the trees on the far bank of the river, 200m beyond Petersham Meadows, is the splendid facade of **Marble Hill House**, a creamy Italianate confection built in 1729 for **Henrietta Howard**, the Countess of Suffolk, who was George II's mistress and lady-in-waiting to his wife, Queen Caroline. The *ménage à trois* was no secret and the two women were said to have "hated one another very civilly". Howard enjoyed a lavish lifestyle here, entertaining the likes of Alexander Pope and Horace Walpole in the extravagantly gilded reception rooms. These rooms are now ornately furnished with some fine period furniture.

Ham House

On the left just before the Hammerton's Ferry sign you'll see a signed path from the towpath leading to **Ham House** (March–Oct Sat & Sun noon–4pm; gardens same days 11am–5pm; £14.60, garden only £6.50; NT). Built in 1610 for the first Earl of Dysart, the house was greatly expanded and lavishly decorated by Dysart's daughter, Elizabeth, and her second husband, the Earl of Lauderdale. The building works left the family heavily in debt, however, and little was changed over the following three hundred years by the cash-strapped Lauderdales, with the result that the house now survives as an unusually well-preserved period piece. In 1948, the National Trust acquired the house and began restoration, while the **gardens** have also recently been returned to their seventeenth-century glory. Features include a cherry garden, a "Wildernesse" (actually a maze-like area of hornbeam hedges concealing four circular summerhouses), a kitchen garden and an orangery, which now serves as a tearoom (10am–5pm) and makes a good place for **lunch**, but only if you want to see the gardens, as you have to pay the entrance fee.

Detour to The White Swan and Eel Pie Island

1.5km If you fancy a pub lunch at this point, catch **Hammerton's Ferry** across the river (Feb–Oct daily 10am–6pm; Nov–Jan Sat & Sun 10am–6.30pm; £1). The ferry runs from a well-marked spot on the river bank by the path to Ham House, crossing on demand between Marble Hill and Ham House. Turn left and go through the park along the river, where you'll soon come to *The White Swan*.

EATING AND DRINKING

The White Swan 26 Old Palace Lane TW9 1PG, 020 8744 2951, http://whiteswantwickenham.co.uk. A terraced seventeenth-century inn that does a roaring trade in pub lunches on summer days (mains such as Cumberland sausages and vegan chilli from £13). Mon–Fri noon–3pm & 6–9pm, Sat noon–9pm, Sun 11am–10.30pm.

Around 500m south past *The White Swan*, a metal bridge leads to the faintly surreal suburbia of privately owned **Eel Pie Island**. Pies and ale were sold on the island in the sixteenth century (Henry VIII is said to have stopped off once en route between Whitehall and Hampton Court to sample the local fare), though the island didn't acquire its present name until the nineteenth century. It had a reputation for revelry and entertainment into the twentieth century, with steamers bringing day-trippers down the river from London – the Rolling Stones played here in the 1960s. Today, the island is home to a community of artists and inventors, each house having steps or ladders leading to a boat. If you're visiting in June or July you may catch one of the island's open studio events. The surrounding waters are surprisingly clear: look out for the eponymous eels.

Backtrack to the ferry and recross the river to continue the walk.

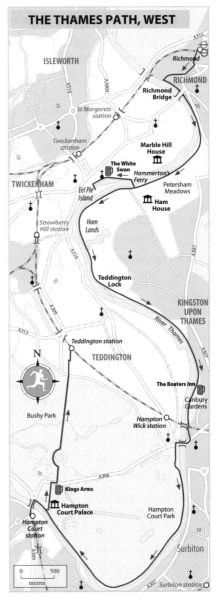

THE THAMES PATH, WEST

1

The Ham Lands
2.5km Beyond Eel Pie Island, the river meanders on, past gently sloping banks where small shingle beaches make ideal sites for a **picnic**. Inland, meadows stretch off to the horizon. There's a sense that the city hasn't yet encroached here, even though you're just a few hundred metres away from the northern reaches of Kingston upon Thames, while the suburbs of Twickenham and Teddington lie on the opposite bank, obscured by mixed woodland and weeping willows.

Surprisingly, this apparently rural landscape is very much a product of its urban surroundings. Prior to World War II, the **Ham Lands** – the stretch of meadow flanking the Richmond side of the river between Ham House and Teddington Lock – was an ugly, industrial landscape, scarred with gravel pits. Land reclamation began here in the late 1940s, using rubble from bomb-damaged sites in central London to fill in the gravel pits. The made-up ground has been carefully managed ever since: looking at it today, it's hard to imagine that there was ever anything here but unspoilt countryside.

Teddington Lock to Kingston Bridge
3km Roughly 2.5km beyond Ham House you come to **Teddington Lock**, the collective name for the series of locks and weirs that mark the end of the tidal river. Some 1km beyond this, you join a paved road which heads past attractive Edwardian houses and, eventually, into the centre of Kingston. Stay alongside the river, following the cycle route through **Canbury Gardens**, where the terraced garden at the riverside *Boaters Inn* is a nice stop for a drink. From the inn, an avenue of plane trees brings you to the far edge of Canbury Gardens. Coming out of the gardens onto the road, go straight ahead past the white clapboard building and take the raised path past the back of John Lewis. Go through the tunnel under the **Kingston Bridge** and then take an immediate left turn up the slope and then left again at the top and onto the bridge.

Hampton Court Park and Palace
4.5km Head over Kingston Bridge and, before reaching the roundabout, turn left to follow signs for the Thames Cycle Route. You're now at the northeastern tip of **Hampton Court Park**, though there's little to see for a while apart from the suburban sprawl on the opposite bank. This corner of the grounds is given over to a golf course, but the deer, which roam freely here as elsewhere in the park, appear unperturbed by the flying golf balls. Across the river, boathouses nestle by the suburban apartments and villas of Surbiton.

The vista opens up with the final bend of the river on the approach to Hampton Court: the palace lies just ahead, with the village green at **Molesey** on the opposite bank. In summer this is a quintessentially English scene, with cricketers playing on the green, people picnicking by the river, and pleasure boats trawling the Thames.

Hampton Court Palace (daily: April–Oct 10am–6pm; Nov–March 10am–4.30pm; £21.30) was built for Cardinal Wolsey in 1516 and purloined by Henry VIII thirteen years later. Oliver Cromwell moved in during the Commonwealth (he died here in 1658), and some of the most ambitious building work was carried out in the late seventeenth century, during the reign of William and Mary, who hired Sir Christopher Wren to remodel the palace. Wren had planned to demolish the Tudor structure and rebuild it in the style of Versailles, though his ambitious plans were brought to a halt by the death of Mary in 1694. The Classical additions that he was able to make to the palace, including the king and queen's own apartments, form a contrast with the original red-brick structure. The palace was opened to the public by Queen Victoria in 1838.

Entrance to part of the grounds is free, but to see the Royal Apartments you'll need a ticket – expensive, but well worth it. You can stroll around at your own pace, or take

1

one of the excellent guided **tours** (price included in entry fee), although these only cover Henry VIII's State Rooms and the King's (William III's) Apartments. It's also worth having a look at the **Tudor Kitchens** and **Wine Cellar**: the workaday underbelly of the palace, these offer a stark contrast to the opulent interiors upstairs. Henry VIII had the kitchens quadrupled to their current size, and they are kitted out as they would have been to cater for the massive banquets for which he was famous.

The palace's **grounds** cover almost seven hundred acres, but the main attraction, the famous **maze** (covered by the ticket to the palace; otherwise £4.40), lies close to the palace itself near the Lion Gate to the north of the complex. The maze is quite tricky – leave yourself plenty of time for getting lost if you plan on giving it a go.

Hampton Court Palace has a café and a restaurant, though both are a bit pricey and overcrowded, and there are plenty of great spots for picnics in the grounds. If you want a drink, go for the *Kings Arms* on Hampton Court Road, by the Lion Gate.

Bushy Park

2km From the palace, you can either catch a train back from **Hampton Court station** (just across the river by Hampton Court Bridge) or head through **Bushy Park**. For the park route, cross the front of the palace and go straight ahead through the grounds. The entrance to Bushy Park is just beyond the *Kings Arms*, opposite the Lion Gate. Bushy Park was Hampton Court's royal hunting park, and today is still home to abundant red and fallow deer, though with more than a thousand acres to lose themselves in, you may see surprisingly few. The route to Teddington takes you along **Chestnut Avenue**, designed by Sir Christopher Wren and lined with 300-year-old horse chestnuts. Exiting on the far side of the park, head straight ahead down Avenue Gardens. At the T-junction at the end of Avenue Gardens bear right then take the first left down Victoria Road; **Teddington station** is in front of you.

The North Downs

NORTH DOWNS WAY SIGN

2

The North Downs

The chalk escarpment of the North Downs stretches from Surrey to the cliffs between Dover and Folkestone. At their western extent, the wooded downs provide dense greenery in an otherwise overdeveloped corner of the southeast, while to the east they are characterized by orchards and farmland, and by almost untouched, prototypically English villages. The first walk in this section takes you from London's fringes through deep countryside to Darwin's House at Downe. The steep escarpment of Box Hill provides unexpected drama, while the walk to the secluded village of Compton takes in the Watts Gallery and Chapel. The shortest route, Gomshall and the North Downs, links a couple of medieval Surrey villages and provides a leg-stretching climb. The final walk, the two-day Pilgrims' Way, ascends the North Downs, leading from Charing to Canterbury. You can easily treat this as two separate one-day trips, although spending a weekend walking does give a satisfying sense of the original pilgrimage.

Downe and around

Chelsfield to Down House via Cuckoo Wood

Distance and difficulty 14.75km; moderate
Minimum duration 3hr 40min
Trains London Charing Cross via Cannon Street and London Bridge to Chelsfield (hourly; 35min); return from Chelsfield to London Charing Cross (hourly; 35min); Southeastern Railway
Maps OS Landranger 177: *East London*; OS Explorer 147: *Sevenoaks and Tonbridge*

This walk covers the territory where the London suburbs end and, magically, the Kent countryside begins. From Chelsfield, the route runs up to **Cuckoo Wood**, which contains some ancient woodland as well as orchids, bluebells, violets and primroses. Emerging from the wood, you come to a country lane that leads to **Downe**, Charles Darwin's home for forty years. There's an excellent **pub** in the village, *George & Dragon*, which does great food, or you can eat at the tearoom in **Darwin's house** itself. The house is a wonderful tribute to the great naturalist, and shouldn't be missed.

From here, the route follows an intricate network of tiny paths that cuts through fields and woodland to the venerable church at **Cudham**. From Cudham you begin to circle back towards Cuckoo Wood, with London's tower blocks shimmering on the horizon.

Getting started

1.5km Exiting Chelsfield **station** on the platform 2 side, walk up the long sloping path to the road. Turn left down the hill. Where the road forks, go left down Windsor Drive and carry on up the wide suburban street. From Woodlands Road onwards, the road heads downhill, with a curve of countryside ahead of you.

Passing Woodland Road on the left, cross Glentrammon Road and carry on, straight downhill on Vine Road. At the end of Vine Road turn right down the hill, then turn left at the red-brick Baptist church. Around 200m further on there's a roundabout – go anticlockwise here, passing the *Rose & Crown*. Take a right off the roundabout down Cudham Lane North. After just 10m the road forks at a red postbox – turn right up

Old Hill. After 20m turn left, follow the battered public footpath sign that leads round the back of no. 17 **Old Hill**, and up the slope. The path leads through a wooden kissing gate by a pylon, and out into open countryside.

Cuckoo Wood

2km The path runs across the field along the telegraph poles for 400m towards **Cuckoo Wood** and then into the wood and gently uphill through a corridor of greenery; you're now in High Elms Country Park.

Go straight ahead past a crossroads with a bench and after 250m you reach a fork in the path. Go straight ahead down Beech Walk. At a second fork a bit further on, bear right and follow the woodland path on the edge of the golf course. After another 250m you come to another crossroads, with the golf course immediately on the right, a bridleway leading downhill to the left signed Green Street Green Circular Walk (which you'll come back up on the return trip) and one straight ahead also marked **Green Street Green Circular Walk** – follow this one, still edging the golf course. This eventually leads downhill to a small car park with some information panels.

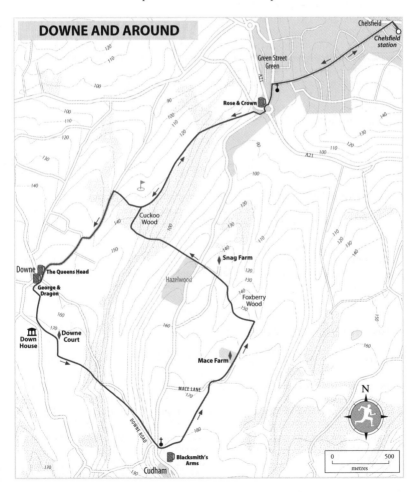

2

Leave the car park and turn left onto the narrow country road heading towards Downe. Watch out for traffic and use the parallel path to the road where available. You'll come to a brown sign pointing left for Down House; follow it on the signed bridleway that parallels the road to the right-hand side.

Downe

1.75km After 1km you come to characterful **Downe** village, composed of a scattering of pretty cottages and grander houses, a thirteenth-century church where Emma Darwin (Charles's wife) is buried, and a couple of pubs. Just past the primary school on the right a narrow passageway leads down to the back of the *Queens Head*, a real-ale **pub** that was apparently frequented by the great man. For pub food, *George & Dragon* is a better bet, though.

EATING AND DRINKING

George & Dragon 26 High St, Downe BR6 7UT, 01689 889 030, http://georgeanddragondowne.com. Serves Sunday roasts, big pies and chicken curry from a recipe by Emma Darwin. The interior is cosy, with a low-beamed roof and bunches of dried hops running round the tiled bar, and there's a beer garden out back. Mon–Sat noon–11pm, Sun noon–10.30pm.

To continue, head on into the village, past the church. Beyond the church, turn left towards **Down House**, passing some brick and flint cottages and a Baptist church. After 150m, take the **public footpath** to Cudham, which leads down to the left. The path runs up the edge of a field, through a hedge into another field where you should turn right (signs to Down House point the way). Go through the metal kissing gate and over the road to reach Down House, which is very well worth a visit, not least for the large cakes in the **tearoom**.

Down House

At last gleams of light have come and I am almost convinced that species are not (it is like confessing murder) immutable.

So wrote **Charles Darwin** to Sir Joseph Hooker in 1844, from his rural sanctuary in Downe. Darwin, his wife (and first cousin) Emma and their children lived here from 1842 until his death in 1882, and it was in this Kent retreat that he crystallized the research and learning from his extraordinary five-year journey on HMS *Beagle* into *On the Origin of Species*, published in 1859.

Down House (April–Sept daily 10am–6pm; Oct & Nov daily 10am–5pm; Dec–March Sat & Sun 10am–4pm; £12.70) was a haven for the invalid Darwin, who avoided a more public life for a studious and family-orientated existence, supported and protected by Emma. At the large former farmhouse where they made their home, he alternated his studies of barnacles, earthworms, orchids and bees with walks, copious letter-writing, village activities and a daily hour dedicated to smoking.

The ground floor of the house is much as it was in Darwin's time, while the first floor features an interactive **exhibition** on his life and work. In the garden there's a wormstone (designed by Darwin to show the movement of soil displaced by the action of worms) and a **greenhouse** containing orchids and insectivorous plants. Darwin's studies of less exotic plant and animal life in the surrounding fields

ON THE ORIGIN OF SPECIES

Charles Darwin's theory of **natural selection** took twenty meticulous years to develop, the same theory flashing upon the naturalist Alfred Russel Wallace in 1858 when he lay in a fever – Wallace developed the theory in two hours, and wrote it up over the course of three evenings. Wallace sent his ideas to Darwin, who was then propelled to publish his own work, though the two men translated their rivalry into friendly support.

were essential to his work – as well as making close observations of grasses and soils, he set his children the task of monitoring the flight path of bumble bees, and studied the seed content of bird droppings, using this as evidence of dispersal in *On the Origin of Species*. It's well worth taking the **audio tours** of the house and garden (included in the price), voiced by David Attenborough and Andrew Marr respectively.

Down House to Cudham

2km From Darwin's house, cross the road and go through the gate back onto the footpath, but turn right instead of coming back the way you came. The path takes you round the buildings of Downe Court – for the moment you're on the **Circular Leaves Green** route, which you follow as it zigzags round the farm buildings and fields.

You come to a **crossroads** of public footpaths on the edge of the field – go left here down the edge of another field. Follow the path right, steeply downhill through the woodland for 250m. The path descends some wooden steps to come out at a narrow country road; turn right to join the lane for just 50m, and then turn right again over the stile, following the sign towards Cudham on the permissive footpath. This section of path cuts across a field to come out at a path alongside a lane; the path runs steeply uphill for 500m to Cudham.

The path emerges onto a road – just keep heading uphill into the village. You soon come to **Cudham**'s eleventh-century flint **church**; take the footpath that leads through the churchyard to the right of the church. You walk past some gigantic yew trees, thought to be a thousand years old. Turn left here beyond the church to continue the walk, or, if you want a **pub** stop, turn right along the playing field to get to the main part of the village. Turning right at the lane at the end of this path brings you to Cudham's *Blacksmith's Arms*, a nondescript but friendly village inn.

Cudham to Cuckoo Wood

3.5km Continuing the walk **from the churchyard**, head left along the playing field and go through the black kissing gate. Cross the lane and go up the public footpath, following the **Cudham Circular Walk** signs. You're now walking across open countryside – the views open out and suddenly you can see London to the north beyond the trees, with Canary Wharf glittering like the Emerald City in *The Wizard of Oz*.

The path cuts through a thin strip of woodland, then joins a narrow lane where you need to turn right. You pass Mace Farm and carry on up the lane; beyond **Mace Farm**, the tarmac peters out and you're on a path, which you follow for 500m downhill into Foxberry Wood.

Some 150m further on, follow the **public bridleway** sign with the yellow arrow that leads left out of the wood and uphill across a field. The path winds between tall hedgerows and light woodland until eventually you come out at a country lane. Go straight ahead here for 200m. At the T-junction cross over the road and take the permissive path that leads down the edge of the field parallel to the road. After 150m, turn left up through the fields, following the sign towards High Elms.

Back to Chelsfield

4km The path goes alongside a field and climbs uphill back into **Cuckoo Wood**, dipping and then running diagonally up through the wood. At the top you cross a path with "no cycling" signs to either side – carry on straight ahead, past a line of tall beech trees. Another 250m further on, you come to the edge of the golf course at the crossroads you encountered earlier in the walk. Turn right to head along the edge of the woodland, the way you came earlier. Just retrace your steps through the wood and at the edge of the woodland head back down the field to rejoin **Old Hill**.

At the roundabout at the bottom of Old Hill, go back the way you came, following the road to Orpington. At the Baptist church, turn right onto World's End Lane. Go up Vine Street and carry on straight ahead to reach the **station**.

Box Hill

Westhumble to Mickleham Downs and Box Hill

Distance and difficulty 8.5km; strenuous

Minimum duration 2hr 30min

Trains London Victoria to Box Hill & Westhumble (hourly; 50min); return from Box Hill & Westhumble to London Victoria (hourly; 50min); Southern Railway

Maps OS Landranger 187: *Dorking & Reigate*; OS Explorer 145: *Guildford & Farnham*

Box Hill has long been one of the famous beauty spots of the south, its popularity soaring with the arrival of the railway here in 1867; Box Hill & Westhumble is a lovely little station, built in gingerbread/Gothic style. The steep folds of the chalk hills are unusually spectacular for southeast England, Box Hill itself soaring to 193m. The area supports varied woodland – oak, beech, ash and yew – as well as the celebrated evergreen **box trees**: more familiar cut into novelty shapes in gardens, they grow wild here. The walk leads across a valley to the village of **Mickleham**, which enjoys a lovely leafy situation in the lee of the downs. You ascend, via an excellent **pub** that makes a good lunch or pint stop (though it gets very busy at weekends), into the woodland of **Mickleham Downs**. From here, the path plunges down to valley level, then up onto Box Hill, where the National Trust servery at the summit, housed in a nineteenth-century **fort**, dishes out tea and cakes.

There are some ear-popping altitudes on this walk, so, though the distances are short, it is strenuous in parts.

Getting started

1.5km Exit the station from platform 2 of **Box Hill & Westhumble station**. Turn left out of the station, cross over the brick railway bridge and, opposite the "Chapel Lane" sign, take the public footpath that leads alongside the **railway**. The path

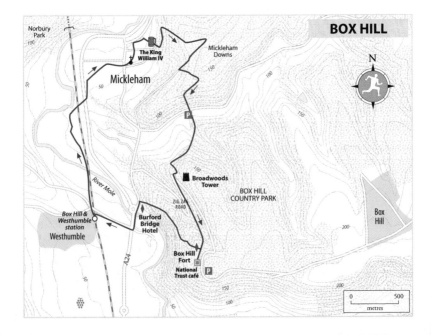

BOX HILL IN LITERATURE

Emma had never been to Box Hill… she wished to see what everybody found so much worth seeing.

Emma, Jane Austen

In the event, the eponymous heroine of **Jane Austen**'s novel has a dispiriting time on Box Hill – the trip is marred by ennui and bad temper. Emma is rude to Miss Bates and the outing ends, quite literally, in tears. Austen may have been inspired to set the scene here by her admiration for the novelist **Fanny Burney**, who lived nearby and was married in Mickleham church.

The novelist and poet **George Meredith** lived near the zigzag road and reflected the sublime element of the landscape, writing, "anything grander than the days and nights in my porch you will not find away from the Alps: for the dark line of my hill runs up to the stars, the valley below is a soundless gulf". The great poet of the sublime, **John Keats**, stayed at the *Burford Bridge Hotel* (then the *Fox & Hounds*), and climbed Box Hill in the moonlight; he completed his epic poem *Endymion* here: "I like this place very much. There is Hill and Dale and a little River. I went up Box Hill this Evening after the moon… came down and wrote some lines."

While both these poets stress the solitary pleasures of Box Hill, **Daniel Defoe** in *A Tour through the Whole Island of Great Britain* (1724–26) writes of crowds and chaos – the clamorous scene he describes might strike a chord with today's summer visitors:

"…every Sunday, during the summer season, there used to be a rendezvous of coaches and horsemen, with abundance of gentlemen and ladies from Epsome to take the air, and walk in the boxwoods; and in a word, divert, or debauch, or perhaps both, as they thought fit, and the game increased so much, that it began almost on a sudden, to make a great noise in the county."

emerges into a field. At the arched brick railway bridge, take the path across the metal pedestrian bridge alongside.

Some 30m beyond the railway bridge, you'll see a path heading underneath the railway but ignore this and carry on through the fields. Ahead you'll see the creamy facade of Georgian manor house Norbury Park on the hill – from 1938 to 1958 it was home to Marie Stopes, founder of the first ever birth-control clinic. You come to some farm buildings after around 400m – facing the corrugated iron barn, bear right up the paved road. This eventually leads under a railway bridge. Emerging at the Swanworth Lane sign, cross the busy **A24** and turn right up the wide tarred path for 100m. Turn left onto the **public footpath** to Mickleham, signed with a yellow arrow.

To Mickleham

1.5km The path leads along the edge of a field – ahead you'll see the stumpy spire of **Mickleham**'s church. Where the path emerges, turn right at the four-way public footpath sign, heading uphill past Box Hill School. You come out at the clapboard-and-brick *Running Horses* pub; cross over to the squat flint and stone **church**, restored in the nineteenth century, though you can still see a Norman arch which divides the nave and chancel. Facing the main door is the grave of Richard Bedford Bennett, an Anglophile Canadian prime minister who died in Mickleham in 1947. There are two very worn ancient tombstones in the porch.

Resuming the walk, go up the path through the **cemetery**, to the left of the church as you face it. The path bears left between a wooden fence and a hedge, then leads along a paddock and onto a narrow paved lane. Cross the lane and go straight ahead up the path towards a clapboard cottage. Facing the cottage, take a right onto the path up the hill – there's a Box Hill Hike sign here. Just after the substantial shuttered villa to your right you come to a gravel track; bear left here, past the Church of England school. You emerge at a lane, with the dual carriageway down to the left – turn right to reach the tile-hung *King William IV* **pub**.

EATING AND DRINKING

The King William IV Byttom Hill, Mickleham RH5 6EL, 01372 372 590, http://thekingwilliamiv.com. An appealing country-cottage, style pub, built in 1790, with an open fire, a bright cosy interior and a sheltered terrace. The hearty grub on offer includes soup, steaks, pies, ploughman's and veggie specials (£6–15), and there are Surrey Hills ales on handpump. Mon–Sat 11am–11pm, Sun noon–10.30pm.

Mickleham Downs

2km Take the steep steps that lead alongside the pub and beyond, taking you up onto **Mickleham Downs**. The path soon emerges at a crossroads by an old flint wall; go up the bridleway ahead of you, the narrow path climbing up through the trees. (As you ascend the hill, look back for the sweeping views of the North Downs to the west.) Follow the Box Hill Hike sign along the secluded, gently winding path through beech woodland.

Where the path forks, bear left, ignoring the Box Hill Hike sign. You'll soon see a post with a blue bridleway sign. Around 50m beyond, you come to a wooden post signed Downs Road. There's a blue arrow pointing you straight ahead, but turn right here, up the track through the woodland; ignore the metal gate to the left, and carry on straight ahead. The track soon begins to lead gently downhill. You're on the **Thamesdown Link**, signed with a yellow arrow on a post.

You come out at a crossroads with the **Box Hill Hike** sign. Turn left, up the hill. After 300m the path, enclosed by dark yew trees, curves round to the right. Where the path levels out, look for an unsigned turning to the right, heading downhill. The path begins an initially gentle descent of the hill, passing a bench to the right in a clearing, before veering left for a precipitously steep descent via wooden steps to the car park. The path comes out on the road, opposite Whitehill car park. Go straight ahead, up Whitehill.

Box Hill

2.5km Go up the track for 300m, then take the right-hand turning onto the **public footpath**. It's opposite a stile with a sign about the beautiful cows that graze these hills: they are hardy and shaggy Belted Galloway steers. The path climbs steeply uphill, through woodland. After 80m you go through a wooden gate. After another 350m take the path to the left that leads up the hill and, another 250m beyond, you come to a T-junction – turn right and carry on up the hill. Eventually you come to a round flint folly, **Broadwoods Tower**.

Go straight ahead past the tower, on the narrow path through the undergrowth. The path soon begins to lead downhill and curves left to join a hairpin bend on the tarred **zigzag road**. Take the right-hand route, downhill for 500m – to your left is a steep bank dotted with box trees, to the right is the sharp incline of **Box Hill**. At the next hairpin bend, you need to climb up the escarpment via the long run of wooden steps. You come out at a flint track where you should turn left to reach the summit and visitor centre. After 600m you come out at the long low walls of Box Hill **fort**, built in 1899 for protection from French invasion. Storage chambers under the fort are now home to a protected colony of bats.

The cream-coloured low brick buildings to the left of the fort contain the National Trust café and shop, and **servery** (11am–6pm), where you can get tea and coffee, home-made cakes, bacon rolls and ice cream. After refreshments, you need to **descend Box Hill** – instead of returning on the flint track, go back to the fort,

keeping it to your right. At the far end of the fort buildings, take a left on a slightly tangled path that leads through undergrowth for a short stretch. You then join a wide clay path that runs along the high ridge for 500m, with wonderfully sweeping views to either side.

Back to the station

1km The path begins its slow descent of the hill. Ahead you'll see a couple of routes that lead straight ahead on the highest part of the hill, running down to solitary box trees. Take the path that veers left, heading down towards a **roundabout**. The path runs down the escarpment, dips into woodland and then takes you onto the road. Turn left, past what is now the sadly bland *Burford Bridge Hotel* – it is said to be the place where Nelson met with Lady Hamilton, and where he spent his last night in England before the Battle of Trafalgar. Wordsworth, Robert Louis Stevenson and Keats (see page 75) also stayed here.

Beyond the roundabout, head along the path next to the busy A24, then after 100m follow the **cycle route** signs to the station via the subway. This takes you onto Westhumble Street, which leads, after 450m, to the **station**.

Guildford and the North Downs

Guildford to Compton and back

Distance and difficulty 9.75km; moderate

Minimum duration 2hr 20min

Trains London Waterloo to Guildford (every 15min; 35min); return from Guildford to London Waterloo (every 15min; 35min); South Western Railway

Maps OS Landranger 186: *Aldershot & Guildford*; OS Explorer 145: *Guildford & Farnham*

This circular route takes you from the leafy fringes of the handsome county town of **Guildford**, through gentle North Downs countryside to the village of **Compton**. Here you can see the Arts and Crafts Watts Gallery, dedicated to the work of G.F. Watts; it's a wonderful showcase for his paintings and sculpture, and has the advantage an appealing **tearoom**, housed in what was the building's pottery. This tiny village is also home to the **Watts Chapel**, its interior designed by Watts' wife Mary in a unique fusion of the homespun and the visionary. From Compton, the route loops through Loseley Park and the hamlet of **Littleton**, back to the edge of Guildford.

Getting started

1.75km Coming out of the station at **Guildford**, follow the exit sign reading "Royal Surrey County". Turn left on the road and walk for 100m to reach the roundabout – cross straight over and follow the path that leads up the hill, passing terraces of red-brick Victorian houses. When you come out onto Mareschal Road, cross over and carry

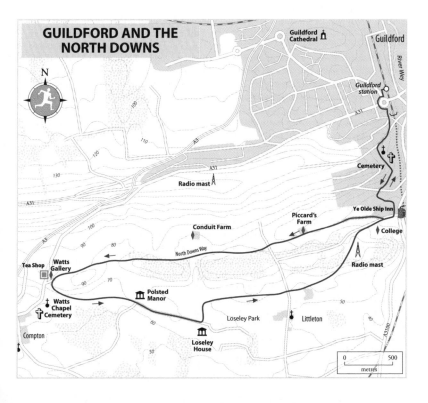

GUILDFORD AND THE NORTH DOWNS

2

ENGLAND'S MICHELANGELO

The reputation of **George Frederic Watts** (1817–1904) is beginning to recover after a long decline; in his time he enjoyed dazzling success, fêted by critics as "**England's Michelangelo**". While this may seem hyperbolic, Watts' portraits, particularly of celebrated women such as Ellen Terry (to whom he was briefly and disastrously married), his patron Lady Mary Augusta Holland and society beauty Lillie Langtry, are both glamorous and sympathetic. His enormous output in oils and later sculpture immortalized his Victorian contemporaries and friends – among whom were Ruskin, Tennyson and Julia Margaret Cameron – but he was also known for more allegorical works and for mystical landscapes.

Born in London in fairly humble circumstances, and a self-taught painter, Watts was politically a radical, though his connections with upper-class patrons gave him crucial access to an intellectual and aristocratic milieu. He married Mary (who was 36 years his junior) in 1886, and in 1890 they moved out of London because of his poor health, settling on Compton in order to be close to friends. They built a mock-Tudor home, Limnerslease, and a few years later work began on the building that was to become the Watts Gallery. It was purpose-built as a gallery, but also housed Mary's pottery students.

Watts' Hall of Fame portraits, begun in the 1850s, include Carlyle, Browning and Rossetti; he left the collection to the National Portrait Gallery in 1895. With the village chapel that he and Mary built (see page 81), Watts Gallery forms an eloquent and intriguing testimony to his ideals.

on up the path straight ahead of you – it leads to a flight of steps; descend these and turn right and carry on up the hill.

After 500m you pass a chapel on the left concealed by a high flint wall; at the end of the wall turn left, following the public footpath that cuts through the **cemetery**. In the upper part of the cemetery (you'll need to make a slight detour to reach it), Lewis Carroll is buried. The author of *Alice in Wonderland* bought a house in Guildford for his six unmarried sisters, and lived here in 1898, at the end of his life.

The path through the cemetery ends at an octagonal tower. From here, follow the gentle curves of the road that takes you downhill, past suburban villas and their well-established gardens.

Another 600m down this road, cross over the wide road ahead and turn right then immediately left down Chestnut Avenue. Initially gravelled, it becomes paved and curves left, past St Catherine's Village Hall, bringing you to a wide busy road. Turn right here before taking the first right onto Sandy Lane, opposite *Ye Olde Ship Inn*. Keep your eyes peeled for the narrow path to the right, 350m further on, signed "North Downs Way".

The North Downs Way

3km Turn onto the **North Downs Way**, which leads straight ahead for an easy 3km to Compton, along tracks and farm lanes and through woodland and pastures. Along the way are a couple of large farms – Piccard's Farm, which you come to after 600m, and, 1km beyond this, Conduit Farm (unsigned). The route is clearly waymarked with yellow arrows.

Some 400m beyond **Piccard's Farm**, the route veers left for just 20m, and then right, through a metal gate and up a sandy track. You'll see the red roofs of Conduit Farm along a track on your right, but take the left-hand fork. From here onwards, although the path is beautifully secluded, leading through beech woodland, your ears will begin to pick up the thunderous roar of the A3, which passes by Compton.

Another 750m after Conduit Farm the path slopes down to a crossroads, cutting over a public bridleway. Carry on straight ahead. From this point the little sandy track slopes downwards between two banks to emerge at some farm buildings. Carry on straight ahead along the track – this section of the walk leads between dense hedgerows towards **Compton**. Through a picket fence on the right, you'll soon see the long low outlines of the Watts Gallery.

Watts Gallery and Chapel, Compton

A driveway sweeps up from the end of the path to the low grey Arts and Crafts building that houses the **Watts Gallery** (Tues–Sun 10.30am–5pm; £12.50; http://wattsgallery.org.uk), purpose-built in 1904 to house the work of G.F. Watts, the prolific sculptor, painter and symbolist who lived in Compton with his wife Mary from 1890 until his death in 1904. The building has undergone a major restoration, and now, as well as displaying Watts' paintings and sculpture against rich red wallpaper and with a green ceramic hanging rail, it is home to special exhibitions about his contemporaries, as well as a commercial gallery and tearoom.

2

EATING AND DRINKING

Watts Gallery Tea Shop Down Lane GU3 1DQ, 01483 810 235, http://wattsgallery.org.uk. Housed in what was Mary Watts' pottery, the tearoom has a barn-like roof and dishes up substantial and tasty snacks such as Welsh rarebit (£6.50), plus scones, traditional cakes and afternoon tea. Daily 10.30am–5pm.

At the entrance to the Watts Gallery, the North Downs Way joins the road into the village. To **continue the walk**, turn left onto the road; after just 10m, turn left again onto a narrow path, which is the return route to Guildford. However, it's well worth continuing for another 500m up the road, to see the exceptional Watts Chapel.

Watts Chapel

Watts Chapel (daily 9am–5pm) sits in the hillside cemetery to the left of the road. Follow the brick path through the cemetery, between tall yew trees, to reach the elongated terracotta-coloured building.

The chapel was built between 1895 and 1898, under the instruction of Watts and his wife, Mary, who designed it. Constructed with the aid of local craftsmen and seventy villagers, it is a rapturous expression of the ideals of the **Home Arts and Industries Association**, which sought to improve social conditions through creative endeavour. Round the door is a cluster of angel heads, modelled from clay in moulds, each one made by a villager.

The **interior**, created under the direction of Mary Watts between 1901 and 1904, achieves a majestic effect that is surprising for a small structure. Her decorative scheme was sculpted in gesso, its sea-greens, reds and golds glowing in the soft light provided by four pairs of tall stained-glass windows. The tendrils of the Tree of Life lead the eye upwards, via cherubim and seraphim and pairs of grave winged messengers, to a pattern symbolizing eternity. Coming out of the chapel and descending the hill, look out for Mary's terracotta **well**, near the lychgate.

To connect to the return path to Guildford, turn right onto the road after you've descended the hill, back the way you came. Then take the public footpath just before red-roofed **Coneycraft Farm**, 200m beyond the chapel – it's a grassy path between sturdy wooden fences. Follow the path round the farm, then follow the wooden public footpath signs up the broad concrete path away from the farm.

To Littleton

2.75km Go out of the wooden gate away from the paddocks and fields of Coneycraft Farm, and follow the public footpath sign that leads straight ahead, rather than the one that points down to the right. Head past gently rolling fields towards the buildings that comprise **Polsted Manor**. At the far edge of the manor grounds, wide wooden steps lead down to a path. Turn right here for 10m, and then left, following the public footpath sign.

The track, flanked by horse chestnuts, leads for 800m beyond Polsted Manor to **Loseley Park**. At the gate to Loseley Park the path leads down to the left, and then right, to skirt the grounds of the house. Cross the stile over a farm track, and carry straight across the field – to the right there are views of Elizabethan Loseley House.

From the pond that borders the park, go through the metal kissing gate and across two fields to the attractive jumble of houses that comprises **Littleton**, passing a timber-framed building to the left. Go straight ahead at the crossroads, down the lane.

2 Back to Guildford

2.25km You pass a turning to a mansion called Orange Grove, to your right. Beyond this, instead of crossing the cattle grid, go left up a grassy public footpath. You soon come to a post with yellow arrows – take the path to the left, which is overhung and narrow at this point, leading uphill along the edge of a **wood**. It emerges onto a road – go straight ahead through the gap in the wall, following the public footpath sign.

This stretch of the path takes you through more woodland, then runs down on to the road – go straight ahead downhill, passing, after 400m, the turn-off to the North Downs Way you took earlier in the day. From this point you need to retrace your steps to get back to the station.

Turn left at the bottom of the lane, opposite *Ye Olde Ship Inn*, a snug, traditional pub where you might fancy stopping for a pint. Otherwise, take a left onto **Chestnut Avenue**. At the top of the avenue cross the road and go left, up **Beech Lane**. Climb the long steady curve of Beech Lane to the octagonal tower, where you turn right, back through the cemetery.

Turn right down the road once you've gone through the cemetery, and head down the hill. At the end of the descending terrace of Victorian houses, go left up the flight of steps. Cross Mareschal Road and then cross over Wodeland Avenue to head down the path, from where you'll have spectacular views of the brick bulk of **Guildford Cathedral**, designed by Sir Edward Maufe and built between 1936 and 1961. When the path reaches the roundabout, go straight back up Guildford Park Road and turn right into the railway station.

Gomshall and the North Downs

Gomshall to Shere and back

Distance and difficulty 9km; easy–moderate

Minimum duration 2hr 15min

Trains London Bridge, London Waterloo or London Victoria to Gomshall (hourly; 1hr 10min); return from Gomshall to London Bridge, London Waterloo or London Victoria (hourly; 1hr 10min); South Western Railway, Southern Railway

Maps OS Landranger 187: *Dorking & Reigate*; OS Explorer 145: *Guildford & Farnham*

This circular walk begins and ends at the village of **Gomshall**, which sits on the Tilling Bourne stream between the green ridge of the North Downs and the Low Weald – given the proximity of Guildford and Dorking, the gentle, rolling countryside is surprisingly unspoilt. The route runs to fabulously pretty medieval **Shere** where *The Dabbling Duck* café is a good lunch stop, and then climbs up onto the **North Downs**. You continue along the forested ridge of the downs before descending back into Gomshall to emerge opposite *The Gomshall Mill*, a picturesque stop for a post-walk pint.

Getting started

1.5km From platform 2 of tiny **Gomshall station**, head down the path to join the road, and then turn right (if you want to go straight into Gomshall to eat, go under the railway bridge and down the road for 500m). To get to Shere take the track to the left, just before you get to the railway bridge – it's marked with a wooden public footpath sign. Cross a stream, and where the track turns sharply to the left, take the signed footpath to the right.

After 400m you join a track and then emerge at a lane; turn right underneath the railway bridge, with a Tudor house ahead. Turn left up the minor road on the other side of the railway bridge and, at the junction 200m ahead, go straight on up Gravelpits Lane, following the National Cycle Network sign. Continue along the road,

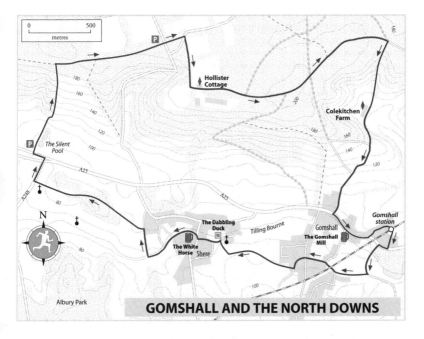

GOMSHALL AND THE NORTH DOWNS

curving round to the left, after which you'll come out at a junction by Gravel Pits Farmhouse. Turn right here, following the sign for the **Shere Parish Millennium Trail**. The path beyond here is narrow and leafy, running through rolling countryside with good views of the downs to the right, and then joins a more open track along a field.

Shere

Follow the path along a line of trees until you come to **Shere**. Turn right and head downhill to **St James' Church**, entered via a handsome lychgate built by Lutyens. The church is mainly Norman, with a fine, plain interior and a beautiful font (dating from around 1200). Inside the church on the north wall is a quatrefoil with a squint, which allowed the local anchoress, **Christine Carpenter**, to see the altar – her only view of the outside world. Christine was walled up in a cell attached to the church in 1329; she was released after three years, but later succeeded in having herself imprisoned again. Contemporary documents describe her desire to evade the "rapacious wolf" outside her cell – it's unclear whether she was guilty of some transgression that caused her to be imprisoned in the first place, or whether it was a self-imposed act of devotion. Christine's cell no longer exists, but its low outline can still be seen on the exterior wall, giving some sense of its claustrophobic proportions. Also worth looking out for inside the church is the thirteenth-century **Crusader chest**, one of a number placed in churches by order of Pope Innocent III to raise money for the Crusades; a small devotional medieval statue of a Madonna and Child is displayed nearby, while fragments of medieval glass adorn the windows.

From the church, head towards the village; the *White Horse* **pub** is straight ahead of you. To the right down the hill is the main body of the village, mostly comprising pretty fifteenth- and sixteenth-century timber-framed cottages. The Tilling Bourne stream, which is usually full of bobbing ducks, runs through the village.

EATING AND DRINKING

The Dabbling Duck Middle St, Shere GU5 9HF, 01483 205 791, http://thedabblingduck.uk.com. Just over the Tilling Bourne, this little café and deli makes an excellent lunch stop – they serve burgers, fishcakes and tarts (from £12), and there's a scenic garden out back. Daily 9am–5pm.

To the Silent Pool

2km Go down **Lower Street** along the stream, passing some allotments on your right. Turn left at the public footpath sign just before the ford. Go straight ahead through the next gate, keeping the stream to your right. Go through signed **Vicky's Gate** and turn right, crossing the stream following the minor road, and turning left onto the path after 200m.

After 100m you come out into a big field which opens up to reveal downland. Cross the field and go through a kissing gate into a stretch of beech and birch wood, before crossing another kissing gate into the field. Off to the left, you can see glimpses of **Albury Park**, a much altered Tudor manor house. After 200m you pass a Saxon church to the left, then go through the gate, and descend towards the A248. At the road, turn right. A narrow path runs along the side of the road, saving you from having to walk on the road itself.

At the end of the road is the busy **A25** dual carriageway. Cross the road and turn left briefly to get to the car park. Keeping the car park on your left, follow the path leading to the Sherbourne Pond, which is on the right after about 75m; you'll see an extensive vineyard up to the left. The path then winds round to the **Silent Pool** – both pools are pretty devoid of atmosphere, thanks to the roar from the A25. According to popular legend, though, a woodman's daughter was bathing in the Silent Pool when a caddish nobleman appeared. He rode his horse into the water to reach her and she drowned

A PUNT RIDE ON THE RIVER STOUR PASSING THE 16TH-CENTURY *OLD WEAVERS HOUSE*

2

trying to escape him. Her father found the body and the nobleman's hat floating on the water, which, in a sinister twist, bore the emblem of Prince John, suggesting that the future king of England was the culprit.

The North Downs

4km To the left of the Silent Pool, wooden steps bring you up to a wire fence along a field; turn right on the narrow path up the hill. It's a stiff and steep climb through the woods – only 500m, but it feels further. Keep going till you reach a four-way fingerpost, then turn right to walk through a beautiful beech wood on a wide path. After 750m you reach a car park; cross the road and go straight ahead, following the signs for the **North Downs Way**. After 150m you reach another road. Turn right and then almost immediately left onto the wide path.

After 250m, take a left onto a curving track, marked with a North Downs Way sign. At **Hollister Cottage**, 250m beyond, turn left through the farm buildings on a wide track. Pass the stables, then go through an access gate straight ahead. Follow the track for 400m to the crossroads, and continue straight on. Just over 1km further on you come to a **crossroads** where you'll see a big circular concrete structure on your left. Turn right on the signed path to Gomshall.

Back to Gomshall

1.5km The path dips down through the trees for 500m. Eventually the trees thin and there's a lovely verdant clearing to the right. Carry on straight ahead, and you'll see picturesque **Colekitchen Farm** to the right, in the lee of a steep hill. Beyond the farm, a tarred road runs uphill and then down through woodland before emerging onto a wider road; turn left to reach, after 150m, *The Gomshall Mill*. To get back to the **train station**, head on past the pub through the village.

EATING AND DRINKING

The Gomshall Mill Station Rd, Gomshall GU5 9LB, 01483 203 060, http://brunningandprice.co.uk/gomshall mill. An idyllic pub, whose rambling series of seventeenth-century rooms sits above the mill stream. They serve filling mains such as venison with redcurrant sausage and beetroot burgers (from £14). Daily noon–11pm.

The Pilgrims' Way

Charing to Chilham and Canterbury

Distance and difficulty day one: 17.5km; day two: 11.5km; moderate

Minimum duration day one: 4hr 25min; day two: 2hr 50min

Trains London Victoria to Charing (hourly; 1hr 15min); return from Canterbury East to London Victoria (every 30min; 1hr 25min); Southeastern Railway

Maps OS Landranger 189 and 179: *Ashford & Romney Marsh* and *Canterbury & East Kent*; OS Explorer 137, 149 and 150: *Ashford, Sittingbourne & Faversham* and *Canterbury*

The route that became known as the **Pilgrims' Way** was an amalgam of country roads and paths leading from Winchester and serving pilgrims from the south and west of England and continental Europe (via Southampton). At Harbledown, just outside Canterbury, this route merged with the much more ancient Watling Street, the route for the main body of pilgrims from London and the north. All were bent on seeing the gold- and jewel-encrusted tomb of **Thomas Becket**, and perhaps, as *The Canterbury Tales* testifies, having a bit of fun along the way.

This two-day walk covers a particularly attractive stretch of the Pilgrims' Way, and takes you to the goal of the pilgrims – the magnificent **Cathedral** itself. The walk begins

---

THE CANTERBURY TALES

And specially from every shires end Of England, down to Canterbury they wend To seek the holy blissful martyr, quick To give his help to them when they were sick.

In **The Canterbury Tales**, begun in 1386, Geoffrey Chaucer rolled together a rich bundle of stories – romances, animal fables, saucy yarns and sermons – by the simple expedient of having a group of characters, himself included, engage in a story-telling competition on a two-day pilgrimage to Becket's tomb. The pilgrims' host at the *Tabard Inn* in Southwark instigates the competition on the eve of the pilgrimage, launching Chaucer into his sparkling and pacey prologue, where he introduces his cast of characters, from the valiant knight, "his bearing modest as a maid", to the coy nun and the greasy pardoner. These vignettes are elaborated when the characters tell their tales, each one infused with the flaws, pretensions and, occasionally, nobility of the teller.

The framing device Chaucer employed for his tales represented a narrative revolution in English literature, as did the use of English in the telling, rather than courtly French or churchy Latin. For all their canonical significance, though, the *Tales*, which seesaw between bawdiness and moral instruction, remain remarkably engaging.

The action of the book turns entirely on the stories themselves and the often tetchy interaction between the characters – one of the most disarming episodes is when the Host interrupts Chaucer's own *Tale of Sir Topaz* and begs him to quit his tedious "doggerel-rhyme" and tell a tale in prose. There's little mention of the topography of the route, except of the most incidental "Oh look, we're at Greenwich!" kind. So it hardly serves as a travelogue, but nonetheless it's quite fun to take the book with you on this walk. There are many versions available, from pared down and often pallid retellings for children to the full and (for most people) incomprehensible Middle English monty. The best choice, which will save you stumbling over too many *wympuls* and *lordynges*, is Nevill Coghill's rhythmic and vigorous modern verse rendering, published by Penguin Classics.

If you are doing this as a **one-day route**, start the walk by turning left out of Chilham station. Follow the curve of the busy road and, after 300m, take the (unsigned) left-hand fork towards the village. Climbing "The Street" beyond *The Woolpack Inn* brings you to the church, where the route starts.

2

at **Charing** in Kent, leading through lovely woods and farmland to **Chilham**, an idyllic village where you can stay overnight, before continuing on to **Canterbury** the next day. You can do either day of this walk on its own, taking the train from or to Chilham, but the most rewarding day in terms of landscape is the first. This is fine, abundant countryside, especially appealing in April – when Chaucer set his tales and when the fruit trees are covered in blossom – or in late summer and early autumn, when you can scrump for apples and pears. Although this is an established walk, the signing (for the North Downs/Pilgrims' Way) is minimal.

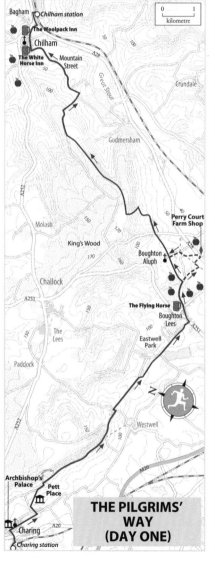

Day one

17.5km Day one links two very pretty and historic Kentish villages: **Charing** and **Chilham**. In between, Boughton Lees is home to a pub that has been serving pilgrims for hundreds of years, though a better **lunch** option on a sunny day is the nearby Perry Court Farm Shop, where you can put together a picnic. The country you walk through is for the most part domesticated but beautiful, with rolling vistas, orchards and the odd scattering of appealing tile-hung or half-timbered cottages. Towards the end of the walk you climb up into dense woodland, before descending into Chilham, where you can either take the train home or stay the night.

Getting started

1km The walk starts at the village of **Charing**, tucked between the North Downs and the Low Weald. From Charing station, turn left onto Station Road and go straight ahead, crossing the busy A20 and continuing up the High Street into the village. Just past the post office, turn right down the lane to the **church** of St Peter and St Paul, which has a beautiful painted tie-beam roof, dated 1592. On the left are the remains of the **Archbishop's Palace**. These substantial and handsome ruins now incorporate picturesque houses, but once comprised a large manor house, built between the twelfth and the sixteenth centuries, which was given to Henry VIII by Archbishop Cranmer. A day's ride from Canterbury, the palace provided accommodation for more prestigious pilgrims.

Exit the church, turn left and follow the paved path behind the church that leads between houses and emerges at a playing field; go straight ahead across the field on the paved path, then walk up the grassy path. Go straight ahead again, following the yellow arrow, across a field. Cross the stile and the field towards **Pett Place**, an early eighteenth-century mansion. Bear left when you reach the road, then follow the path to the right, marked with a green footpath sign, which leads via wooden steps into a field.

Pett Place to Boughton Lees

6.5km The path climbs across the field, crosses a minor road, then cuts diagonally across another field to bring you to a huge beech tree. Turn right along the road here – you are now technically on the **Pilgrims' Way** itself. Follow the track ahead and then round to the right; it soon passes a quarry.

The route, marked with **North Downs Way** signs (also with acorns), runs for 1.5km through beautiful woodland; where it eventually forks, go to the left. It then joins a paved road; go left and carry on for nearly 1km until you come to a T-junction; cross the stile and turn left, then almost immediately right to cross the field. The path widens to become a track and dips through the fields, then climbs gently uphill. Turn right just before the white no entry sign then turn left to continue on the Pilgrims' Way.

Cross the stile and go through the field, with a large house up to the left. Coming out of the field, go straight ahead on the paved road, with the lake down to the right. At the T-junction, follow the footpath straight ahead across the field for 100m to reach a **National Trail** sign; after 600m you join the drive that leads down to a boundary wall of the nearby hotel and the A251.

Boughton Lees to Boughton Aluph

1.5km Turn left onto the busy road and then take the right fork, along the village green. You'll see *The Flying Horse* pub across the green.

EATING AND DRINKING

The Flying Horse Boughton Lees TN25 4HH, 01233 620 914. This was one of a chain of pubs designed to feed and water passing pilgrims. It's located in a fine old building right on the village green, where in summer you can sit outside and watch local cricket matches, and they serve good pub grub (mains from £13). Mon–Wed & Sun 10am–midnight, Thurs–Sat 10am–1am.

To continue, turn left out of the pub and then take a left, marked with a Pilgrims' Way sign, continuing down the road for 750m to reach a footpath sign that points in three directions: to continue on the Pilgrims' Way to Boughton Aluph, take the path to the left; to detour to the farm shop (see below), carry on up the road for 100m, then turn right and go through the gate with a yellow arrow.

The Pilgrims' Way leads across the fields for 750m, emerging in the tiny village of **Boughton Aluph**.

Detour to Perry Court Farm Shop

1.5km If you don't fancy a pub lunch, the **Perry Court Farm Shop** is well worth a detour. To reach the shop, having left the Pilgrims' Way and gone through the metal gate on the right-hand side, marked with a yellow arrow, follow the line of trees to your left; turn left and then right to cut through the field towards the busy A28 road. Cross the road to reach the shop, which is clearly signposted.

EATING AND DRINKING

Perry Court Farm Shop Canterbury Rd, Ashford TN25 4ES, 01233 812302, http://perrycourt.farm. You can put together a great picnic from the home-baked and locally grown goodies – cheeses, fresh bread, pear and apple juice, beers and all kinds of cakes, plus coffee and tea – and eat it in the adjoining orchard. Daily 8am–6pm.

2

To **continue to Boughton Aluph**, without retracing your steps, go back to the footpath but go straight ahead, not left. Cross the field, heading towards the church, then turn left onto the minor road. After 50m turn right up the fenced path by the cattery, crossing the field towards the church.

Boughton Aluph and King's Wood

6.5km The fourteenth-century church of **All Saints** in **Boughton Aluph** is not in regular use, and as a result has an attractively ramshackle and solitary air. The church is sturdily built of flint, with brick buttresses and a stocky tower, though it's surprisingly lofty inside. Look out for the fourteenth-century glass in the east window, and for the memorial to the men of the Wye Fire Brigade, who saved the church from destruction by incendiary bombs in September 1940 at the height of the Battle of Britain.

To continue the walk, exit the main gate, cross the road and go over the stile. After 500m you come to a narrow path through an arch of greenery. Ignore the stile on the left and carry on straight ahead, passing through a metal kissing gate onto a road; cross the road and head down a track towards a picturesque **farmyard**. After you pass the farm, turn left and head up the steep field.

Go through a metal gate, with hedgerows to either side, and into **King's Wood**, particularly spectacular at bluebell time in April/May. At the crossroads, follow the marked path to the right (a signed detour from what the Ordnance Survey map designates as the Pilgrims' Way). The track descends the hill for 100m and then forks; take the route to the left and, after 500m, follow the signs back up to the left, then, after 1.5km, bear right to rejoin the Pilgrims' Way, following the red arrow. You'll see a stone waymarker here. The path continues through the woods for 2.5km, then drops down off the ridge, and curves round to the left. After 250m you come to a wooden gate that leads you onto a small road: **Mountain Street**.

Chilham

2km Head left along Mountain Street, passing the first of **Chilham**'s timbered houses. After 1.5km or so you reach the village proper, a high wall to the left marking the boundary of Chilham Castle. At the end of Mountain Street, School Hill leads up the hill to the left to the village square; to reach *The Woolpack Inn* (see below), turn right.

Chilham is a perfect English village, the main street climbing from *The Woolpack Inn* past picturesque timbered houses to the flint church and a handsome central square. Tall and forbidding gates at the far end of the square all but conceal **Chilham Castle** – actually a Jacobean manor house.

PLACES TO STAY AND EAT IN CHILHAM

Chilham has a few places to stay, including some good Airbnb options – just make sure you book well in advance, especially in summer.

Homelea Canterbury Rd, Chilham CT4 8AG, 07951 496 836, http://nickonslow.com/homelea. Just out of Chilham on the Canterbury Road, with comfortable modern rooms and a self-contained studio/chalet. Doubles from £89

The White Horse Inn The Square, Chilham CT4 8BY, 01227 730 355, http://thewhitehorsechilham. uk. For a quiet drink, go up the hill to this welcoming fourteenth-century inn in the village square where you

can sample a pint of bespoke White Horse Ale, home-cooked food and live music on Saturdays. Mon, Wed, Fri & Sat noon–midnight, Tues & Thurs noon–11.30pm, Sun noon–10.30pm.

The Woolpack Inn The Street, Chilham CT4 8DL, 01227 730 351, http://woolpackchilham.co.uk. Rooms in a converted stable block at the friendly village inn. The food is decent and the atmosphere lively. Doubles from £85

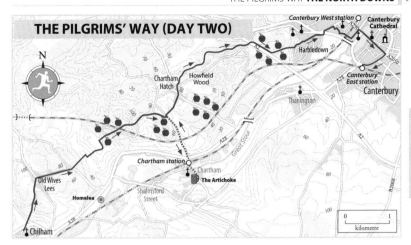

THE PILGRIMS' WAY (DAY TWO)

2

If you're only doing this as a one-day walk, at the eastern end of the village take the main road toward Bagham to reach Chilham **train station**, with regular services to Waterloo, Charing Cross and London Bridge (hourly; 1hr 35min); it's a right-turn past the cluster of B&Bs.

Day two

11.5km Day two is less bucolic than day one, and the orchards you pass through are on a rather commercial scale. There are some lovely sights along the way, though, and as the walk is relatively short there's time to meander around Chilham in the morning and still get to **Canterbury Cathedral** in time to have a look round. There's a decent pub at Chartham for **lunch**, which adds another 3.5km to the day's walk.

Chilham to Old Wives Lees

2km The second day's walk starts from the **church** in **Chilham**. Go round to the left-hand side of the church and follow the path that leads behind it, cutting down through the graveyard. Where the path forks, go left down the slope and onto a narrow track. Turn right, and follow the track until you come to a busy road. Cross the road and carry on up the lane directly opposite.

When you reach **Old Wives Lees** (which isn't nearly as pretty as Chilham), you come to a junction; cross the road and go up Lower Lees Road. This leads through straggling houses for 750m until you come to a couple of oast houses on the left. Just beyond, a sign points you off to the left. Go to the end of the road and turn right for a few metres – there's a kissing gate on the opposite side that leads you back onto the Pilgrims' Way.

To Chartham Hatch

3km From here, a wonderful **avenue** of lime trees leads downhill, forming a dense, leafy tunnel. At the end of the avenue, cross the stile leading into a field, where you'll see tall poles used for growing hops. At the bottom of the hill turn right, then almost immediately left, climbing up the hill ahead, with the line of huge beech trees to your right.

At the top of the ridge continue straight on, then follow the yellow arrow on the wooden post which leads you left along the field. Then go right, down the field in the direction of the wooded hill. The path ascends a slope, then dips to a sprawling fruit farm. At the farm, turn left under the **railway bridge**.

Go up the track towards the tiled oast houses. Before you reach them, take a right up the gravel track. As you continue, the path becomes paved. Follow it until the path forks; take the right-hand fork, signed with a wooden post. Carry on past some houses, towards the electricity pylon. Just before you reach the pylon, a paved road leads to the right; there's a detour of 3.5km there and back into Chartham, if you fancy a country pub lunch at The Artichoke. Otherwise, carry on into the smaller settlement of Chartham Hatch.

EATING AND DRINKING

The Artichoke Rattington St, Chartham CT4 7JQ, 01227 738316, http://artichokechartham.co.uk. This beautifully timbered and flower-hung boozer is a venerable 700 years old, and dishes up mains such as artichoke pie (£9.95) and burgers (£8.95). Food served Mon 5–11pm, Tues–Sat noon–2.30pm & 5.30–8.30pm, Sun noon–4.30pm.

Chartham Hatch and Howfield Wood

2.5km Continue down the road into **Chartham Hatch,** turning left onto Howfield Lane when you reach a T-junction. Soon after, follow the public footpath sign that leads away to the right. The narrow path emerges onto a road – cross this and continue on the path ahead, signed "The North Downs Way".

Go along the edge of the playing field, continuing along the path and into **Howfield Wood**. You eventually emerge in a clearing, with an orchard on your right and an avenue of trees ahead; ignore the stile to the left and continue straight ahead. At the end of the avenue of trees, in **No Man's Orchard**, you'll see a large, weatherbeaten wooden sculpture of a snake curving through the grass. Coming out of the orchard, follow the sign that points down to the left: just keep following the yellow arrows. Go straight ahead; the path comes out at a junction onto a short paved section of path; turn right, and walk a few steps until you reach the North Downs Way signpost and a road. Turn left and cross the bridge over the **A2**.

Harbledown

1.5km Turn right at the end of the bridge, following the bridleway sign. The path leads up the hill, running alongside the A2. After 500m the path curves left into woodland, and through an orchard. Cross a little bridge over a stream, and then follow the steep path up into **Harbledown**, mentioned in *The Canterbury Tales* as "Bob up and down", presumably for its hilly geography. The route joins a tarmac path; bear left and go straight ahead.

Into Canterbury

1.5km The path comes out at a large roundabout; cross the road via the subway and go straight ahead, following the blue cycle-path sign to the city centre (you are now diverging from the official Pilgrims' Way to follow a more scenic route into the city). After 800m, go through the gate into **West Gate Gardens**, just right of the sign for Whitehall Road. Cross the footbridge over the Stour, turn left and walk through the gardens to emerge at the medieval **West Gate**. Many pilgrims ended their journey at a canter – the word derives from the phrase "at a Canterbury pace" – to reach the West Gate before dusk, when the portcullis descended. Turn right here and go straight up **Canterbury**'s main street, where there's an all-pervasive smell of fast food from the grotty selection of kebab and burger joints that has colonized the otherwise appealing mixture of old buildings. About 200m up the street, the road crosses the river – look up to the left and you'll see a **ducking stool**. Turn left at Boots, down narrow Mercery Lane, for the cathedral.

The Cathedral

Mercery Lane leads into the Buttermarket, where pilgrims once bought religious relics. Before you is the wonderfully elaborate sixteenth-century **Christ Church Gate**, and beyond that lies **Canterbury Cathedral** itself (Easter–Sept Mon–Fri 9am–5.30pm, Sun 12.30–2.30pm; Oct–Easter Mon–Fri 9am–5pm, Sun 12.30–2.30pm; £12.50). Canterbury Cathedral has been central to the history of the English Church since St Augustine's sixth-century mission from Rome to establish Christianity in the country. The original Saxon church was rebuilt by **Archbishop Lanfranc** in the eleventh century, but was severely damaged by fire a hundred years later. The choir was then rebuilt by William of Sens, a French master-mason, and extended by his successor, William the Englishman, in the 1180s. The rebuilding and remodelling of the nave and aisles continued into the early fifteenth century.

From a distance the cathedral appears rather ethereal, but close up what impresses is its colossal physical presence. The bulk and length of the Gothic **nave** is lightened by the soaring Bell Harry tower, added in the late fifteenth century. Inside, the stately nave is full of light, the ribs of its roof fanning out to join the long, central rib, punctuated by gold ceiling bosses. A flight of steps leads to the elaborate fifteenth-century choir screen, and beyond that another flight of steps ascends to the altar.

The **choir**, one of the longest in England, was built by the two Williams in transitional Norman style, with both round and pointed arches. It is separated from the aisles by ornate screens and canopied **tombs**. Among them are the splendid tomb of Henry IV (d.1413) and his second wife Joan of Navarre (d.1437), and a portrait effigy of Edward, the Black Prince (d.1376), hung with his flamboyant armour.

To the left as you face the choir screen is the area of the cathedral called "**Martyrdom**", where Thomas Becket was hacked to death as vespers were sung on December 29, 1170. A jagged modern sculpture symbolizes the bloody instruments of his murder. Becket, the Archbishop of Canterbury, had been chancellor and friend to Henry II, but they argued about the king's jurisdiction over the Church – few contemporary or modern commentators can explain Becket's belligerence in reviving tensions between Church and state. Henry launched a furious outburst against Becket, supposedly exclaiming, "Will no one rid me of this turbulent priest?" This, perhaps the most famous rhetorical question in English, prompted four knights to cross the Channel to kill the archbishop.

Stricken with guilt, Henry II did penance for the murder in the cathedral, and shortly afterwards the English defeated the Scots at the battle of Alnwick, the first of a series of "miracles" which were associated with the shrine. Becket was **canonized** three years after his death, and his lavish tomb became the most significant pilgrimage site in England. The tomb was destroyed by Henry VIII during the dissolution of the monasteries, but the cult of Becket survived. To the east of the cathedral lies the spacious fourteenth-century chapterhouse where T.S. Eliot's austere verse play *Murder in the Cathedral* was first performed in 1935.

The lofty arched **crypt** features lively Norman carving on its capitals – the stonemasons, perhaps as a form of spiritual insurance, incorporated some distinctly pagan figures into the mix. The **Great Cloister** features beautiful Early English arcading; beyond it is a series of rambling buildings belonging to the King's School, a monastic foundation established in the seventh century – the Elizabethan playwright Christopher Marlowe was a pupil. Evensong (during which admission is free) is at 5.30pm Monday to Friday & 3.15pm Saturday and Sunday.

Leaving Canterbury

1km There are two train stations in Canterbury – Canterbury West, just outside the West Gate, from where trains leave for London Bridge, and **Canterbury East**, where faster trains leave for Victoria (change at Ashford for a quicker journey). To reach Canterbury East, go up the High Street till you reach the roundabout and the city walls. Turn right and walk round the walls, with the handsome **Dane John Gardens** down to the right. After 700m, a footbridge leads to the left, over the busy road that circles the walls, taking you right into the station.

The Weald

IGHTHAM MOTE

The Weald

The quintessential image of the Weald – the low, rolling stretch of wood and farmland between the North and South Downs – is of orchards, country cottages, oast houses and hop gardens. The system of medieval land tenure used in the area meant that estates were divided rather than inherited wholesale, with the result that this fertile land was split into smaller and smaller plots, creating a patchwork of fields and orchards enclosed by dense hedgerows. A correspondingly modest architectural style predominates, with tile-hung and timber-framed cottages giving the landscape a domestic appeal that is hard to resist. The name "weald" derives from the Anglo-Saxon word for forest, and remains of ancient woodland can be seen on the walk through the Eden Valley, where great oak trees dot the landscape. A longer route, from Borough Green to Knole, climbs a ridge on to the Greensand Way. The High Weald Walk takes you from picturesque Tunbridge Wells to the spectacular sandstone rock formations around Groombridge.

The Eden Valley

Penshurst to Chiddingstone and back

Distance and difficulty 12km; moderate
Minimum duration 2hr 45min
Trains Cannon Street/London Bridge or London Charing Cross to Penshurst (every 30min; 1hr); return from Penshurst to London Bridge/ Cannon Street or London Charing Cross (every 30min; 1hr); Southeastern Railway
Maps OS Landranger 188: *Maidstone & Royal Tunbridge Wells*; OS Explorer 147: *Sevenoaks & Tonbridge*

This walk leads in a satisfying circle through rolling Kent countryside, across fields and meadows and past orchards, vineyards and great solitary oaks, remnants of what was once thick forest. The route takes you from **Penshurst station** to the amazingly intact Tudor village of **Chiddingstone**. From here, paths and farm tracks lead across the **Eden Valley** to Penshurst, home to a recommended **afternoon tea** stop and the mighty manor house **Penshurst Place**, which has a spectacular medieval hall, an intriguing art collection and extensive gardens. From the house, the route runs through parkland and finally by road back to Penshurst station. Start walking early to see Penshurst Place as last entry is at 3pm, and check return times in advance: there are no evening services from Penshurst during the week.

Getting started

3km Exit the station opposite the *Little Brown Jug* pub and turn left. Walk down the road for 250m, then take the path to the left marked by a green **public footpath** sign; it's just before the post office and red phone box. The path leads along the edge of a field and crosses the railway via wooden steps. Walk along the edge of the next field, with the line of trees on your right, until you get to a gate after about 200m; go through the gate on your right and straight across the next field and over the stile.

Walk across the following field. Go round the right-hand side of the **oast houses** and over the stile at the far end. Cross the driveway that leads to the farm. Continue straight ahead on the track for 10m, then over the stile and down the edge of the field (ignoring the stile on your left). Go into the next field – diagonally across it you'll see a house with chimneys sticking up through the trees. Head across the field towards the house, then, with the little brook on your left, veer right to the metal gate and stile.

Cross the stile and turn left up the **tarred road**, heading uphill. After 100m, take a right onto a track: on the left of the track is a red-brick house and, on the right, a crumbling tiled garage. You soon come to a stile on the left; cross over and go up the right-hand edge of the field. At the end of the field is another wooden stile; carry on straight ahead and cross a fence, continuing straight ahead, with a long avenue of ash trees to your left. At the end of this field cross another stile to emerge onto an oak-lined **track**. Turn left onto the track, with North Cottage on your left-hand side.

Following the track for 500m, you'll come to a tile-hung house on the left, with lattice windows and with the date 1601 over the door. Shortly beyond the cottage, the track narrows, leading to a bridge over the **River Eden**. Carry on up the path, keeping the little wood to your left, until you emerge onto the road – turn right for Chiddingstone.

3

Chiddingstone

1km Just before you get to **Chiddingstone**, a marked path to the left makes the short detour to the **Chiding Stone**, the much-graffitied and weathered rounded outcrop for which the village is named. The stone itself was, according to legend, an altar for **druids** (see page 174). It then became the place where villagers brought their grievances against each other and were "chided" for their transgressions.

The village itself was very prosperous, first thanks to pig farming – the pigs grew fat on acorns in the nearby oak forest – and then through a basic form of iron

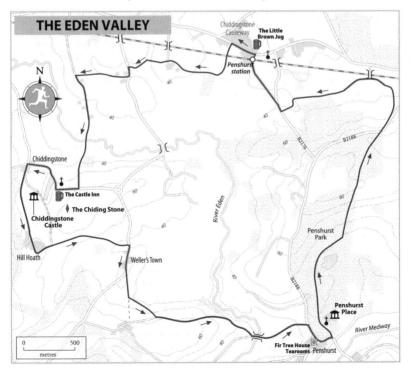

OAST HOUSES

You can't go far in the Weald without seeing **oast houses**, the distinctive brick towers with conical tiled roofs that are so characteristic of the area's landscape and agricultural heritage. Oast houses were originally used for the drying and packing of **hops**, whose flowers imbue beer with its bitter tang. Most have been converted into homes, though with the revival in small-scale brewing a few are now being used for their original purpose.

The eccentric design of the oast house was imported from Flanders in the sixteenth century, when hops first began to be widely used in brewing in England. A **kiln** (in old English, oast) was located at the base of the tower, with a drying-room floor set a few metres above it, spread with a horsehair cloth onto which the hop flowers were laid. Smoke from the kiln was released from the building via a cowl surmounting the cone of the roof. Almost all oast houses were connected to a two-storey building: hops were cooled on the upper floor then stamped down into long sacks that dangled through holes in the floor. As well as accommodating the dangling sacks of hops, the ground floor also provided access to the kiln, which was stoked and serviced from here.

Nearly all the surviving oast houses date from the nineteenth century, when the growth of a drinking culture in the expanding cities created a huge demand for **beer**. The consumers of most Kentish beer – Londoners – augmented the huge workforce needed for harvesting; indeed, until the 1950s harvesting was the closest thing that most working-class Londoners had to a holiday. Hops are still integral to the beer-making process (though they are mostly now processed into pellets rather than being laboriously dried), and the starkly regimented lines of tall chestnut poles on which they're grown are as much a feature of the Kent countryside as the converted oast houses themselves.

smelting. The timber-framed and tile-hung **houses** dating from the village's heyday in the sixteenth and seventeenth centuries are perfectly preserved and, although the place swarms with tourists in summer, it retains great beauty and character. Look out for the 1452 post office building, and the fourteenth-century **Church of St Mary**, its tower decorated with stone gargoyles, which stick their tongues out at the village below. There are many memorials inside the church to the Streatfeilds, who owned Chiddingstone Castle and whose eighteenth-century sandstone mausoleum sits in the churchyard.

Across the road from the church is the half-timbered *Castle Inn* **pub**, which has occupied the Tudor building since 1730. From the pub you can detour left through the gates to **Chiddingstone Castle** (Mon–Wed & Sun 11am–5pm; £9.50; http://chiddingstonecastle.org.uk) – it's really just a house, originally medieval but rebuilt in the seventeenth century and renovated and castellated in 1805. Inside there's a tearoom, and a diverse collection of objects, from an ancient Egyptian funerary boat to Japanese lacquered boxes and some body parts of James II.

To continue the walk, go straight ahead from the pub and, after 200m, follow the road as it curves round to the left. At the crossroads, take the signed left-hand fork which goes round the back of Chiddingstone Castle.

Across the Eden Valley

4km To reach the **Eden Valley**, continue on the road past the turn-off to the castle. After 500m, the road meanders into the appealing hamlet of **Hill Hoath**. Instead of turning right into the tiny heart of Hill Hoath – marked by a rickety sign that says "private road" – take the left-hand track up the hill. At the top of the hill, turn left on the farm track, passing Hill Hoath cottages on the left and a black wooden converted barn on your right; you'll be able to see Chiddingstone down to the left.

Go straight ahead, and cross the stile with a yellow arrow into a field and take the path straight ahead through fields and woodland. Cross the open field towards the large oak tree. Go straight ahead; you'll see the conical towers of four oast houses over to the left. Follow the path, which curves slightly to the right. At the bottom of the field, turn right onto the road. Ignore the green public footpath sign that points to the left and carry on up the hill through the hamlet of **Weller's Town**. Go past a long row of terraced cottages to the right, then, 50m further on, follow the green footpath sign to the left through the field.

Take the path down the middle of the field. At the bottom of the field, cross the small wooden plank bridge and go through the metal kissing gate. Instead of heading up to the pinkish corrugated-iron barns at the top of the hill, turn left, with the trees on your left. Go over the double stiles to emerge into another field; turn right and go up the hill. At the top right-hand corner of the field you come out onto a narrow farm track. Turn left here – the track, which runs along a ridge and has lovely views, leads all the way to Penshurst. After just over 1km the track comes to a T-junction at a little paved road; turn left and cross the bridge over the River Eden.

Penshurst

4km Five hundred metres beyond the river crossing, the road joins the much busier B2176; turn right for **Penshurst**. Just beyond the excellent *Fir Tree House Tearooms* at the T-junction, turn left to visit the partly twelfth-century **Church of St John the Baptist**, which has a distinctive squat tower, topped with pinnacles. The church is tucked away beyond a courtyard of ramshackle but appealing half-timbered buildings, and houses a chapel dedicated to the Sidney family, owners of Penshurst Place. Also worth looking out for is the damaged, late thirteenth-century marble effigy of **Sir Stephen de Penchester**, Warden of the Cinque Ports and one-time resident of Penshurst Place, who is depicted drawing his sword.

3

EATING AND DRINKING

Fir Tree House Tearooms Penshurst Rd, Penshurst TN11 8DB, 01892 870 382. The timbered tearooms serve up tea, sandwiches, tasty home-made cakes and scones; tables in the back garden are set among flower beds and under a willow tree. Wed–Sun 2.30–6pm.

PENSHURST PLACE

Penshurst Place (April–Oct house noon–4pm, last entry 3pm; £12.50, gardens & grounds 10.30am–6pm; £10.50) was built by the London draper and merchant Sir John de Pulteney in the 1330s, and in 1552 became the home of the Sidney family, whose most famous son is the Renaissance poet and statesman **Sir Philip Sidney**. Sir Philip – who died aged 32 from a wound received at the Battle of Zutphen, where he famously refused a drink of water in favour of another wounded man – praised the "firm stateliness" of the house in his pastoral romance *Arcadia*. The original house was much extended in Tudor times and again in the nineteenth century, but the overall impression of the crenellated exterior is coherent and majestic.

The first view of the interior is unforgettable: you enter via the 18m-high **Baron's Hall**, built in 1341 from huge chestnut timbers, propped up by life-size wooden statues depicting local characters. In the centre is an open octagonal fire, and to the side two massive oak trestle tables. Upstairs in the Solar, alongside family portraits including the young Sir Philip, is a famous painting thought to depict Queen Elizabeth I dancing a lively volta with the Earl of Leicester, possibly in the room you're standing in. The caption describes the complex politics of the scene, including the role of Sir Philip, the furthest figure to the right.

Outside, don't miss the colour-coordinated herbaceous borders, topiary and orchards of the extensive grounds. To **rejoin the walk**, go back up the drive away from the house and pick up the route from the church.

To visit Penshurst Place, go back onto the road leading to the church, turning left to reach the long drive into the park. But to rejoin the walk, take the path to the left of the church into the grounds. Cross the narrow road that leads to the house. Keeping the cricket pitch and pavilion to your right, go straight ahead through the gate, then curve around the edge of the large **pond** to the right.

You pass the blasted **Sidney Oak**, reckoned to be a thousand years old, on your left. Continue diagonally across the field heading towards the gate at the top right-hand corner. Go through the gate and up the hill. From the ridge at the top of the hill take the path straight ahead directly away from Penshurst. Turn left onto the gravel track at the bottom of the slope.

Reaching the road, turn right and follow it with caution for 75m before turning left down on to a quiet single-track country lane. Follow the lane for 400m before taking a track labelled Little Moorden immediately before the railway bridge. Where the Little Moorden track bears left, cross the stile on the right into the field. Keeping the hedge to your immediate left, walk along the edge of the field towards the woodland. Keeping the woods to your left, go through a gate and follow the edge of a second field to pass through a gateway, then follow the gravel track round the back of the houses to the road. Turn right at the road and follow it for 100m, before taking the left-hand fork back for the final 500m to Penshurst station.

3

The Greensand Way

Borough Green to Knole via Ightham Mote

Distance and difficulty 12.5km; moderate

Minimum duration 3hr 50min

Trains London Victoria to Borough Green (every 30min; 45min); return from Sevenoaks to London Bridge/Waterloo (every 20–30min; 25min); Southeastern Railway

Maps OS Landranger 188: *Maidstone & Royal Tunbridge Wells*; OS Explorer 147: *Sevenoaks & Tonbridge*

This rewarding walk takes you down narrow country lanes, through lush orchards and across fields, from the village of **Borough Green** to tiny **Ivy Hatch**. From this point, the walk becomes not just pretty but spectacular. First you pass the atmospheric medieval and Tudor manor house of **Ightham Mote**, which looks like a quaint half-timbered cottage writ large, ringed by a moat: make an early start in order to visit the house. There's a café/tearoom at the house that makes for a good lunch break. From Ightham Mote, the walk ascends a high ridge, following part of the established **Greensand Way**, with terrific views south to the High Weald. From the ridge you enter the magnificent deer park at **Knole**, walking past the high ragstone walls of Knole House itself. As the house closes early in the day and is huge (it has 365 rooms – one for every day of the year), it's best saved for a separate visit, so isn't described in any detail here.

3

Getting started

1.5km Turn right out of the station, past the Co-op, and take a right across the railway bridge. Carry on straight ahead, down **Borough Green**'s main street, going straight ahead where the road curves right. After 350m you come to a busy intersection; cross over and carry on straight ahead, up Quarry Hill Road. Continue for another 250m to a roundabout, then go straight ahead on Thong Lane. The road leads downhill, under a disused railway bridge, before curving left to Basted, running alongside a stream.

Basted to Ivy Hatch

3.5km After 800m the stream widens into a picturesque weir at the village of **Basted**, which has some pretty eighteenth-century houses alongside modern pastiches.

Go straight through the village and follow **Plough Hill**, which leads up to the left. Immediately beyond *The Plough* pub, follow the public footpath sign to the right. Head straight across the field ahead of you. Continue along the bottom of the field and turn left along the hedge to the corner, where a path leads down to the right and joins a narrow lane.

Turn right onto the lane, which leads through apple orchards for 750m to a junction. Turn left and follow the road, which curves to the right onto Bewley Lane. Turn right onto the busy A227, then left after 150m onto Back Lane, which leads to the edge of **Ightham Common**. Follow the turning to the left for Ivy Hatch.

To Ightham Mote

1.5km Some 750m further on you reach the picture-book village of **Ivy Hatch**; at the junction at the end of the lane turn left onto the bigger road, then after 100m take a right opposite the oast house to Ightham Mote. After 200m, take the turning to the house if you're planning to visit – otherwise you skirt the outside. The lane leads downhill between high banks scattered with wild flowers in summer, and provides a stunning view of the house.

Ightham Mote

Ightham Mote (daily 10.30am–5pm; £17.20; NT) is a gem of an English manor house, its stone tower and half-timbered Tudor walls set prettily in a square moat. The interior is a warren of relatively small-scale and intimate rooms. Sensitive preservation reflects the house's eight hundred years of occupation (which only ended when its American owner bequeathed the house to the National Trust in 1985): the Victorian billiard room with its

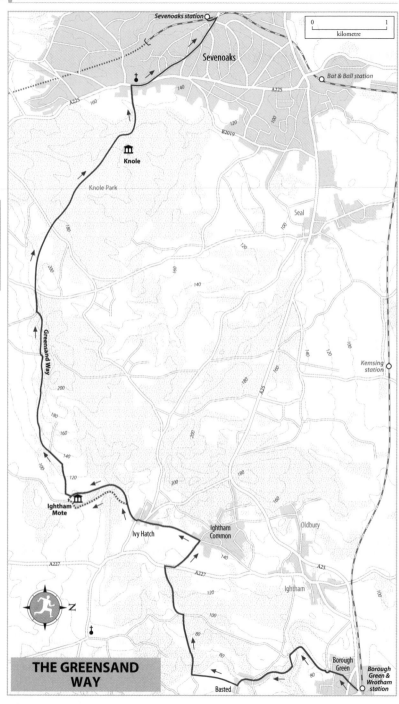

3

THE GREENSAND WAY

massive table and flounced lamps has been restored, as has the 1880s housekeeper's room and the parts of the house that date back to the fourteenth century.

The entrance, from the internal courtyard, takes you into the oldest part of the house: the outer hall and panelled **Great Hall**, built in the 1320s. Look up to the beams in the Great Hall, where the face of a green man is carved. A passageway built in the 1340s takes you past the Victorian **housekeeper's room**, into the **butler's pantry**, with its huge fireproof safe and system of bells. The adjoining **crypt** was also built in the 1320s, and is the only part of the house to retain its original appearance.

A handsome wooden staircase takes you from the Crypt to the **Oriel Room**, named for its projecting window. Beyond is the barn-like **Old Chapel** – looking up, you can see it was originally split into two floors (the line of what was a ceiling is above you). Next you come to a series of attractive bedrooms with Victorian furniture, and then to the well-preserved **New Chapel**, with pews carved with poppyheads and a ceiling painted with Tudor roses, stylized castles and quivers full of arrows. In the long **drawing room** the exquisite eighteenth-century Chinese wallpaper is alive with exotic birds and dragonflies. From here you descend, via the library, back into the courtyard, from where you can access the billiard room.

The *Mote Café* (10am–4pm) dishes up snacks, home-cooked lunches, cakes and tea.

3

The Greensand Way

4km Pass Ightham Mote and continue up the road, turning right after 50m at Mote Farm and heading towards some oast houses. The track curves to the right in front of the oast houses and continues up the hill: follow the waymarker with a blue arrow. At the second fork, after 750m, continue to the left, following the signs for the **Greensand Way** – this leads all the way to Knole. You pass an idyllically sited cottage; the path leads around it to the right, via a flight of wooden steps, before continuing into beech woods and then emerging on a lane after 750m. Turn right up the lane, following the signs for the Greensand Way, and soon afterwards picking up the path opposite Rooks Hill Cottage.

The path forks 100m beyond the stile at One Tree Hill: take the unmarked left-hand fork downhill into the woods. You come to a little clearing with wonderful views across the **Kent Weald**. Pick up the path to the far left across the clearing, following the yellow arrow and heading downhill, bearing left again where the path forks. At the next road, turn left, then take a right opposite Carter's Hill House. The path is narrower at this point. It emerges onto a track; turn right, following the yellow signs, and cross the stile on the left into a field. Walk to the far edge of the field and then skirt round it; about three-quarters of the way along you'll see signs for the Greensand Way. Follow the path until it comes to a road; cross this and go through the metal gate into Knole Park.

Knole Park

0.5km The path leads for 200m through **Knole Park** to a crossroads – go straight ahead to reach **Knole House** (mid-March to Oct Wed–Sun noon–4pm; £17.10; NT) – carry on to a T-junction in the track, then go straight on, following the Greensand Way yellow arrow. You'll soon see the long wall enclosing the house to your right.

The hundred-acre park was created for the archbishops of Canterbury to hunt in (the house itself was built in 1456–80 as an archbishop's palace, but was seized by Henry VIII). The **deer**, residents of the park for centuries, look cute, but shouldn't be approached as they can be dangerous.

To Sevenoaks station

1.5km To leave the park, take the paved drive that leads from the front of the house and then curves to the left facing the car park. The drive winds through parkland for 500m to twin gatehouses; go to the top of the lane and turn right, then keep going till you come to ornate signposts in the middle of a traffic island. Take the left-hand fork for the 1.5km trek through **Sevenoaks** to the station.

The High Weald Walk

Tunbridge Wells to Groombridge and back

Distance and difficulty 24.5km; moderate

Minimum duration 4hr 30min

Trains London Waterloo or Cannon Street/London Bridge to Tunbridge Wells (every 30min–1hr; 50min–1hr 15min); return from Tunbridge Wells to London Waterloo or London Bridge/Cannon Street (every 30min–1hr; 1hr–1hr 15min); Southeastern Railway

Maps OS Landranger 188: *Maidstone & Royal Tunbridge Wells*; OS Explorer 135: *Ashdown Forest*

This circular Kent/Sussex route mostly follows the well-signed **High Weald Walk**, which links a chain of pretty, secluded villages via dense woodland and more open, gently hilly countryside. An unexpected feature of the walk is imposing sandstone cliffs, including Harrison's Rocks and High Rocks, more *Picnic at Hanging Rock* than what

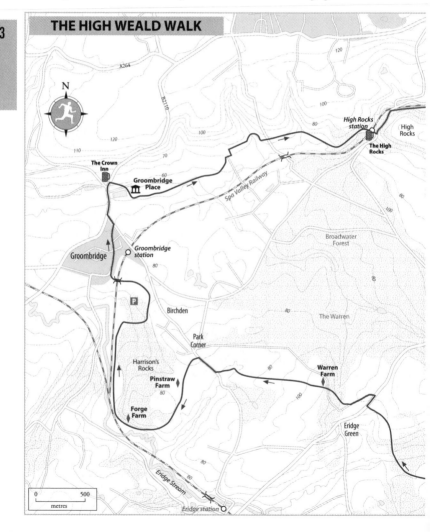

THE HIGH WEALD WALK

you'd expect in southeast England. The walk takes a while to leave the spa town of Tunbridge Wells itself, but it's no hardship to explore its handsome pastel-coloured villas, quirky boutiques and cafés. There are plenty of food shops for **picnic** supplies, or you can have lunch at the *Abergavenny Arms* **pub** in Frant; there's also an excellent old boozer at the lovely village of Groombridge.

Getting started

3km Coming out of **Tunbridge Wells** station, turn right and go straight ahead at the roundabout, down the attractive sloping **High Street**. After 350m, at the bottom of High Street, go straight ahead down narrow Chapel Place, with its Georgian houses and boutiques. Descend the steps to emerge opposite a red-brick building with a sign for **Cumberland Walk**. Turn left here, up the brick path.

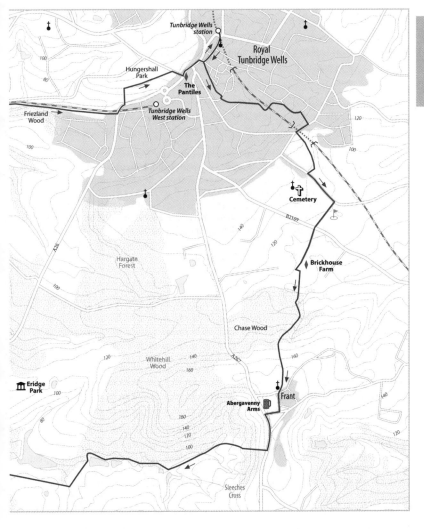

The leafy path leads you past some magnificent tall villas; you come out onto a suburban street – turn right for 20m, then left onto **Upper Cumberland Walk**. This emerges onto a quiet suburban lane – go straight ahead, between the houses. After 200m this narrows to a path – keep on straight ahead. The path leads up beyond a wooden house to your right, through some woodland, with a fence to the left. Cross the bridge over the railway line and follow the narrow path, which emerges onto a street of low brick villas. Turn right and carry on down Delves Avenue for 400m. Where Delves Avenue begins a gentle curve to the left you'll see a green **public footpath** sign to your right, between the houses. Follow this and at the end of the path go through the wooden gate and straight ahead along the line of trees, up the grassy hill to the road.

Go through another wooden gate at the top of the hill, up the steps and cross the road, then follow the pavement to your right for 100m. Tucked away to the left is a little lane with a green public footpath sign. You go through some trees, the path running gently downhill, and then curving right and uphill to join a paved lane, where you need to turn left. After 350m there's a golf club on your right, with stone cows' heads on brick pillars to either side of the drive. Immediately before it, and easy to miss, is a narrow path signed **The Tunbridge Wells Circular High Weald Walk**: this is where the walk proper begins.

Towards Frant

2km The path initially runs along the back of the golf club. Head down the edge of the golf course; the route crosses the B2169 and resumes immediately across the road, on the track to **Brickhouse Farm**. Go straight through the farm buildings and left for 10m, after which you turn right, following the sign through the trees.

The path runs along the treeline, towards a wooded dip and a little stream, crossed by a footbridge. You are now in **Chase Wood** – the path splits 100m beyond the footbridge at a woodland clearing. Take the narrower left-hand fork, initially unsigned, down the hill. After just 30m the path crosses a stream and you'll see a High Weald sign, indicating that you're on the right track. The path leads steadily uphill, through the tall fir trees and holly bushes. At the edge of the wood, a gate and stile with the High Weald sign takes you into a field. Turn left up the edge of the field, then up some stone steps into a second field – keep going straight ahead. At the end of this field, a gate and stile brings you out into the churchyard at Frant.

Frant

0.5km Skirt early nineteenth-century **Frant** church, with its unusual castellated exterior, and exit the churchyard via the pavilion-like gate and go up the main street, with *The George Inn* **pub** on your left. The village features an attractive jumble of Victorian cottages, clapboard houses and mock-Tudor homes. You emerge after 150m at the sweeping village green – take the right-hand fork round the green, passing a tiled pavilion on your left. Just 30m beyond here, at the curving brick wall with the High Street sign, take a sharp right towards a clapboard house with tall chimneys. Turn right onto the major road for the *Abergavenny Arms*, or left to continue the walk. After 200m, 50m beyond the edge of the green, on the right-hand side of the road you'll see a narrow path leading downhill, marked with the High Weald Walk sign.

EATING AND DRINKING

Abergavenny Arms Frant Rd, Frant TN3 9DB, 01892 750 233, http://abergavennyarms.co.uk. This friendly boozer is located in an old coaching inn, and serves real ales and good food (mains £14–20). The pub has a long history: in the mid-fifteenth century the site was occupied by a timber-framed hut serving ale. Daily noon–11pm.

Whitehill Wood

7km Head downhill, into **Whitehill Wood** and the fenced deer park, which you enter via the gate; this is the oldest enclosed deer park in the country and was mentioned in the *Domesday Book*. Descend the hill, with the trees of Whitehall Wood to the right and gently rolling hills to your left: you're now on the **High Weald Landscape Trail**.

After 2km, following the High Weald Landscape Trail signs, you come to a large pond to the left; just beyond the pond the path bears left to cross the stream via a wooden **footbridge**. Some 200m beyond, you emerge on the edge of parkland. Take the path through the woodland to the right, which runs along the edge of the park. After 400m you come out at a metal cattle grid: don't cross the grid, but instead turn right, crossing the stream and following the path straight ahead up the field. From the top of the field, you can look out to your right to see a lake, the grasslands of **Eridge Park**, and the house itself, rebuilt in Georgian style in the 1930s.

At the edge of the field you come out at a track – go straight ahead for 20m and then follow the sign to the right, into the wood. A raised path leads through woodland, across a wooden footbridge. You emerge onto a track: cross it, then turn right along the track to cross a second bridge. You come out into a field – go up the field, towards the village of Eridge Green.

Eridge Green to Harrison's Rocks

4.5km Head diagonally up the next field, towards the track that leads up to a major road through **Eridge Green**. At the main road, turn right and continue for 100m. Just past the Washington Hill bus stop turn left, up the lane, following the High Weald sign. Ahead of you is a wood called The Warren, and the smooth, high **Eridge Rocks**, distinctive sandstone formations which shelter rare mosses, liverworts and ferns. Just beyond the car park, the signed path leads right off the track, running up through the woodland for 100m. Coming out of the wood, turn right up the paved track and, after 200m, where the track bears right, turn left at the sign. Warren Farm is to your right.

The route leads straight across two wide fields, sloping gradually downhill. At the edge of the far field turn right and go down for 20m to the corner, where you bear left. Cross the wooden footbridges over the stream. At the end of the next field, cross the stile, join the lane and turn right for 300m into the hamlet of **Park Corner**. At the top of the lane, opposite the Eridge Road sign, take the track to the left. It's marked as the private road to Pinstraw Farm, but it is a public footpath.

You pass Pinstraw Farm to your right and carry on up the track, which eventually becomes a path, curving to the right. You then take the left-hand track through another stretch of woodland for 300m, emerging at Forge Farmhouse and a converted oast house – these and the neighbouring tile-hung houses make a very appealing cluster, with the rail line and the river running close by. Go straight ahead at the wooden gate, at the sign reading Birchden Forge. The path starts climbing above the railway – up to the right are the smooth outcrops of **Harrison's Rocks**, popular with climbers. A gap in the fence allows you to detour uphill to see the rocks up close. The path follows the course of the railway for 1km – across the meadow to your right are long and dramatic sandstone steps, threaded with the roots of tall trees.

The path leads away from the rail line and back into woodland, with a huge oak tree to the left. Ascend the hill for 100m, with a car park to your left; beyond the car park, turn left up the track to join a tarred road. You emerge at the edge of **Birchden** village; just before the road beyond take a left at the metal gate, following the High Weald sign.

Groombridge

1.5km A narrow path leads for 400m to **Groombridge**, crossing a wide wooden bridge over the railway cutting. At the end of the path, turn right into the village. Head down Corseley Road for 400m, past Victorian terraces. At the end of Corseley Road, opposite the village hall, turn left. At the roundabout, bear right up the B2110. After

350m you come to the village green, and its picturesque mixture of clapboard, tiled and chequered-brick cottages. At the corner of the green, the tile-hung sixteenth-century *The Crown Inn* makes for a snug and attractive stop.

EATING AND DRINKING

The Crown Inn The Green, Groombridge TN3 9QH, 01892 864 742, http://thecrowngroombridge.com. The atmospheric *Crown Inn* has flagstoned, low-beamed rooms, and a terrace out front on the green. There's IPA and Greene King Abbot on handpump, and they do decent and reasonably priced bar food (£13–20 for mains). Mon–Fri 11am–3pm & 5–11pm, Sat 11am–11pm, Sun noon–10.30pm.

Back to Tunbridge Wells

6km Opposite the pub and just beyond the chapel, a narrow path with a wooden fingerpost sign leads right off the B2110. Follow it down a field and towards mid-seventeenth-century **Groombridge Place**; continue on the grassy path between the lake and the house. With its latticed attic windows, weathered brick and narrow portico, the moated house combines vernacular Kentish architecture with a grander aesthetic; it was built on the site of a thirteenth-century castle, and it's thought that Christopher Wren had a hand in the architecture. Arthur Conan Doyle stayed in the house to take part in seances, and made it the setting for the Sherlock Holmes mystery *The Valley of Fear*. In 2005, Groombridge Place was used as a location for the film *Pride and Prejudice* starring Keira Knightley.

Go along the side of the house, between the moat and a small stream, along a rusty metal fence. Beyond the house, go between the wooden picket fences, crossing a stream, and out of the gate. Carry on straight ahead, up a long meadow. The route runs north of and parallel to the **Spa Valley Railway** (http://spavalleyrailway.co.uk) line – during summer weekends, you may see little steam trains puffing along the track.

At the edge of the meadow cross the stile, go along a stream and over a little wooden footbridge. Go over the next field to emerge onto a lane; cross the lane and go straight ahead, following the **Tunbridge Wells Circular Link Route** signs. There's a sewage works down to your right, but you're mostly shielded from it by woodland. Beyond the works, cross the road and go straight ahead up the track. After 200m this joins an expanse of grass. Go straight ahead through the metal gate and follow the path as it curves right, into a patch of dense woodland. You come out of the woodland at a wooden stile – go straight ahead here, with the barbed-wire fence to your left. The path leads downhill; turn left at the wooden post under a huge oak. After meandering through woodland for 500m, the path crosses a wooden footbridge and runs under the stone railway bridge at **High Rocks station**. The route joins a road for 150m at the *High Rocks* pub (Wed–Sun), an ivy-clad building with Alpine-style additions and an oak-framed barn. Just beyond the pub, turn right up the path into Friezland Wood, under the impressive sandstone **High Rocks**, which were settled in the Stone Age.

From here, the secluded path runs through woodland, hugging the right-hand side of the rail line. Some 2km beyond High Rocks, the path opens out and then goes through some suburban houses. At the busy A26 bear left, under the railway bridge. Just past the entrance to the **Wyevale Country Gardens**, take the narrow path left off the road into Hungershall Park on the edge of Tunbridge Wells. The path climbs steeply – opposite the tile-hung cottage, take the first right along the path that runs above and parallel to the A26. You emerge onto a busy road – cross over to have a wander up the colonnaded **Pantiles**, built in the town's eighteenth-century heyday, before making your way back up High Street to the train station.

The South Downs

PRETTY VIEW OVER THE SOUTH DOWNS WAY

The South Downs

All the walks in this chapter are in Sussex, around the less-developed eastern part of the South Downs. The first route leads between the steep walls of the downs, following the lush banks of the Arun River towards Arundel's extraordinary castle and cathedral. Goring-by-Sea is the starting point for a downland hike which takes in a couple of pretty villages as well as mighty Cissbury Ring, the second-largest hillfort in Britain. The Mount Caburn walk ascends the downs from Lewes, dipping into the villages of Gynde and Firle, and including a detour to Charleston, the home of Vanessa Bell and Duncan Grant. The final walk in this chapter is a two-day one (though you can treat it as two separate one-day walks) along the South Downs Way, from Lewes to Southease on day one, and then on to dramatic Beachy Head, via Alfriston and the Cuckmere Valley, on the much more strenuous second day.

Along the Arun

4

South Stoke via Burpham to Arundel

Distance and difficulty 11.5km; moderate
Minimum duration 2hr 50min
Trains London Victoria to Amberley (hourly; 1hr 10min); return from Arundel to London Victoria (hourly; 1hr 25min); Southern Railway
Maps OS Landranger 197: *Chichester & the South Downs*; OS Explorer 121: *Arundel & Pulborough*

Winding through the lush Arun Valley, this route links three ancient Sussex settlements: picturesque **South Stoke**, tucked in a bend of the Arun, with its lovely Saxon church; **Burpham**, which sits above the river and was fortified during the Danish invasions of the area during the tenth century; and **Arundel** itself, whose fantastic Gothic castle dominates the valley. You can time your walk to have lunch at *The George at Burpham*. Bear in mind that the path can become waterlogged after rain – wellies are a good option for this walk.

Getting started

2.5km Coming out of **Amberley** station, turn left down the road, past the telephone box, and take another left on to the main road towards the long stone bridge; to the right are some little shops and cafés – the *Riverside Café and Bistro* (daily 9am–5pm, http://dinebytheriver.co.uk) has outside seating by the river and is a good place to fuel up before you start the walk.

Cross the bridge over the Arun. At the far side of the bridge you'll see a yellow public footpath sign to the left – go through the kissing gate into a **meadow** which borders the right bank of the river. Keep going straight ahead across the meadow, to an overgrown area on the far side, where a bridge leads over a brook. From here the partially boardwalked path runs along the gently flowing **Arun**, bordered on either side by nettles, elderflower trees and – in June – banks of dog roses, irises and buttercups mixed in with the wild foliage. Dense reeds run along the river side of the path. Eventually you emerge from the undergrowth on to a wider path. Turn left and continue along next to the wooded chalk escarpment. In a clearing just over 750m from the start of the path, a large beech tree stands on the slope to the right, with intricate exposed roots and a rope swing.

To South Stoke

1.5km Around 200m beyond the swing you'll reach the flint boundary wall of **Arundel Park**, created in 1806 by Charles, Duke of Norfolk, out of common land. Farmers lost the right to graze their sheep here, with the result that prosperity – and eventually the local population – declined sharply. You eventually come to a gate into the park, but ignore this and carry on along the path, keeping the flint wall to your right. The path begins to climb away from the river, zigzagging upwards to a wooden gate where you go through into a field.

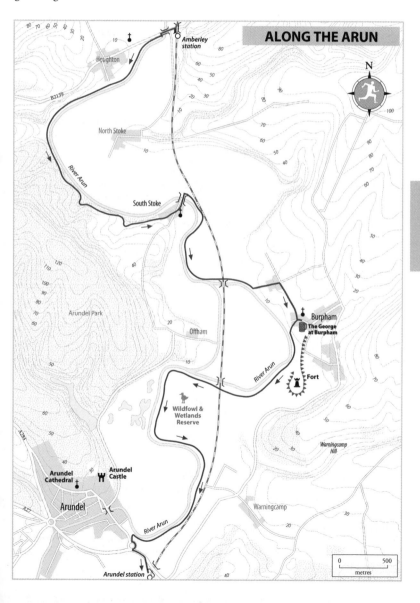

ALONG THE ARUN

The view now opens out, with a sloping field to the right and the South Downs beyond. Carry on down the field and follow the farm track to the left, through a gate where you'll see a wooden public bridleway sign. The path climbs up through woodland then continues through another field to reach a farmyard. You're now in the village of **South Stoke**, which was owned by the earls of Arundel from the Norman Conquest until the reign of Elizabeth I. When Earl Philip Howard (later St Philip) refused to renounce Catholicism, his possessions – including South Stoke – were seized by the Crown. After years of imprisonment, he eventually died in the Tower of London.

Go past the mid-Victorian Chapel Barn, just beyond the farmyard, and turn left on the tarred road. The road bends to the left; follow it and take the footpath on the right just beyond the postbox (set into the side of a wall) to reach the beautiful flint church of **St Leonard's**. Although restored in the nineteenth century, St Leonard's is essentially Norman. The interior is appealingly rudimentary – the church has no electricity – and features a wonderful wooden-beamed ceiling. The churchyard is exceptionally pretty; the Georgian facade of the **rectory** conceals a house dating back to the fifteenth century.

To Burpham

2km Rejoin the road, turning right onto the road and ignoring the "Private no entry" signs – these relate to the field on the left – and continue along the macadam path which takes you over the Arun on a little metal bridge. Then take a right over the wooden stile immediately beyond. You're now walking along the raised left bank of the river, which is wide and fast-moving. Cross a wooden stile and pass through dense foliage; if it's too overgrown, just climb down the bank and carry on through the metal gate – either way you'll emerge over another stile onto a stretch of **pasture**.

Continue along the bank of the river for around 500m. Where the river splits, head up to another wooden stile where the route crosses the railway line towards Burpham. On the other side there's a meadow; the river is much narrower and slower moving at this point. When you meet the track, take the left-hand fork up the **hill**, passing flint houses on the left-hand side. Carry on up the track, which merges with a tarred road; follow the road and, where it divides, turn right into the village.

From here you'll see the fairy-tale shape of **Arundel Castle** to the right across the valley.

Burpham

0.5km Carry on along the road to enter **Burpham** (pronounced "Burfam"); turn left at the bottom of the road for the **pub**. Like South Stoke, Burpham is an extremely old settlement and the site of one of the five **forts** built by King Alfred (see page 162) to repel Danish invaders who used to sail up the Arun Valley, which was then a tidal estuary.

Burpham Church was substantially rebuilt between 1160 and 1220, the vaulted chancel being French in style, though the north wall of the nave and parts of the walls between the arches predate the Norman Conquest. In the churchyard you'll find the grave of the writer **Mervyn Peake**, who lived in the village; Gormenghast Castle in Peake's outlandish Gothic fantasy *Titus Groan* was inspired by Arundel Castle. Just up the road from the church is *The George at Burpham*.

EATING AND DRINKING

The George at Burpham Main St, Burpham BN18 9RR, 01903 883 131, http://georgeatburpham.co.uk. This heavily spruced-up pub makes a good lunch stop, serving fine snacks as well as Sunday roasts from £14). Wash it all down with a pint of Harvey's Best Bitter. Mon–Sat 11am–11pm (closed 3–6pm winter), Sun noon–4pm.

Across the Arun Valley

5km From *The George at Burpham*, head back past the church, but instead of turning right and retracing your steps, go straight ahead down the road with the dead-end sign.

Turn left where the wooden public footpath sign points in two directions and follow the path through the woods; the river now lies to your right and the raised ground up to the left conceals the remains of Alfred's **fort**. Excavations here have revealed the foundations of Saxon buildings, as well as the remains of a mint, which operated up until the Norman Conquest, but there's little to see now – just a wooded mound.

Beyond here, the path emerges at a stile. Cross this, ignoring the track that climbs up the hill to the left, and follow the path as it heads down a meadow and across the **Arun Valley**, with Arundel Castle straight ahead. Over to the left you'll see the terraces of **Warningcamp Hill**, possibly built and named by ancient Britons who feared Roman invasion.

The path continues, passing over dykes via a series of stiles and bridges, and crossing the railway line once more. Ahead, across the river, is the *Black Rabbit* pub at Offham, idyllically situated with a white cliff rising up behind and boats moored in front; Turner painted a mist-shrouded Arundel Castle from this point. Beyond here the path continues to run alongside the river – which is very wide at this point – as it curves away from Arundel, back towards Warningcamp. The surrounding area belongs to the Wildfowl and Wetlands Trust and is home to several unusual species, including the blue duck and the world's rarest goose, the nene, a black-and-grey short-winged Hawaiian bird.

You approach the railway line again but, instead of crossing it, veer right and go through the kissing gate marked by a post with yellow arrows, and continue round to the right. You're now heading back towards the castle. Up ahead, the busy **A27** breaks the peace – the path skirts it, curving round towards the town. Approaching Arundel, the river lies to your right, with little boats in various states of decay moored to fragile wooden jetties.

4 Arundel

The castle and nineteenth-century cathedral lose much of their Gothic glamour on closer inspection, being evidently faux-medieval, but nevertheless **Arundel** is a pretty little town, sitting on a hill in the middle of the Arun valley. Once an inland port linked to the sea by the Arun, Arundel's current staid atmosphere belies the fact that it was a vibrant shipbuilding centre until the Edwardian period, and was also the scene of fights between smugglers and excisemen.

If you want to skip the town and head straight for the **train station**, cut through the field just before the dilapidated tiled building immediately before the moorings. Turn left at the roundabout and follow the A27 to the left. The station lies 200m up the A27 on the right-hand side.

Arundel Castle

Arundel Castle (April–Oct Tues–Sun noon–5pm; £23, gardens £13; http://arundelcastle.org) was originally a Norman structure but was blown up during the Civil War and lavishly reconstructed in the 1860s by Henry, fifteenth Duke of Norfolk, an immensely wealthy eccentric who dined on swans but dressed like a tramp. Inside the castle, make a beeline for the lofty **Baron's Hall** and the **library**, which is hung with works by Gainsborough, Holbein and Van Dyck. The fourteenth-century **Fitzalan Chapel** contains the tombs of past dukes of Norfolk, including two effigies of the seventh duke – one depicting him as he was when he died, the other his emaciated corpse. The chapel adjoins the fourteenth-century parish church of **St Nicholas**, entered from London Road; the chapel is, very unusually, separated from the altar of the Anglican church by a glass screen and an older iron grille.

Arundel Cathedral

West from here along London Road is **Arundel Cathedral** (daily 9am–6pm; http://arundel cathedral.org), gorgeously romantic from a distance, but a bit dull close up. Built in the 1870s by Duke Henry, the cathedral's spire was designed by John Hansom, inventor of the hansom cab. Inside is the tomb of St Philip Howard, exhumed from the Fitzalan Chapel after his canonization in 1970.

Cissbury Ring

Goring-by-Sea to Worthing

Distance and difficulty 14km; moderate–strenuous

Minimum duration 3hr 30min

Trains London Victoria to Goring-by-Sea (every 30min; 1hr 25min); return from Worthing to London Victoria (every 20min; 1hr 20min); Southern Railway

Maps OS Landranger 198: *Brighton & Lewes*; OS Explorer 121: *Worthing & Bognor Regis*

This route starts from **Goring-by-Sea**, at the far edge of the sprawling seaside town of Worthing, west of Brighton. It runs via a small hillfort and the village of **Clapham**, through woodland to attractive **Findon**, where *The Gun Inn* is a reliable pub lunch stop. From here you climb up to **Cissbury Ring**, a vast hillfort with sweeping sea views. The path then descends to **Worthing**, with some urban sprawl to get through before you reach the station.

The route doesn't give you the feeling of unspoilt isolation common to the other South Downs walks in this chapter – aside from Cissbury Ring the downland here has been cultivated and its long contours divided into strips of field. But there are plenty of attractions: the thirteenth-century church at Clapham; the venerable boozer with its World War II associations; and the majesty of Cissbury Ring itself. Plus, if it's a sunny day, you finish up with a swim from **Worthing Beach**.

Getting started

1.5km From **Goring-by-Sea** station, come out onto the road by the railway crossing and follow the green public footpath sign on the path parallel to the railway track, leading away from the station and along the edge of the field. After 700m follow the three-way wooden **public footpath** sign that points up to the right, along a line of trees. Some 200m further on the path comes out onto the bend of a road – cross over onto the pavement and turn right, following the curve of the road towards the downs – you pass some flint cottages to the right. After 200m you come to the dual carriageway, which you need to cross. Turn right and, after only about 10m, follow the green bridleway sign that points to the left up the road.

Highdown Hill and Highdown Garden

2km The track now begins the ascent of **Highdown Hill** – at the top of the track to the right of the metal gate, enter the signed National Trust boundary. Head uphill here along the fence. To the right you'll see a worthwhile detour to **Highdown Garden** (daily: Jan–March 10am–4pm; April–Sept 10am–6pm; Oct–Dec 10am–4pm), an ideal picnic stop. To reach the garden, go through the kissing gate and follow the track, which curves round to the right for 300m to the car park. The garden was created from a chalk pit in the early twentieth century and features many unusual plants and trees, including a Handkerchief Tree and a rare Afghan form of the Judas Tree. It's especially good in early spring, carpeted in daffodils, anemones, snowdrops and bearded iris.

Retrace your steps, and head straight uphill towards the fingerpost. (Down to the left you will now be able to see the sea – and you may also be able to see and hear skylarks above you.)

At the fingerpost, follow the public bridleway sign, which points to the right and skirts the eastern side of Highdown Hill's **Bronze Age fort** – it was once thought to be an outpost of Cissbury Ring, but in fact long predates it. Go straight ahead downhill to continue the walk, or make the short detour to the left to explore the fort. Steps cut into the bank take you to the centre of the small ring-shaped structure from where you can see what a good strategic position this was, with 360° views of the surrounding countryside. A Saxon cemetery was found inside the fort, with cremations and burials, spearheads, knives and glass drinking horns – these finds can be seen in Worthing Museum.

4

Back on the route of the walk, the path veers left into woodland at the three-way fingerpost. It then curves right and begins a gentle descent of Highdown Hill. After 500m, the track emerges from the woodland; the **A27** is audible ahead. Just beyond the substantial house to your right, the path joins a wider track – carry on straight ahead, continuing on the **bridleway** down the hill to the busy tarred road.

This section is little short of hideous due to busy roads – turn left towards the roundabout and then right, crossing one roundabout and the bridge over the A27, towards a second roundabout. Go straight ahead here, on the road signed towards Clapham and Findon. Stay on the left-hand side of the road where there's a pavement but, after a mercifully brief 150m, turn right on the narrow road signed for the Clapham depot – there's also a green public footpath sign.

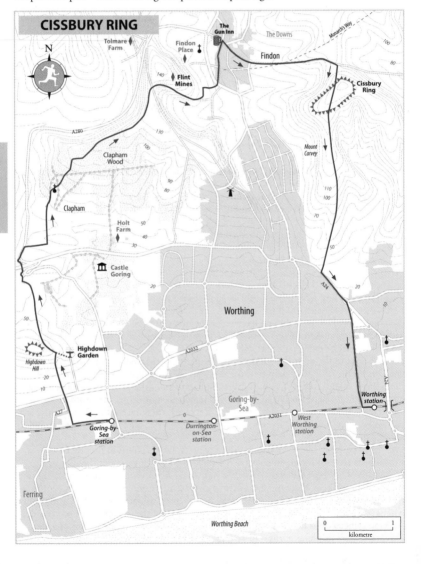

Walk past brick and flint cottages, straight ahead towards the depot. Just before the entrance gates of the depot you'll see a scrubby area to the right, with a faded yellow arrow on a post. Follow this, down the side of the depot. At the end of the buildings turn immediately left through the **woodland**, with the green metal fence to your left. Head down the hill – you soon come out of the woodland and you'll see Clapham village ahead of you.

Clapham village and wood

2km At the bottom of the hill you come to a wooden kissing gate and then a metal gate – the path leads from here up the field to the village of **Clapham**. At the end of the field a wooden gate at a long flint wall takes you up the track into the village. You emerge onto a paved road, with a picturesque thatched building down to the right. Go straight ahead here, following the public footpath sign for the church, **St Mary the Virgin**.

A tiled lynchgate leads to the church – if the gate is locked just go through the portcullis-style gate to the right. The substantial flint church with its bulky tower is mainly thirteenth century and was sympathetically restored by Sir Gilbert Scott, the brilliant Gothic Revivalist architect of St Pancras station and the Albert Memorial. Inside, look out for the lovely **William Morris tiles** over the altar depicting the archangels, and the sixteenth-century brasses and tombs that commemorate the Shelley family, ancestors of Percy Bysshe.

To continue the walk, circle round to the back of the church and you'll see a wooden stile with a yellow arrow – go over the stile and cross the field. Go over a second stile into **Clapham Wood**, which mainly consists of oak and hazel trees. After just 200m you come to a clearing in the wood – go over the stile and cross the clearing. Carry on up the path, which in spring is carpeted to either side with bluebells, celandine and primroses. The path curves right – follow the yellow arrow, which leads along a clearing, with the woodland to your left. Some 200m beyond, cross a stile and another clearing. On the far side there's another wooden stile – continue on the path, which leads gently downhill through the woodland.

You cross another clearing – through the light woodland to your left you'll be able to see rolling downs and hear traffic noise from the A280 at the bottom of the hill.

Towards Findon

2km The dirt track leads straight ahead, exiting the woodland – the views suddenly open out and you can see the soft but dramatic contours of the surrounding **downs**. Carry on straight ahead for 850m. You come out at a track – turn right and, after 20m, take a left, following the blue arrow.

The track leads through light woodland, heading downhill along the side of a ridge; to the left is the site of an ancient **flint mine**. The track runs on for a slow, steady kilometre downhill, with a low flint wall to the left. It comes out at South Lodge. Go straight ahead down the hill, with South Lodge to your left. Turn left after 100m onto the wide track, and keep heading downhill towards the road and the cluster of buildings that comprise Findon.

Findon

2km You come out at a dual carriageway – cross here and bear left and then bear right to head on up Findon's **High Street**, passing *The Black Horse* **pub** to your left. The village is a handsome and affluent little place, with a mixture of 1930s bungalows, Victorian Gothic houses, Georgian mansions and terraced cottages. You pass the *Findon Manor Hotel* on the right and eventually, on the left, you come to the fifteenth-century *Gun Inn*. A plaque outside the pub commemorates the Glengarry Fencibles, a Canadian D-Day division who, while drinking in the pub, originated the popular battle cry "up the Glens".

CISSBURY RING

Epic in scale, **Cissbury Ring** has an enclosed area of 65 acres, with an inner bank 1.5km in circumference. It was constructed some time before 300 BC and would have been surmounted by a timber palisade. The sea views, from Beachy Head to the Isle of Wight, made it a wonderful vantage point, but the fort may have been used to protect livestock rather than for military purposes. The site is dotted with deep flint mines of even greater antiquity: they were mined by Stone Age people using antler-horn tools around 3000 BC. Cissbury Ring was abandoned and then farmed by the Romans, later becoming an Armada beacon site and an anti-aircraft emplacement during World War II.

EATING AND DRINKING

The Gun Inn High St, Findon BN14 0TA, 01903 872 235, http://thegunfindon.co.uk. A low-beamed traditional village inn with a good lunch-time menu featuring chestnut pie, rib eye steaks, roasted plaice and so on for £12–19, plus puds like trifle for £6.50. Mon–Fri 11am–11pm, Sun 11am–10.30pm.

Coming out of the pub, go straight ahead, following the sign to Stable Lane. Head up the road for 500m; at the edge of the village, at a bend in the road, follow the blue pedestrian sign for Cissbury Ring. Go up the paved road for 1km, ignoring the Monarch's Way signs to either side.

Cissbury Ring

0.5km You soon get views of **Cissbury Ring**, the unmissable vast oval mound to the right. Turn right off the road at the National Trust sign. Go straight ahead through the wooden gate to ascend to the top of the **fort**. Head up the stepped path till you reach the top – ahead is a stone that marks the **summit**. From the summit, head south along the length of the inner part of the fort, along the broad grassy path that runs gently downhill.

You come to two mounds at the far side of the fort, with steps built into their inner edges. Exit the fort through the gap in between the mounds.

To Worthing

4km Some 250m beyond the ring, you come out at a National Trust sign and a fingerpost pointing to Steyning Bowl. Ignore this and go straight ahead, through the wooden gate where you'll see a blue arrow and a National Trust sign. The fenced path heads gently up the rounded hill called **Mount Carvey** and then slopes downhill. Ahead you'll see a gas tower in Worthing, and beyond this the sea. Eventually, the path leads along a golf course. Keep heading downhill till you reach a wide road, where you need to turn left. After 500m you come to the Grove Lodge roundabout – take the right-hand turning on the A24 towards Worthing.

Go down the right-hand side of the expansive triangular green, and head down South Farm Road for 1km to reach **Worthing station** – once you cross the rail line bear left on Cross Street for the station. To get to the beach, go straight ahead on Clifton Road for another kilometre.

Mount Caburn and the South Downs

Lewes to Southease via Firle

Distance and difficulty 14.5km plus 5km detour; strenuous

Minimum duration 3hr 40min plus 1hr 15min detour

Trains London Victoria to Lewes (every 30min; 1hr); Southease to Lewes (hourly; 8min); return from Lewes to London Victoria (hourly; 1hr 5min); Southern Railway

Maps OS Landranger 198 and 199: *Brighton & Lewes* and *Eastbourne & Hastings* (the latter is only needed if you do the detour to Charleston Farmhouse); OS Explorer 122 and 123: *Steyning to Newhaven* and *Newhaven to Eastbourne*

This walk takes in the most pleasing features of the Sussex countryside: unspoilt villages, undulating chalky downland and a couple of decent pubs. From the handsome and prosperous town of **Lewes**, it climbs **Mount Caburn**, with its Iron Age earthworks, then descends to the idyllic villages of **Glynde** and **Firle**, both complete with cricket greens and delightful seventeenth- and eighteenth-century buildings. The **Ram** at Firle can provide **lunch** or you could pick up a **picnic** in foodie-heaven Lewes. From Firle there's a great **detour** through the grounds of Firle Place and across the fields to **Charleston Farmhouse**, the country retreat of the Bloomsbury Group. Beyond Firle, a steep path leads up onto the downs, with the **South Downs Way** running east for 5km along a high ridge to the village of Southease, from where there are trains to Lewes. Alternatively, to **shorten the walk**, return to Glynde from Firle and take the train back to Lewes from there.

Getting started

1.5km From the main entrance of **Lewes station** turn right to cross the railway bridge. At the *Landsdown Arms*, go uphill on Station Street then turn right on to the High Street and go straight ahead for 750m. You'll see plenty of places here to pick up a picnic. Carry on to the junction with South Street and then go straight ahead up steep and narrow Chapel Hill. At the top of the hill, with the golf club on your left, is a wooden waymarker with yellow arrows. Follow this through the gate and go straight ahead, following the fence for 50m, then go straight ahead across the field, to a wooden post where you head down into the valley.

Over Mount Caburn

3km This is where the walk proper begins, through the valley that bisects **Mount Caburn**. There are no views from here, but the enclosing valley walls create a wonderfully still atmosphere, which intensifies the sound of lark song. Look out for yellow cowslips in April and May. Head downhill, through two gates, then continue down across a field following the yellow arrow. Go straight ahead at a third gate by some feeding troughs, then follow the bottom of the slightly ridged hill round to your right. Cross a stile by the green sign that welcomes you to Mount Caburn, after which the path begins to climb steeply.

At the top of the hill you cross another stile, from where there's a panorama of the long ridge of the South Downs, the route of the second half of the walk. A short detour to the right leads to the fort itself, whose encircling **defensive ditches** are still clearly visible. Caburn (from the Celtic *caer bryn*, or "fortified hill") was the site of an Iron Age fort, erected around 500 AD. The fort is thought to have contained about seventy wattle-and-daub houses, gathered around a great hall.

Glynde

3km Back at the stile on the top of the ridge, go right and down the hill to the village of **Glynde**, following the path that leads straight ahead down the field. Cross a stile to descend a second field.

Entering the village, you emerge from the path onto a paved road, with an attractive pink cottage opposite. Turn left then right onto Glynde's main street where, among the beautiful flint cottages, there's an Arts-and-Crafts-era working **forge**, fronted by a giant horseshoe (visitors are welcome). Glynde lies just to the south of the world-famous **Glyndebourne Opera House**, and is also home to Glynde Place, a privately owned Elizabethan mansion. Pass Glynde **train station** on the right, cross the bridge over Glynde Reach, a tributary of the Ouse. Cross the busy A27 and take the narrow paved track directly ahead of you.

4

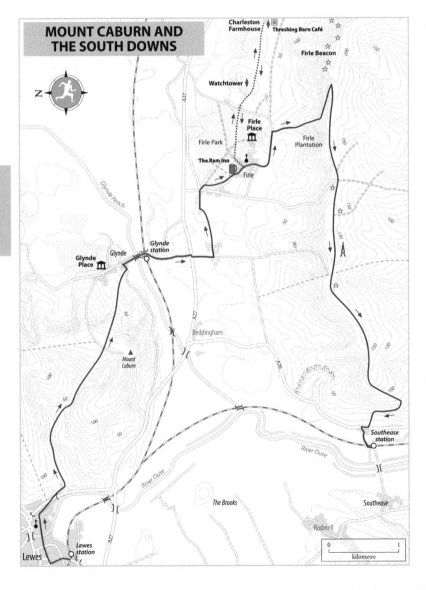

THE SOUTH DOWNS

The "blunt, bow-headed, whale-backed" **South Downs**, as Kipling described them, run from Winchester in the west, terminating in the east at the spectacular high white cliffs near Eastbourne. Walking along the ridge of the downs, with the crescents of smooth, green-gold hills ahead, the sea to one side and the winding rivers to the other – and maybe a trilling skylark above – you can feel an exhilarating sense of space and isolation. The vegetation is low and from a distance appears sparse, lending the landscape an austere quality – the beauty, as far as plant life goes, is in the detail, from butter-coloured cowslips to tiny, delicate orchids. The downs are cut through by a series of river valleys – the Arun, the Ouse, the Adur and the Cuckmere – dotted with wonderful medieval villages which, partly owing to the economic depression that characterized the area until intensive farming was begun after World War II, remain remarkably unchanged and unspoilt. They offer plenty of diversions, from Saxon churches to excellent old country pubs.

Turn left when you come to a wall marked Preston Court. Continue along the track, passing a flint barn and some outbuildings on your left. Just beyond this is a stile – cross it, turn right and walk through the field. Go through two sets of gates and cross the field ahead of you, then swing round to the left, past a barn. Here you join a wider farm track; turn right towards Firle. After 300m, at the five-way junction, cross the road to the public footpath leading into the grounds of **Firle Place**. This picturesque house was built in the late fifteenth century, tucked in the lee of the downs to protect it from strong winds and furnish it with well water; it was later remodelled and given an elegant Georgian facade. Follow the paved path for 50m, then cut off to the right towards the playground. Go through the gate by the playground and follow the path between the cricket ground and the tennis courts into the village.

Firle

The route brings you out at the back of the seventeenth-century *Ram Inn* at **Firle**, a decent **lunch** or pint stop, though a boutique-style makeover has diminished the atmosphere. The oldest part of the building is thought to be medieval, and there is a resident ghost, that of an old washerwoman with a wooden leg who lived in an attic in the eaves. She was found dead one day in her laundry basket; it's claimed she can sometimes be heard stomping across her tiny room.

EATING AND DRINKING

The Ram Inn The Street, Firle BN8 6NS, 01273 858 222, http://raminn.co.uk. This historic but heavily restored pub has a large orchard at the back and serves decent gastro- pub lunches (from £12 for a main) plus Harveys Bitter, guest ales and cider on tap. Mon–Sat 11.30am–11pm, Sun noon–10.30pm.

To rejoin the walk, carry on up Firle's main street following the sign for St Peter's Church, past rows of neat seventeenth- and eighteenth-century cottages. Just before you come to St Peter's at the top end of the village, there's a detour (2.5km each way) left off the main street to **Charleston Farmhouse**, the painter Vanessa Bell's immaculately restored home, which was a focus for the activities of the Bloomsbury Group.

Detour to Charleston Farmhouse

5km Go through the gate into the grounds of **Firle Place** and head to the right, passing the house, which lies to your right. There are a couple of wooden posts with yellow arrows in the field showing the route through the estate, though they're easy to miss; you need to head for the high ground to the right, which is surmounted by a tower. At the edge of the estate go through the wooden gate, up the driveway between two **flint cottages**, and then through a metal gate. Carry on ahead along the thin chalk path that leads up the field, to the right of the flint wall. At the top go through the wooden gate (a chalk track heads left to the tower, which is a private house). From the wooden gate, carry on straight ahead on the second track that leads across the fields. From here you can see the barns and orange roof of Charleston ahead of you.

Charleston Farmhouse
In 1916, on the recommendation of her sister Virginia Woolf, Vanessa Bell moved to **Charleston Farmhouse** (April–Oct Wed–Sat 1–6pm, Sun 1–5.30pm, last entry 1hr before closing; obligatory 1hr tours run every 20min; £16; http://charleston.org. uk), along with the painter Duncan Grant, her two children and the writer David Garnett. The house initially provided a rural retreat from World War I, but soon became the country home of the **Bloomsbury Group** and a social and artistic stimulus for the Woolfs and other intellectuals including the artist and curator Roger Fry, the biographer Lytton Strachey and the economist John Maynard Keynes.

EATING AND DRINKING

Threshing Barn Café Charleston Farmhouse, Firle BN8 6LL. Charleston's café, located in some outbuildings, serves simple seasonal meals (tart of the day £6.50) and cream teas (£5). Wed–Sat 10am–5pm.

Grant and Bell decorated every surface of Charleston – both were admirers of the emphatic lines and bold colours of the postimpressionists – so that the house became a work of art in its own right. However, by the time Duncan Grant died in 1978, Charleston had become dilapidated, and a reverential **restoration** of the house and garden was undertaken in the 1980s by the Charleston Trust. The Mediterranean colours of the wall paintings were revived, the loveliest perhaps being the cockerel and hound above and below Bell's bedroom window, which Grant painted to wake her in the morning and guard her at night. Other experiments in the decorative arts were less successful, as the rather wobbly pottery of the offshoot **Omega Workshop** testifies. But the house is still permeated with sensuous colour and light, and the lush gardens, with their quirky statuary, are enticing too; all can be seen on the impressively informative tours.

On to the downs

1.5km From the front of the pub, go straight up the main street, passing the drive to St Peter's Church and the tradesmen's entrance to Firle Place, following the bridlepath signs. (If you've made the detour to Charleston Farmhouse, you could simply turn left up the track on the eastern edge of Firle Park and climb up onto the downs from there).

Plain **St Peter's** itself is well worth a look; a stained-glass window designed by John Piper depicting the Tree of Life features strong, sinuous lines and dazzling colour, and there's also an Elizabethan tomb with a sombre double effigy.

Follow the track, which curves round to the left, for 500m till you come to a beech tree in the middle of the track. Go along the gravel path up the hill to the right, skirting the aspen and silver birch woods of **Firle Plantation** on your right. The path makes the dizzying ascent up the escarpment of the South Downs, eventually joining the **South Downs Way** at the fence at the top. Looking back, you'll see a crenellated flint tower, built in the early nineteenth century as a watchtower for the gamekeeper of Firle Place. When you reach the top, the English Channel is revealed to the south; you might see a cross-channel ferry from Dieppe nipping into the port of Newhaven.

The South Downs Way

5.5km At the top, take a right onto the **South Downs Way**, and continue for 300m till you come to a car park. From here the South Downs Way leads through a wooden gate marked with a sky-blue arrow and runs along the top of the ridge. There's no chance of losing your way here: just keep to the highest ground. After 700m you pass some radio masts on the left; from here the fort surmounting Mount Caburn is clearly visible.

After 1.5km, you start to descend, with Newhaven visible to the left. The track then plunges steeply, down Itford Hill towards **Southease**, to emerge near the A26. A footbridge takes you across the road to **Southease station**, from where trains make the short run back to Lewes. Alternatively, you can call a **taxi** on 01273 477567, http://gmtaxislewes.co.uk to take you back to Lewes (around £12).

4

The South Downs Way

Lewes to Eastbourne via Alfriston

Distance and difficulty day one: 8km, moderate; day two: 29.5km; strenuous

Minimum duration day one: 2.5hr; day two: 7.5hr

Trains London Victoria to Lewes (every 15min; 1hr 38min); return from Eastbourne to London Victoria (every 30min; 1hr 30min); Southern Railway

Maps OS Landranger 198 and 199: *Brighton & Lewes* and *Eastbourne & Hastings*; OS Explorer 122 and 123: *Steyring to Newhaven* and *Newhaven to Eastbourne*

The **South Downs Way** runs for 160km from Winchester to Eastbourne; the two-day section described here covers the spectacular eastern extent of the route. It starts from **Lewes** and ends at **Eastbourne**: each day's walk can be done separately, or you can stay at **Southease** and make a two-day walk of it. On **day one** you walk across the Ouse valley, crisscrossed with water channels, via a couple of ancient Sussex villages – Iford and Rodmell. You can eat and stay at the YHA **hostel** in Southease, or return to Lewes from here by train. **Book in advance** for the hostel. On **day two** you ascend the downs for a longish hike before descending to picturesque Alfriston. The route then leads through the lush Cuckmere Valley to the undulating cliffs at Beachy Head and on to Eastbourne. This second day should only be undertaken if you're fit: there are some fantastically wiggly contours to contend with.

Day one

8km The walk starts gently, from **Lewes** and down onto the watery plain of the Ouse River – this can be a very muddy stretch. Surrounded by downland views, you walk alongside water channels before climbing briefly onto the downs and dropping down into **Rodmell**, where the *Abergavenny Arms* is a good stop for a pint and lunch. It's well worth exploring Rodmell, to see **Monk's House**, the home of Leonard and Virgina Woolf, and to look at the twelfth-century church. The route continues to Southease, where there's an excellent youth hostel, or take the branch-line train for the eight-minute journey back to Lewes (check times in advance as they stop early evening).

Getting started

1km From the main entrance of Lewes station, turn left down Station Road, then right onto **Priory Street**. Turn left beyond the church, down **Cockshut Road**. You go underneath a bridge over the minor road; 50m beyond here, turn left and follow the sign if you want to detour to see the remains of the Cluniac St Pancras Priory. It was founded in the eleventh century by William de Warenne, builder of Lewes Castle, and his wife Gunrada, and destroyed in 1538 during the dissolution of the monasteries.

Back on the route, head down the path and, with the bank ahead of you, turn right following the cycle sign to Kingston, through the **concrete tunnel** under the major road. Turn right and then left, following the **public footpath** sign on the fingerpost. Go across the field then through a wooden kissing gate, and climb up the bank immediately to your right.

To Itford and Rodmell

5km Walk along the bank, with the water channel to your right and playing fields beyond. After 800m, go through the wooden gate and, just after the playing fields peter out, the path draws close to the road. Take the path that cuts across diagonally and up to the left. You're heading for the **wooden gate** at a gap in the hedge.

Go through the gate, and straight across another field. At the edge of the field you go through a gap in the hedge onto a **narrow dirt path**, with trees to the left and gardens with rabbit hutches to the right. You pass a small sewage works to the left and come out onto a track. Turn right for just a few metres, then left up the bank via some wooden steps. You go over a stile at the top of the bank and go to the summit of the field and straight ahead, eventually following the **yellow arrow** on the post you will see in front of you; go straight ahead here, not to the right.

You emerge, 700m beyond the sewage works, at the hamlet of **Itford** – approaching, go over a stile at a metal gate with a yellow arrow and cross a second stile. At Itford, head up the track between a converted barn and a flint cottage. Cross the tarred road and the stile, marked with a public footpath sign. Go through the field, with the long flint wall to your left – behind the wall is a beautiful white villa. Go across a drive,

4

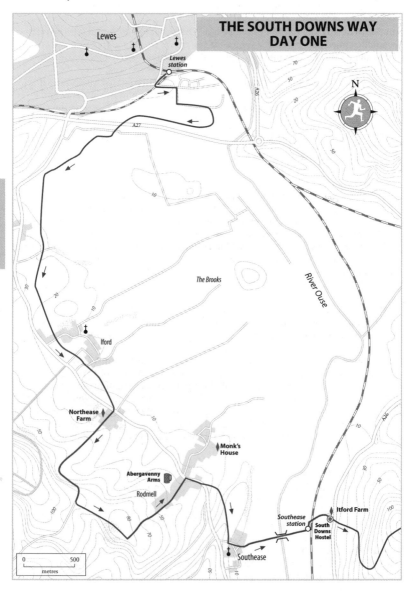

THE SOUTH DOWNS WAY
DAY ONE

MONK'S HOUSE

Leonard and Virginia Woolf bought **Monk's House** (April–Oct Wed–Sat 2–5.30pm; £5.25; NT) in 1919 when Virginia was 37, and the "unpretending house, long & low, a house of many doors" became their country retreat from London. They painted it in shades of pomegranate and pistachio green, and filled it with painted tiles, drawings and oils by Virginia's sister Vanessa Bell and her partner Duncan Grant, who lived at nearby Charleston (see page 123).

It's hard not to be moved by the house, which, despite the charm of its colour scheme and decoration, strongly conveys the austerity of the Woolfs' lives – when E.M. Forster stayed here he got so cold that he burnt his trousers on the bedroom stove trying to get warm. The colours of the **garden** are as bold and striking as those inside the house, and it's cleverly divided into intimate sections that feel like separate rooms. Beyond it is an orchard with, as Virginia wrote, "the grey extinguisher of the church steeple pointing my boundary". The little wooden lodge was Virginia's writing room, and its loft was used to store apples.

It was from this paradisal place that Virginia Woolf, fearing another onset of mental illness, walked to the Ouse and drowned herself in 1941. Leonard stayed on in the house until he died in 1969.

through a couple of gates and then you emerge with a pink villa to your left under an arched pine tree. You join the road for just 20m, then go over the stile on the right, back into the fields.

Across another couple of fields you join a track where you turn right to join the road. It's possible to turn left along the road here for a quicker route into Rodmell, but it's not recommended as there's no verge to walk on. Instead, cross the road and turn right for a few metres, then turn left on a paved **farm track**. Follow the farm track for 1km – it curves round to the left with a bank rising up to the right and impressive open views to the left. Eventually you come to a fingerpost marking a crossroads with the **South Downs Way**. Turn left here, and after 75m you'll see a wooden cross marking the meridian line (the line of longitude); after another 600m you come out at a little road. Turn left down the hill, following the sign to Rodmell. After 700m you come to Rodmell with its appealing jumble of flint, brick and clapboard cottages and villas. You come to a wider road; cross over for the *Abergavenny Arms*, a good pit stop for a **pint**. Coming out of the pub, either turn left along the road to continue the walk to Southease or, for an enticing detour, take a sharp right following the sign to **Monk's House** (see above), a white clapboard cottage that you reach after 550m.

Coming out of Monk's House, turn left and immediately left again onto the public footpath that leads up to **St Peter's church**, which dates back in part to the twelfth century; it features medieval glass and an 800-year-old font. Coming out of the church, turn left up the street into Rodmell. Back at the pub, turn left along the road to get to Southease.

To Southease and the downs

2km Go along the road past the bus stop, and look out for the footpath sign on the left which points to Southease. The path meanders through some fields, and emerges onto a track; turn right and go through the wooden gate, then head left down the tarred lane. You'll see Southease church through the trees to your right.

Southease is a small and extremely pretty settlement, distinguished by a round-towered Saxon church. Inside are faint traces of thirteenth-century wall paintings depicting scenes from the life of Christ. From the church, follow the minor road that leads straight down through the hamlet and over the River Ouse. At the station, cross the railway line and go through the gates. A track leads up towards some farm buildings which house the YHA's flagship *South Downs Hostel*.

EATING AND DRINKING

South Downs Hostel Itford Farm, Beddingham BN8 6JS, 0345 371 9574, http://yha.org.uk. State-of-the-art hostel with good communal facilities: you can sleep in the restored farmhouse or barns, or in a bell tent, land pod or camping pod (for the last option you need to bring your own sleeping bag). The in-house *Courtyard Café* provides a filling dinner (mains £8.95) and breakfast (£6.50). Dorms £18, camping pods £59 per person

Day two

29.5km This is a hugely rewarding and hugely long walk, initially along a high ridge of the downs before a descent to Alfriston. You then take in the verdant **Cuckmere Valley**, secluded forest, and the undulating chalky cliffs of the **Seven Sisters** and **Beachy Head**. To do this as a **one-day walk** from London, take the train to Lewes, then the branch line to Southease.

Along the downs to Alfriston

10km From the youth hostel, cross a wooden bridge over the busy A26 to join the South Downs Way. Make the steady, steep ascent of the downs, until you reach the top of the ridge, with good views north to **Mount Caburn** (see page 121). For the next 10km, the path sweeps along the top of the downs, and you get a real sense of quiet and isolation. Apart from the radio mast ahead, the other features you'll notice on this stretch are the tumuli that lie to either side of the path. These rounded grassy burial mounds are **Bronze Age barrows** – the largest would originally have stood up to 6m high, but all have been eroded over the centuries and opened either by thieves or antiquarians. The barrows were built by a people known as the **Beaker Folk**, named for their custom of placing a drinking vessel beside entombed bodies – bronze daggers and spearheads were left, too, suggesting that the Beaker Folk were preparing their dead for the afterlife. The bodies were arranged in a curled, foetal position, as if the rounded barrow was the womb that would carry them into the next world.

Eventually the path begins to descend towards Alfriston. You come to a **crossroads**, with paths radiating out in five directions. Carry on straight ahead on the South Downs Way itself. The chalky track drops down into the village.

Alfriston

0.5km Once in **Alfriston**, you join a wide tarred road called King's Ride. Go straight ahead until you see the Tudor *George Inn* ahead of you; the *Star* is on the left – you are now in the heart of the village, on the High Street. This handsome village has more the feel of a small town, with good eating options (see below) and some great independent shops, including an award-winning bookshop, Much Ado Books, on the High Street. The main sights are the church and the **Clergy House** (see page 134). There are two fine, timber-framed, fourteenth-century buildings in Alfriston housing pubs – the *Star* and *The George*, mentioned above, but for eating you're best off at the brilliant *Badger's Tearoom*.

EATING AND DRINKING

Badger's Tearoom North St, Alfriston BN26 5UG, 01323 871 336, http://badgersteahouse.com. The extremely pretty tearoom is housed in a 1510 building, and provides amazing home-made cakes which you can eat in the walled and flower-filled garden. Mon–Fri 9.30am–4pm, Sat & Sun 10am–4.30pm.

The walk continues from the square at the east end of the High Street in Alfriston, where you'll see the village's market cross. Opposite the little post office building there's a road off to the right, marked with a South Downs Way marker. This leads to the **Cuckmere River**. Turn right here, down towards the unexpectedly imposing **Church of St Andrews** – known as the "Cathedral of the Downs", it dates from the mid-fourteenth century and has a spacious cruciform interior.

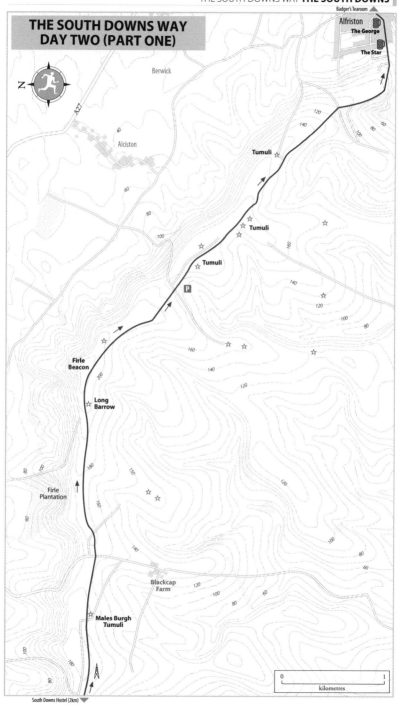

**THE SOUTH DOWNS WAY
DAY TWO (PART ONE)**

Badger's Tearoom

Alfriston
The George
The Star

Berwick

Alciston

Tumuli

Tumuli

Tumuli

P

Firle
Beacon

Long
Barrow

Firle
Plantation

Blackcap
Farm

Males Burgh
Tumuli

4

0 ——— 1
kilometres

South Downs Hostel (2km)

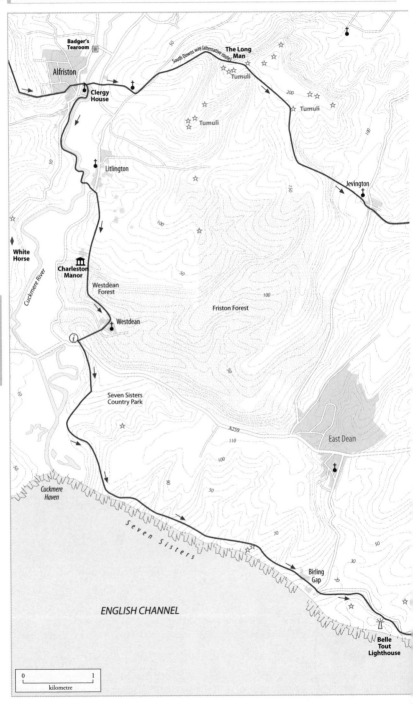

Badger's Tearoom

Alfriston

Clergy House

South Downs way (alternative route)

The Long Man

Tumuli

Tumuli

Tumuli

Litlington

Jevington

White Horse

Cuckmere River

Charleston Manor

Westdean Forest

Westdean

Friston Forest

Seven Sisters Country Park

East Dean

Cuckmere Haven

Seven Sisters

Birling Gap

ENGLISH CHANNEL

Belle Tout Lighthouse

0   1
kilometre

4

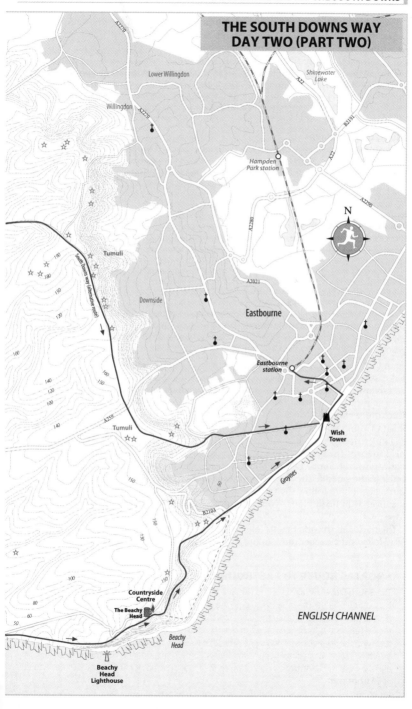

**THE SOUTH DOWNS WAY
DAY TWO (PART TWO)**

Shinewater Lake

Lower Willingdon

Willingdon

Hampden Park station

N

Tumuli

Downside

Eastbourne

South Downs way (alternative route)

Eastbourne station

Tumuli

Wish Tower

Groynes

Countryside Centre

The Beachy Head

ENGLISH CHANNEL

Beachy Head

Beachy Head Lighthouse

4

From the church, head through the graveyard towards the fourteenth-century **Alfriston Clergy House** (early to mid-March Sat & Sun 11am–4pm; mid-March to end Oct Mon, Wed, Thurs, Sat & Sun 10am–5pm; end Oct to mid-Dec Mon, Wed, Thurs, Sat & Sun 11am–4pm; £6.90; NT). This is a Wealden "hall house" – the central hall is flanked by two-storey bays that jut out to the front – and the whole building is surmounted by a thatched roof. Turn left before you reach the house, then go straight ahead, with the church behind you. Turn right and you're back on the bank of the Cuckmere, which skirts the cottage garden of the Clergy House.

Along the Cuckmere

1.5km Beyond the Clergy House, the **Cuckmere** winds through an exceptionally pretty and lush valley – it's hard to believe that contraband goods were once run up this lazy little river from the sea (see page 135). Just before you reach the wooden bridge over the Cuckmere at Litlington, you can see a white **chalk horse** on the hill ahead, created in 1924 by three brothers who secretly cut the horse by moonlight one night.

Litlington to Westdean Forest

3km Once over the bridge, turn right. After 150m the path joins a road opposite a huge thatched house; turn left into **Litlington** and then take the first right. Immediately to the right, a South Downs Way sign points you onto a narrow path, through a kissing gate. The path climbs steeply up a field and through another kissing gate. Carry on up the field and over a stile into another field – then head downhill, keeping the fence to your right, towards **Westdean Forest**.

At the very edge of the forest, turn left to follow the South Downs Way – handsome thirteenth-century **Charleston Manor** is visible ahead through the trees. A little further on, wooden steps lead up into the trees. South Downs Way signs direct you through the forest to the secluded medieval village of **Westdean**. Ignore the road that curves round left to the church and go straight ahead to continue on the South Downs Way. Go past the green phone box on the left, climb the steps ahead of you through the trees and follow the public footpath sign towards Cuckmere Haven.

Cuckmere Haven

2.5km Coming out of the forest, you'll see the Cuckmere River ahead of you, snaking through the silted estuary at **Cuckmere Haven**. Go straight ahead down the field towards the visitor centre. Across the busy road and over the cattle grid, the path splits, the South Downs Way climbing high up the valley wall and a second track leading beside the river. If you want to save yourself a strenuous climb, it's quite possible to follow the track along the river, picking up the South Downs Way just over 1km further on – you can make a little detour on to the beach from the lower path.

The track and the other paths join and then diverge once more; the South Downs Way follows the steeper route to the left, taking you onto the downs again.

SHORTER ROUTE TO EASTBOURNE

The **South Downs Way** splits into two at Alfriston, with one route (10km) taking you to Eastbourne over the downs and avoiding the spectacular but testing (and longer) cliff walk described on page 135. To join this branch of the South Downs Way, cross the bridge over the Cuckmere shortly before you reach the Church of St Andrew and turn left after 100m, following the South Downs Way signs. After 2km you pass **the Long Man of Wilmington**, a 70m-high ancient chalk giant cut onto the hill. Some 3km further on you go through the ancient village of **Jevington**, beyond which the route descends for 5km to the western edge of **Eastbourne**.

JEVINGTON JIGG

Smuggling has a very long history in Sussex – wool-running, known as "owling", started in the thirteenth century following the imposition of a severe tax on wool under Edward I, and continued into the eighteenth century. By this time, smuggling had developed into a serious industry, with goods, from brandy to lace and tea, being smuggled in from the continent.

Many gangs of smugglers were bankrolled by City of London financiers, and whole villages, from estate owners to innkeepers, were involved. One such innkeeper was James Pettit, known as **Jevington Jigg**, who operated out of the *Eight Bells* in Jevington, running contraband from Birling Gap. Jevington Jigg was a kind of Sussex Ned Kelly, and he led a lawless and incident-packed life – when once trapped in an inn surrounded by armed constables, he managed to escape by changing into a petticoat and feigning girlish hysterics. In 1789 he was arrested with his friend Cream Pot Tom for stealing a mare in Firle. Tom was hanged at Oxford, but Jevington Jigg was released, leading people to suspect he had betrayed his friend. He was later nearly lynched at Lewes for informing on other associates. Eventually Jevington Jigg's luck ran out: he was convicted of horse theft and transported to Botany Bay in Australia, and probably died there.

Today the exploits of the smugglers, including a small gang that operated out of Alfriston, are much romanticized, despite their violent and sometimes murderous treatment of excisemen. Traces of tunnels beneath inns and manor houses – and even the church in Jevington – built to hide contraband goods from the excisemen, are the last reminder of the trade.

4

The Seven Sisters, Birling Gap and Beachy Head

7km From here on, brace yourself for the dramatic walk over the switchback sequence of cliffs known as the **Seven Sisters**. The path runs close to the edge of the chalky cliffs, with the only break in the clifftop walk provided by **Birling Gap**, a small settlement with a row of nineteenth-century coastguards' cottages. Beyond, the clifftop walk takes you on a further rollercoaster ride to **Beachy Head**, the highest point of the cliffs (160m). The wildness of the surroundings helps to explain why Debussy came here to complete **La Mer**, his masterly evocation of the sea; he stayed at the *Grand Hotel* on the front in nearby Eastbourne. Look out for the red and white candy stripes of the gorgeous **lighthouse**, built in 1902, just off the coast at Beachy Head.

Into Eastbourne

5km At the *Beachy Head* pub just to the left of the route, you begin to descend into Eastbourne. Take the tarred path that leads off to the right, via a viewpoint. Cross the metal gate and descend the narrow wooded path for 1.5km. Below you is **Eastbourne**, whose Edwardian villas can look unexpectedly glamorous in the evening light. The last gasp of downland walk takes you down a steep grassy slope, and lands you right on Eastbourne's seafront. Follow the seafront for just over 1.5km, heading towards the pier; turn left onto Terminus Road for the station. If you're flagging at this point, a taxi (01323 725511) to the station from the seafront will cost around £7.

The Saxon Shore

WINCHELSEA BEACH

5 The Saxon Shore

Leading along the coast from Hastings in Sussex to Gravesend in Kent, the Saxon Shore Way is named for the string of late Roman fortifications that protected the coast against Saxon invasion, as at Anderida, which features on the second walk in this chapter. This stretch of Sussex shoreline remained vulnerable to invasion though – it was at Anderida that William the Conqueror landed. The first walk leads along part of the Saxon Shore Way, starting with a hike along the cliffs at Hastings, then descending to the lovely town of Winchelsea. The second (and longest) walk, the 1066 Country Walk, takes you along the route followed by the Normans from their landing place through wooded hills to Battle. The Chichester Harbour walk leads from Fishbourne Palace, with its fine Roman mosaics, through marshland and pasture to the appealing village of Bosham. The fourth walk in the chapter explores the cliff-circled Isle of Thanet, with a route running from Ramsgate to Margate via Broadstairs.

The Saxon Shore Way

Hastings to Winchelsea via Cliff End

Distance and difficulty 17km; strenuous
Minimum duration 4hr 15min
Trains London Charing Cross to Hastings (every 30min; 1hr 20min); return from Winchelsea to Hastings (hourly; 15min), then Hastings to London St Pancras (every 30min; 1hr 20min); Southern Railways
Maps OS Landranger 199 and 189: *Eastbourne & Hastings* and *Ashford & Romney Marsh*; OS Explorer 124: *Hastings & Bexhill*

This glorious walk is very much a day of two halves, starting as a strenuous hike along the clifftops near Hastings before descending to the pancake-flat "levels" beyond. The route follows part of the **Saxon Shore Way**, a long-distance path that runs for 260km in its entirety, from Hastings all the way round the coast to Gravesend. Starting in tattily charismatic **Hastings**, a funicular takes you up to the sandstone cliffs that soar above the town into the pristine downland of the **Hastings Country Park**. From here, the route follows the clifftops for 5km, taking in sweeping sea views and dipping down into lush wooded glens before terminating at the prosaically named village of **Cliff End**; a short detour leads from here to a long sandy **beach**, where it's sometimes safe to swim. From Cliff End, the walk runs across **Pett Level**, reclaimed from the sea and crisscrossed by water channels. Though the scenery is less obviously dramatic than along the clifftop walk, the levels have an enticingly still atmosphere and are prettily framed by hills to the north and the long bank of the sea wall to the south. The walk ends at **Winchelsea**, an attractive little town with a fascinating history.

There are lots of **picnic** spots along the way, but you'll need to wait till Winchelsea for a good **pub**. It's cheapest and quickest to return from Winchelsea via Hastings, taking either the bus or the train, meaning that you can buy a return ticket to Hastings. Alternatively, infrequent trains run from Winchelsea to London **via Ashford**, but if you go for this option you have to buy two single tickets rather than a return.

Getting started

2km From **Hastings station**, go down Havelock Road, then straight ahead down Wellington Place, through a pedestrian underpass and towards the old town. Turn left along the seafront and continue for 700m, past Hastings' appealingly shabby jumble of Regency and Victorian buildings, amusement arcades and fish 'n' chip shops. Follow the signs towards the East Hill Cliff Railway.

This picturesque part of town is known as the **Stade**, from the old English for "landing place" – Hastings still has a working fleet and you'll see brightly coloured boats on the beach, among the unusually tall black wooden fishing huts that lend the area a quirky Gothic air. These were built in the nineteenth century to store nets and ropes – as the sea came in much further at that time, fishermen were forced to capitalize on the available space by building up rather than out.

Hastings Country Park

5km Opposite the cluster of fishing huts, the East Hill **funicular railway** (April–Sept 10am–5.30pm; Oct & Nov 11am–4pm; £1.70), Britain's steepest at 39 degrees, runs up the cliffside at surprising speed. If you want to start walking before the funicular starts running, or if it's not functioning, you'll have to climb the cliff via Tamarisk Steps to the left of the train tracks, by *the Dolphin Inn* pub. The funicular provides tremendous views of the town and lands you in **Hastings Country Park**, whose cliffs tower up to 90m above the sea and are bright with yellow gorse in the summer. You pick up the Saxon Shore Way here, though it's not signed; follow the brown signs towards Firehills. If in doubt at any point in the park, head for the path closest to the cliffs.

Go straight ahead and up the hill, which is surmounted by a low, circular-banked structure, the remains of an **Iron Age fort**. The views are tremendous, with the sea to the

THE SAXON SHORE WAY

5

THE LEVELS

The **levels** are the defining physical feature of the first two walks in this chapter: a landscape of fields and banks, reclaimed from the sea and crisscrossed by little man-made channels (known as "sewers"). Reclamation was an expensive and therefore very gradual process, begun by the Romans, revived in the eighth century by monastic houses that owned tracts of marshland, and continued into the eighteenth century. The result of this piecemeal development is a landscape of small and irregularly shaped fields, scattered with shells, offering a reminder of the land's watery origins. The marshy, reed-fringed **peninsula** near Fishbourne Palace illustrates how the levels must have looked before they were reclaimed.

right, Hastings to the left and the cliffs you'll walk along ahead. Just beyond the fort, head right to the long wooden fence that runs along a field. From here, simply follow the path as it hugs the cliff edge and dips down first into **Ecclesbourne**, **Fairlight** and **Warren Glens**, wooded clefts in the cliffs, following the brown signs to Fairlight and/or Firehills. There's a nudist beach at Fairlight, although the council recommends that you avoid it because of recent cliff falls.

Coming out of Warren Glen, follow the wide grassy path that leads up the hill and veers left, away from the cliffs, following the signs to Fairlight Church and Firehills. Some 400m beyond here you'll pass a radio mast on top of the hill; carry on straight ahead to Firehills on the cliffside path to the right, not the one that leads inland.

Fairlight to Cliff End

3km From the country park, you emerge into staid **Fairlight**. Go straight ahead along Channel Way, a track that leads between the rows of bungalows and the sea. Some 500m along Channel Way, turn left onto Shepherd's Way, and after 100m turn right onto Bramble Way. After 250m turn left onto Smuggler's Way then, after 200m, take a right onto Lower Wait's Lane. This lane cuts through the village for 750m; at the T-junction, turn right. About 100m further on you'll see a National Trust sign. Go through the gap in the hedge here, onto the path that leads through a field and climbs away from Fairlight.

The cliff-top walk resumes from this point. Out of the National Trust area, follow the yellow arrow on the fence post – you'll see a gorgeous golden strand ahead. You're now in **Cliff End**. Head down the hill for 400m, past two pretty thatched cottages – ignore the turn-offs and go straight ahead downhill until you get to the road. Turn right and keep going for 300m to get to the **beach**, but don't swim if the red flag is flying.

Pett Level

4km To continue along the Saxon Shore Way, turn right at the point where the path joins the road through Cliff End and head towards the beach. After 100m, where the road curves, take the footpath to the left along the **Royal Military Canal**, built by William Pitt for defence against a Napoleonic invasion that never materialized. After 200m you come to a little bridge – don't cross over here, but go straight ahead up the left bank of the canal, on a narrow path. After another 200m you'll see a brick pillbox on the left – just before you reach it, turn right over a second bridge to cross the canal. (The official route continues on the left bank here and crosses at the third bridge, but the path can be very overgrown so it's better to cross here.) Continue up the right bank of the canal. At a third bridge, cross the road and carry on up the canal.

From here you're on **Pett Level** and the views open up – the canal heads gradually away from the sea and the noisy seafront road, drawing closer to the hills to the north, where you'll see a windmill. At a kink in the canal the Dimsdale Sewer (actually a water channel) appears on your right, so you're walking between the two stretches of water. Where the canal curves to the right there's a bridge – don't cross over here, but continue for another 700m until you begin to draw near to a white clapboard house on the left.

Cross at the **concrete bridge**, marked with yellow public footpath arrows. Go straight ahead across the field towards the road, then follow the curve of the track up the hill to the left. Go through the gate and turn right onto a minor road. After 100m you come to **New Gate**, one of the medieval entrances to Winchelsea. Go through it, then look back – you'll see that the arch of the gate perfectly frames **Wickham Manor**, a fine early sixteenth-century farmhouse. Follow the road for 700m and bear right at the T-junction for Winchelsea.

Winchelsea
3km On your right as you enter the main part of town is the great **Church of St Thomas**. The transepts and nave were entirely destroyed by the French, but the

---

WINCHELSEA: FROM STORMS TO SACKING

The now sedate town of **Winchelsea** originally sat on a long shingle spit that poked out from Fairlight cliffs. However, by the thirteenth century the spit was being eaten away by erosion. A huge **storm** in 1252 and a freak high tide swallowed up three hundred houses, while another storm in 1288 converted it into an island. It was decided to move Winchelsea to higher and safer ground – the remains of the old town are now submerged, their exact whereabouts unknown.

Edward I employed a French architect, who designed the new town along the lines of a French *bastide* (fortified town) on a neat grid plan. It was built primarily for commerce and was a vital link in the wine trade with Bordeaux, as well as being a place from where fish, wool, cheese and salt were exported, plus iron and wool from the Weald. There was a good road to London, and each merchant was given wharf space on the then wide and flourishing River Brede. The king imposed a perpetual rent on the town in return for the building costs, and a sum of just over £14 is still collected annually.

Prior to the rebuilding, the strategic significance of Winchelsea had already been recognized by its inclusion in the **Cinq Ports** confederation. This was a grouping of five towns – Hastings, New Romney, Hythe, Sandwich and Dover – to which Winchelsea and Rye were later added. At a time when Britain had no navy, the Cinq Ports were the only line of defence against a possible invasion of southern England. In exchange for providing ships and men for a certain number of days a year, the ports were granted freedom from taxation and the governance of their own affairs. This arrangement was open to abuse, however: Winchelsea carried on a lively trade in the **smuggling** of tax-free goods and also engaged in piracy.

The town's wealth and strategic location made it vulnerable to **attack**. In 1359, while the inhabitants were at Mass, the French stormed Winchelsea, killing forty people, and burning and looting the town. They returned exactly a year later, and again in 1380 and 1449, on similarly violent missions. But it was natural forces that were to prove the town's undoing. Early in the sixteenth century, great masses of shingle from the Channel caused the River Brede to silt up and narrow, and its days as a port were finished.

Winchelsea went into economic decline for more than three centuries, the gaps in its grid of streets caused by the French attacks leading both Daniel Defoe and John Wesley to liken it to a skeleton. Yet this air of romantic decay began to draw **writers and artists** from the late nineteenth century: Turner and Millais painted here; Henry James, Thackeray, Conrad, Ford Madox Ford, Rumer Godden and Radclyffe Hall visited; and the actress Ellen Terry lived in Tower Cottage at the town's north end. Ironically, their attraction to this melancholy shade of a town undoubtedly contributed to its transformation into the prosperous little place you see today.

5

scale of the remaining chancel is still grand and the detail ornate. To either side are fourteenth-century effigies – two depict admirals of the Cinque Ports and the others are generic, representing a knight, a lady and a civilian. The 1920s stained glass adds splashes of colour.

Opposite the church is the *New Inn*, a scenic spot for a pint, and nearby is a descendant of **Wesley's Tree**; John Wesley frequently preached at Winchelsea and delivered his last sermon, against smuggling, under the original tree in 1790. The town mainly consists of well-proportioned sixteenth- to eighteenth-century townhouses, with some harmonious early twentieth-century imitations. The only surviving medieval building work, apart from the much-damaged church, is in the wine cellars concealed beneath many of the houses.

From the church, turn right facing the pub onto German Street then left onto Mill Road, crossing Robert's Hill. Continue on the path straight ahead. If you follow the path for 900m you can avoid walking on the main road and there are good views across the marshes – this was a lookout point during the medieval wars with the French. The route leads you in a loop down to the minor road that runs to the station. Otherwise, turn right down German Street, and then left at the end of the street, heading through Pipewell Gate. At the hairpin bend, follow the minor road signed towards the station, which zigzags for 1km to **Winchelsea station**, from where trains depart to Hastings (hourly; 15min) or on to London St Pancras, changing at Ashford (every 30min; 2hr).

The 1066 Country Walk

5

Pevensey to Battle via Brownbread Street

Distance and difficulty 26km; strenuous

Minimum duration 6hr 30min

Trains London Bridge/Charing Cross to Pevensey and Westham (every 30min; 1hr 50min, change at St Leonard's Warrior Square); return from Battle to London Bridge/ Charing Cross (every 30min; 1hr 10min); Southern Railways

Maps OS Landranger 199: *Eastbourne & Hastings*; OS Explorer 124: *Hastings & Bexhill*

This long and wonderfully varied walk is part of the **1066 Country Walk**, which follows the route taken by the Norman army from Pevensey, where they landed and established a castle within the walls of a Roman fort, to Battle, where they defeated King Harold's army (the official route then continues for another 28km through Winchelsea to Rye). The walk starts at **Pevensey and Westham station** – a little further down the line there's a station simply called Pevensey which is slightly closer to the castle and the start of the walk proper, but trains don't run there at weekends. **Pevensey** was the landing place of Duke William of Normandy (although the sea receded over time, leaving the town high and dry), who established himself in the great circular Roman fort of **Anderida** – the ruins of the Roman fort and the Norman castle constructed within it are well worth a wander. From the castle, 1066 Country Walk leads across the Pevensey Levels, where you're likely to see a mass of water birds.

Leaving the levels, you climb uphill to the edge of **Herstmonceux**, whose castle grounds are a good place for a picnic. Beyond Herstmonceux, the route runs across fertile hilly country to the village of **Brownbread Street** where there's an excellent pub, the *Ash Tree Inn*; from here paths and minor roads lead through verdant, undulating countryside, punctuated by small settlements such as **Ashburnham Forge** and **Steven's Crouch**. Eventually the walk heads uphill, skirting the site of the most

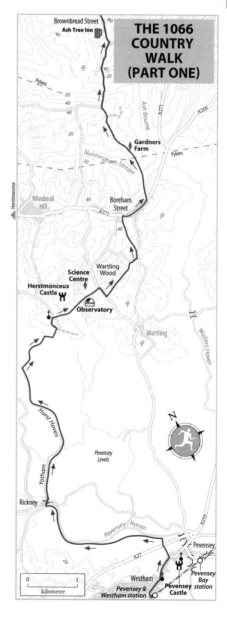

THE 1066 COUNTRY WALK (PART ONE)

5

WILLIAM THE CONQUEROR IN PEVENSEY

Duke William of Normandy landed in Pevensey in September 1066 intent on claiming the English throne, promised to him by Edward the Confessor fifteen years previously. William arrived with a fleet of five hundred ships carrying seven thousand men and 2500 horses. Less impressively, it was said that he fell flat on his face when he disembarked at Pevensey; with a sharpness that was to characterize his leadership during the battle a month later, he salvaged the moment by saying he had "seized England with both hands". William erected a prefabricated wooden defensive tower within the mighty walls that once encircled the Roman fort of **Anderida**, which itself had been built to withstand attack from Saxon pirates. In the month leading up to the fateful battle (see page 148), the Normans waged a campaign of systematic terror against the locals, probably designed to goad Harold into attack.

---

momentous battle in English history, and lands you at the fine fortified gatehouse of **Battle Abbey**.

The route is easy to follow – just look for the circular red **1066 signs**, whose stylized Norman arrows point you in the right direction.

Getting started

1km From **Pevensey and Westham station**, follow the signs towards the castle then turn right onto the High Street, passing two timber-framed Tudor cottages on the right. Just beyond the cottages is the **Church of St Nicholas**, built in 1080 and claimed to be the first Norman church in Britain, though it was later substantially altered, and what you see now is Early English in style. Beyond the church, follow the curve of the road round to the right, past a row of cottages, to reach the ruins of **Pevensey Castle** (April–Sept daily 10am–6pm; Oct 10am–4pm; Nov–March Sat & Sun 10am–4pm; £6.80; EH).

The combination of the Norman stone castle (built in the early twelfth century, probably by William's half-brother, Robert of Mortmain) and the ancient Roman walls provides an evocative start to the walk; you can get a good look at both the Roman walls and the ruined castle without having to pay the entrance fee. Information boards erected around the site provide a good context for what you're looking at, and include a representation of a panel of the Bayeux tapestry, on which the name "Pevensae" can clearly be seen.

From the castle, go back past the row of cottages and turn right, following the road as it curves round past the rugged outer walls of the castle – from here you can see a couple of pillboxes, constructed in 1940 in response to the threat of German invasion.

Pevensey Levels

6km After 600m, at a tiled house called "The Gables", follow the brown **1066 sign** to the left, down a narrow path. After 250m, the path comes to the thunderous A259 – cross the road and follow the path as it resumes on the other side, running along the left bank of **Pevensey Haven**, one of the many channels cut to drain the levels. You should begin to spot some birds: herons, ducks, redshanks, warblers, swans, grebes and sandpipers. Plants line the havens, including great reed mace and yellow water iris.

The path follows the gentle curve of the haven for 3km to the quiet hamlet of **Rickney**. You come out onto a lane through the village; take the 1066 fingerpost straight ahead (not the Jevington route). The lane curves to the right, crossing a bridge over a little stream. Follow the 1066 sign soon after, and you're back in open country. From this point the character of the **Pevensey Levels**, framed by the South Downs to

5

the south and wooded hills to the north, is much more apparent: a network of streams and ditches reflects the light, and herons and swans can be seen in profusion. The path runs for 3km through a series of gates, along the right bank of the wide and fast-flowing haven. Alongside the pedestrian gates that dot the route you'll see wider farm gates and, between them, horse jumps – this is horse country, and you're likely to see a few riders out and about.

Towards Herstmonceux
1km A couple of kilometres ahead is the green dome of Herstmonceux observatory, which you pass later in the day, and the spire of the church at **Herstmonceux** – the name is a combination of the Saxon *herst*, meaning forest, and de Monceux, the name of the Conqueror's grandson, though it's now pronounced in an English style as "Herst-mont-zoo".

Keep your eyes peeled for the 1066 sign and follow it away from the haven to the right (there's another post with a 1066 sign just beyond to confirm that you're on the correct path). The path curves round to the left, over a stile, and then turns into a broad, grassy track, running between two ditches. The path joins another wide grassy track – turn left onto it and follow it round to the church.

Looking out over the Pevensey Levels from the southeast fringes of Herstmonceux village, **All Saints Church** was built around a century after the Conquest, although the dormer windows – which give the long nave roof a gingerbread-cottage look – were a Victorian addition, designed to bring more light to the interior. Inside, look out for the sturdy medieval trussed roof and the long brass on the chancel floor (it may be concealed by a carpet) depicting Sir William Fiennes and dating from 1402 – he wears a mail shirt and sword and his pointy feet rest on a lion.

The Gothic **Dacre Chapel** to the left of the altar was built with funds provided in 1534 by the Dacre family, who were then living at Herstmonceux Castle (see below). The chapel shelters an unusual double effigy, restored in brilliant colour, which commemorates Thomas, the eighth Lord Dacre (1470–1533), with his feet resting on a bull representing the Dacres, and his son, Sir Thomas Fiennes, whose feet are supported by a wolfhound, the symbol of the Fiennes family (now of actor and explorer fame). It's thought that the carving originally represented a pair of half-brothers, but was brought from Battle Abbey following the dissolution of the monasteries and adapted to represent Lord Dacre and Sir Thomas.

Herstmonceux to Boreham Street
3km Go straight ahead across the road from the gate by the churchyard and follow the 1066 sign towards Herstmonceux Castle. The path goes downhill through some pine woods before emerging into an open field. From here, you can see the green dome of the observatory looming ahead of you and **Herstmonceux Castle** to the left. The beautifully symmetrical castle, really more of a manor house, was one of the earliest brick structures in England. It was built by Sir Roger Fiennes, who obtained the necessary "licence to crenellate" in 1440, but it fell into disuse and disrepair and was dismantled in 1777, before being reconstructed in 1932 by Sir Paul Latham. In 1946, the estate was purchased by the Admiralty as a home for the Royal Observatory; and, in 1993 both the observatory and castle were purchased by a Canadian university.

Head towards the **observatory**, up the steepish enclosed path through some woodland. On the left at the top of the hill you'll see smaller steel and copper domes belonging to the Herstmonceux Science Centre; the place is now run as an education facility rather than a serious observatory (the main telescope was shifted in the 1980s to the Canary Islands, where the weather is obviously more reliable). The path goes straight ahead through beech and pine wood, then joins a minor road. Turn right onto the road for 200m, then left just before the orange-tiled cottage.

5

The path runs down the edge of a field, with Wartling Wood on the left, then climbs up a field and curves to join another minor road. Turn right on the road and then almost immediately left over a stile into a field, then go through a series of gates over paddock fences as you head diagonally across the field towards a black barn. The path then curves left towards a line of trees – cross the stile on the far side of the field, and you'll soon see a farm and some houses. Cross the stile leading onto the road on the right, just before you get to the barn. Head down to the road and turn right into **Boreham Street**, an attractive village with some fine Georgian houses and cottages.

Towards Brownbread Street

4.5km Just outside Boreham Street, a 1066 sign points left to **Brownbread Street** – the path heads very steeply down a field, with superb views ahead made more dramatic by the line of giant pylons that marches across it. At the bottom of the hill you come to a stream; cross this and carry straight on up the hill, following the 1066 sign, past **Gardners Farm**, where the path becomes a farm track. A kilometre beyond the farm the track joins a minor road. Go right and continue for another kilometre to come out at a grassy triangle with a red-brick house on the right-hand side. Turn left and follow the sign to Brownbread Street for 200m, where you come to the *Ash Tree Inn*.

EATING AND DRINKING

Ash Tree Inn Brownbread Street, Ashburnham TN33 9NX, 01424 892 104, http://ashtreeinn.com. A free house which makes an excellent stop for a pint, with outside tables in a pretty garden. Mains such as beef bourguignon and steak and kidney pudding start at £13. Tues–Sun 11am–2.15pm & 7–9pm.

To Ashburnham Forge

2km Some 500m beyond the *Ash Tree Inn* you come to **Ashburnham Village Hall**; just beyond this, on the right, follow the 1066 sign that points away from the road towards Ashburnham Forge. The path leads through a wooden kissing gate, then down the field and on to the road – turn left for a few metres, then right onto another minor road. Continue for a couple of kilometres along this very quiet minor road as it rolls up and down through fields. Descend the hill and you'll see a red post box; on the right is Forge Cottage. You're now in the hamlet of **Ashburnham Forge**. Cross the brick bridge over the weir and climb the road up the hill. Follow the path that leads off the road to the right, passing a red-brick house and pond before heading across a wide field.

To Catsfield via Steven's Crouch

5km Go down the field, then cross two little plank **bridges** over streams and pass through some woodland. Climb the steep hill ahead of you, heading for the signed wooden posts. The path levels out and emerges into a large open field. Cross the faint track ahead through the field: it leads diagonally left towards an island of woodland, to the right of which there's a fingerpost (further to the left is a Victorian Gothic stone cottage). Head towards the post at the long line of woodland ahead. You go through the tip of the woodland and then up through the field – there's an enormous horse chestnut ahead, with heavy branches that touch the ground and look as if they're rerooting themselves. Follow the 1066 sign on a post to the left of the tree, which points you up the hill, towards the road. Just to the left is a stone gatehouse and a set of gateposts topped by statues of greyhounds.

A hundred metres beyond, you join a road at the village of **Steven's Crouch** – you'll see some picturesque thatched, timber-framed cottages to the right. Cross a stile and turn left onto the road, then cross the road almost immediately and follow the sign that leads away from the road towards Catsfield. This leads down an avenue lined by tall Wellingtonia trees. After 350m you reach a junction. Go through the gate on

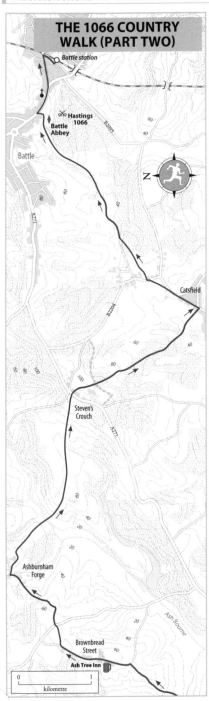

THE 1066 COUNTRY WALK (PART TWO)

the left, then turn right down the track towards Catsfield, rather than curving up to the left. The track leads downhill into pine woodland, passing a couple of lakes on the right after 800m. Some 800m further on, go through a gate, with a pond on the left, and join the lane towards **Catsfield**.

On to Battle

3.5km At the junction turn left and walk along the road for 400m through the village. On the far side of the village you'll see a **1066 sign** on a fingerpost. Turn left off the road at this sign and cross the field to the road. Cross the road and turn left for 50m, then follow another 1066 sign that points off to the right along a track. Follow the track for 100m, continuing straight ahead over a stile and into a field. Go through a pine plantation – beyond the pines in the corner of the field is a stile; follow the sign here that points through some woodland and, after 100m, leads sharp left.

The path leads steeply downhill for 200m. Cross a stile onto a little gravel track and turn right, then eventually go through a metal gate and up the path. Go through another metal gate and the path opens out into a field. Follow the sign that points ahead up the steep grassy hill. At the far side the path joins a gravel track – the houses at the top of the hill are in Battle, while the line of trees to your right conceals the site of the battle beyond. At the top of the track, immediately ahead of you, lies Battle Abbey.

Battle

Battle is a small and inoffensively touristy town, dominated by the gatehouse of the abbey around which it was built. The entrance fee to **Battle Abbey** (daily: April–Sept 10am–6pm; Oct–March 10am–4pm; £12.30; EH) allows

5

you to explore the ruined monastery buildings and also to tour the battle site – and the *Battle Abbey Tearoom* provides refreshments. The papal authorities insisted that William build the abbey as penance for the deaths resulting from the battle; building started in 1070 and the abbey was consecrated in 1094. You enter via the turreted gatehouse, built in 1338 in an elegant synthesis of form and function. Of the complex of buildings beyond the gatehouse, the most intriguing and best preserved (with the exception of the Abbot's Hall, which is now a school and not open to the public) is the airy dormitory, its three chambers descending to accommodate the sloping ground and its long lines punctuated by slender lancet windows. You can also see the foundations of the abbey church, whose high altar is supposed to mark the spot where Harold fell.

The most intangible feature of the site – the **battle** itself – is nicely evoked by an audio tour. You look out over the battle site from the high ground occupied by the shield wall of the Saxons, or you can take an extended version of the tour and walk round the battle site. The Saxon army was famously exhausted by its victory over the Norwegians at the Battle of Stamford Bridge, and by the hasty march south to take on the Normans. The tactics of the Normans – as recalled by the outraged audio thane – included faked retreats by the mounted knights and the consequent slaughter of the pursuing Saxon foot soldiers. The Saxon line was broken and Harold was killed, though he's more likely to have been bludgeoned to death than killed by an arrow in his eye as shown in the Bayeux Tapestry.

Turning right out of the abbey gatehouse, you soon come to the **Church of St Mary the Virgin**, which features a Romanesque nave, Norman font, rare fourteenth-century wall paintings and the gaudy gilded alabaster tomb of Sir Anthony Browns (to whom Henry VIII granted the abbey).

To reach the **train station**, follow the road beyond the church for 500m, then take the signed road down the hill to the left.

5 Chichester Harbour

Fishbourne to Bosham

Distance and difficulty 9km; easy

Minimum duration 2hr 15min

Trains London Victoria/Waterloo to Fishbourne (every 30min; 1hr 40min; change at Havant); return from Fishbourne to London Victoria/ Waterloo (every 30min; 1hr 55min; change at Havant); Southern Railways

Maps OS Landranger 197: *Chichester & the South Downs*; OS Explorer 120: *Chichester*

The short stretch of land covered by this walk is rich and distinctive. The route leads from **Fishbourne**, site of **Fishbourne Palace**, one of the grandest Roman villas in Britain, across a sheltered peninsula to the Saxon settlement of **Bosham**. There are no open seascapes, but water is a constant presence, from the marshland south of Fishbourne, where dense clumps of reeds tower above you, to salty Bosham itself. Here the houses cluster together as if to resist the tide that races up Bosham Channel – one of a series of inlets that comprise **Chichester Harbour** – and then recedes to leave a tangle of seaweed, shells, tiny crabs and other marine detritus.

To get to Bosham in time for lunch, you'll probably need to leave a visit to Fishbourne Palace to the end of the walk. Bear in mind also that the route can get extremely muddy.

Getting started

0.5km From platform 2 of **Fishbourne station**, turn right, crossing the railway line, and go straight ahead down the road in the direction of **Fishbourne Palace** (see page 152); you'll see the palace signed off to the left, up Roman Way. To carry on to Bosham, go straight ahead, turning left at the end of the road onto the A259 towards Chichester. After 300m, cross to *The Bull's Head* pub. Immediately beyond the pub, take a right onto Mill Lane.

South along Chichester Channel

0.75km Mill Lane leads to **Mill Pond**, opposite a thatched cottage. Take the right-hand path that goes past the pond and then winds through the high, rustling reeds, crossing a series of wooden bridges and trackways. This section is very waterlogged at high tide – you may have to wait a little for it to recede. Eventually you come out onto a high bank on the edge of the mud flats that border the Chichester Channel. The landscape opens out and you can see boats either resting on mud or bobbing in the water, depending on the state of the tide. You eventually descend from the bank and the path winds through a glade of low oak trees with a pond on the right – a good place for a **picnic**.

Across the peninsula to Bosham

3km Just beyond the glade, the path veers off to the right to cross the **peninsula** that separates the Chichester and Bosham channels. The path is wide and grassy at this point; where it reaches a T-junction between two fields, turn right and, 200m further on, turn left at the line of lime trees. After 500m, you cross a minor road; continue straight ahead, through wide, flat fields, broken up by patches of woodland. After passing a white cottage, the path joins a rough road. Where it curves round to the left, continue straight ahead. Cross the field ahead, towards a flint cottage.

Steps lead down to a minor road – cross this and carry on straight ahead between a house and a garage. The path leads through the back gardens of Bosham and emerges at the harbour. Go straight along the edge of the harbour to the heart of Bosham.

Bosham

0.75km The seventeenth- and eighteenth-century cottages of **Bosham** (pronounced "Bozzum") have a wonderfully organic quality, more like a Cornish village than anything you'd expect to find in southeast England. The road round the harbour, **Mariner's Terrace**, takes you past terraced cottages and comes out at Beach Cottage (1708) – head straight up the road to reach *The Anchor Bleu* pub, and look out for the protective panels at the doorways of the houses you pass, which slot into stone grooves and protect against flooding at high tide.

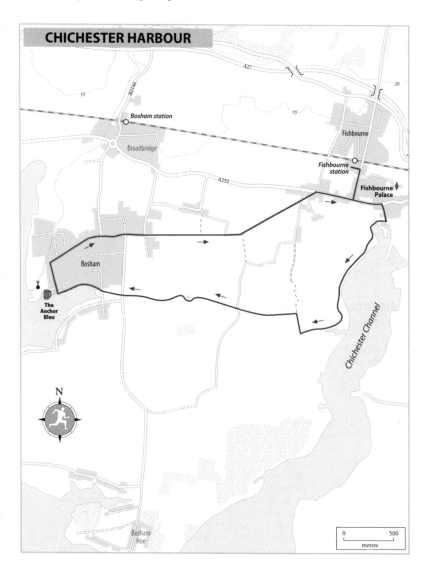

5

EATING AND DRINKING

The Anchor Bleu High St, Bosham PO18 8LS, 01243 573 956, http://anchorbleu.co.uk. Licensed since the 1700s, *The Anchor Bleu* features low beams, flagstones and a wheel-operated bulkhead door (for protection from high tides) leading to a little terrace with sea views. It serves good fish and chips, scampi and crab salad; mains from £10. Mon–Sat 11.30am–11pm, Sun noon–10pm.

Turn left out of the pub to reach **Holy Trinity Church**, which sits on Quay Meadow facing the water. The church is thought to be the oldest Christian site in Sussex, with an unbuttressed Saxon tower. Inside the church, the wide chancel arch gives the structure unexpected scale. The remains of an 8-year-old girl discovered in a tomb in the church in 1865 are thought to be those of **King Canute**'s daughter, who drowned in a mill stream behind the church. (It was also at Bosham that Canute famously ordered the sea to retreat. Contrary to popular belief, Canute knew he would fail, his purpose being to demonstrate both his limited powers as king and his humility as a convert to Christianity.) The church's antiquity is also reflected by its appearance in a panel of the **Bayeux Tapestry**, a replica of which hangs in the church, depicting King Harold leaving Bosham for Normandy in 1064, with the church in the background, so stylized as to be unrecognizable. It was an ill-starred trip, which ended in shipwreck and Harold being forced to swear an oath of allegiance to William, the future conqueror of England.

Back to Fishbourne

4km If you're in a rush to get back to Fishbourne to see the palace before it closes, you could take the short but rather uninspiring circular return route from Bosham described on page 153. However, if you're not in a hurry, the recommended **return route** is the way you came, for the views of Chichester Cathedral and the intricate track through the marsh.

To **return directly to Fishbourne** from the church, turn left past *The Anchor Bleu* back down to Beach Cottage. Turn left again and carry on straight ahead through the village. At the *Millstream Hotel*, follow the road round to the right. If you want to

FISHBOURNE PALACE

Fishbourne Palace (Jan Sat & Sun 10am–4pm; Feb, Nov & Dec daily 10am–4pm; March–July, Sept & Oct daily 10am–5pm; Aug daily 10am–6pm; £10) was one of the very few Roman villas in Britain whose size and grandeur bore comparison to its continental counterparts. Originally a supply depot for the Roman army, the site was developed in the second half of the first century as the grand palace of the Romanized Celtic aristocrat **Cogidubnus** (the villa may have been granted to him in reward for his loyalty to Rome during the onslaught of Boudicca). The villa was similar to those in Pompeii, featuring gardens and a courtyard surrounded by a colonnaded walk, and a vaulted audience chamber where the owner would receive guests. It also featured baths and pools, and was decorated with mosaics, stuccowork, marble panels and frescoes, all thought to have been the work of highly skilled foreign craftsmen, though only the mosaic floors survive in anything but fragments. The villa was destroyed by fire in the third century; charred door-sills are still visible between the mosaic floors. Bodies were buried in the ruins some time after the fire, and the skeleton of one still lies *in situ* in a shallow grave.

The palace's highlight is its series of **mosaic floors**, by far the most flamboyant and beautiful being the one that depicts Cupid riding a dolphin, surrounded by fantastic sea creatures. A jumble of artefacts is displayed in the palace **museum**, including roof tiles which acquired imprints of human and animal feet as they dried two thousand years ago, and a delicate intaglio onyx ring, engraved with a tiny image of a horse, a palm-frond waving above it.

get to **Bosham station** (which, confusingly, is actually in the neighbouring village of **Broadbridge**), take a left up Delling Lane at *The Berkeley Arms*, 600m beyond the point where the road curves; the station is just over 1km up the road. Otherwise, keep going up the road for another 500m.

Where the road curves round to the left, head along the path straight ahead, between the flint cottage and Rectory Farm – it's marked with a public footpath sign. Go straight ahead across the fields.

Where the path ends, continue ahead up the track along a row of high lime trees. After 600m, at the end of the track, go straight ahead up the road for 200m. Turn right at the busy road and, after 300m, turn left on Salthill Road to reach the **station** and **Fishbourne Palace**.

The island of Thanet

Ramsgate to Margate via Broadstairs

Distance and difficulty 15km; moderate

Minimum duration 4hr

Trains London St Pancras to Ramsgate (every 20min; 1hr 15min–1hr 40min); return from Margate to London St Pancras (every 20min; 1hr 30min–1hr 50min); Southeastern

Maps OS Landranger 179: *Canterbury & East Kent*; OS Explorer 150: *Canterbury & Isle of Thanet*

This walk is a tale of three seaside cities (okay, towns), with a strong Dickensian association. Ramsgate, Broadstairs and Margate perch on the coastline of the **Isle of Thanet** which was once, as the name suggests, an island. In the early medieval period the channel separating Thanet from Kent silted up, but the cliff-girt and densely populated area still has a distinct and quirky identity. The route hugs tight to the sea and runs via the front at **Ramsgate** via sandy beaches to **Broadstairs**, a stylish holiday town which perches above *Viking Bay* – Dickens made his summer home here in a fortified villa with a prime location, and Deco ice cream parlour *Morelli's* provides a gorgeous stop for lunch. From here the cliff path takes you to **Margate**, with its contemporary art gallery, enticing pubs and cafés and scenic harbour. It's well worth spending a night in the town to explore its pleasures the next day. And if you're walking in good weather take **swimming** gear – there are plenty of great beaches along the way.

The route is well signed and easy to follow, following a section of the **Viking Coastal Trail**, a 25-mile route which circles the Thanet coastline. The name refers to the fact that the island fell prey to Viking attacks in the ninth century, with its coastal monasteries being requisitioned as feasting halls.

Getting started

1.7km From the station turn right onto Wilfred Road following the green sign to the seafront, then take the first left onto Park Street which is lined with fantastical turn-of-the-century homes with wooden balconies, stucco decorations and circular brick porchways. Turn right off the busy road to take the sloping **High Street** down to the seafront. You pass an old flint cottage on the right, and head on past the mix of thrift stores, fish bars and empty shops. After a kilometre the High Street deposits you on the picturesque **harbour**, crammed with sailboats.

Ramsgate to Dumpton Gap

2.5km Go down to the seafront and head for **Ramsgate Maritime Museum** (Easter–Sept Tues–Sun 10am–5pm; £3), located in an 1817 clockhouse. Amongst other stories, the museum tells the gripping tale of the town's contribution to the evacuations at Dunkirk – this was the assembly point for the flotilla of small boats that rescued over 300,000 British and Allied troops from French beaches in 1940. Across from the museum sits the grand *Queen's Head* pub, a glorious concoction of tiles, red brick and wrought-iron balconies fronted by a sculpted head of Queen Victoria.

From here, continue along the esplanade, with the steep sea wall to the left, and above it a crescent of Georgian houses; to your right are Ramsgate Sands. You pass a castellated building and a row of sea-facing balconied and tile-hung houses. Carry on along the sea under the cliffs for around 800m. Just before the sea path runs out at the cliffs, take the long flight of steps – you emerge at a derelict band stand, and carry on walking by the railings, along the sea. Pass through large metal gates into the King George VI Memorial Park. Beyond the park you come out to an extraordinary house with an octagonal turret topped by a weathervane. There's a view ahead of more idiosyncratic houses, and the high **East Cliff** down to the right.

5

Some 500m beyond this you reach **Dumpton Gap**, where there's a footpath detour down to the sea below the houses – this is a great swimming spot, with an arc of beach and a row of weatherbeaten chalets. Around 900m beyond the gap you reach a pretty wrought-iron shelter where you're treated to the first view of the splendid villas and hotels at Broadstairs, which sits above the sandy crescent of **Viking Bay** with its lines of primary blue and lemon-yellow beach huts.

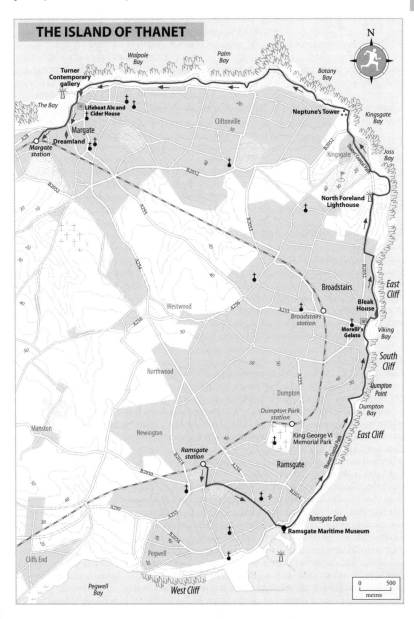

THE ISLAND OF THANET

N

Walpole Bay

Palm Bay

Botany Bay

Turner Contemporary gallery

The Bay

Lifeboat Ale and Cider House

Neptune's Tower

Kingsgate Bay

Cliftonville

Margate

Margate station

Dreamland

B2052

Kingsgate

Joss Bay

B2052

Thanet Coastal Path

B2052

North Foreland Lighthouse

B2053

B2053

Broadstairs

East Cliff

Westwood

A256

A255

Broadstairs station

Bleak House

Morelli's Gelato

Viking Bay

A255

South Cliff

Northwood

Dumpton

Dumpton Point

Dumpton Bay

Dumpton Park station

King George VI Memorial Park

East Cliff

Manston

Newington

A254

Ramsgate station

Ramsgate

B2050

Thanet Coastal Path

B2054

B2054

A299

Ramsgate Sands

Ramsgate Maritime Museum

A255

Pegwell

Cliffs End

Pegwell Bay

West Cliff

0   500
metres

5

Broadstairs and Viking Bay

1.7km Broadstairs is the queen of Thanet's resort towns, whose surrounding chalk cliffs still shelter tunnels and caves built by local smugglers; later the town became a popular spot to convalesce and to vacation, particularly when the railway arrived in 1863. There's still an upbeat holidayish air to the place, even in the depths of winter.

Cut up through the handsome municipal gardens to reach the main drag, Victoria Parade, where you can't miss **Morelli's Gelato**, a great stop for a snack or ice cream. From Morelli's, carry on through the town above the bay, turning right at the flint wall and heading through the 1540 York Gate archway towards the sea, passing The Palace Cinema. Down on the harbour, the wooden **lifeboat station** is adorned with curving whale ribs. From here, head up steeply away from the harbour and the car park, following the green public footpath sign. You'll see a huge anchor embedded into the wall; turn right onto the public footpath. To your left, around 300m from the turning, is a fanciful fortress style building built in 1801; this is **Bleak House**, where Charles Dickens spent his summers in the 1850s and 60s. Here, in his "airy nest," Dickens wrote David Copperfield.

EATING AND DRINKING

Morelli's Gelato 14 Victoria Parade, Broadstairs CT10 1QS, 01843 862 500, http://morellisgelato.com. With a bird's eye view of the town and gelato-inspired vintage decor – look out for the brass ice-cream cone lights – Morelli's is a gem. This family business dates way back to Scotland in 1909, with the Rochester parlour being built in 1932. The decor is quintessentially 50s though, with neon lighting, a soda fountain and sorbet-pink leatherette seating, and they dish up classic sundaes and milkshakes, as well as hot drinks, pastries, sandwiches and crêpes.

East Cliff and North Foreland

3.6km Carrying on along the path, you soon see a huge sea windfarm in the distance; carry on along scenic **East Cliff** for 1km. At the large Wainwright building (once a convalescent home, now private flats) the route runs up the street away from the sea. Turn right opposite Stepping Stones cottage, following the blue **Viking Coastal Trail** sign. After 75m there's a green footpath sign leading down to the beach – another possible detour for a swim. Otherwise, continue along the road for 800m – it turns into North Foreland Road. Turn right, following the coastal trail signs. Take Cliff Road, downhill towards the sea; the route curves through a large private estate.

To Margate

5.5km Soon after you leave the houses of North Foreland you pass a wastewater pumping station – go straight ahead, following the clifftop path. After another 500m you reach sandy **Joss Bay**. Head down the hill and you see a sea arch ahead – you're now at **Kingsgate Bay**, whose main feature apart from the sea arch is a white wedding cake Georgian mansion (now holiday apartments) flanked by two stone lions – ahead is a castellated eighteenth-century folly housing a pub called the *Captain Digby*.

Beyond the pub, you follow the path between wooden fences. The flint ruin on the cliff edge is **Neptune's Tower**, built by whimsical folly creator Lord Holland, who also built the *Captain Digby* building. You pass Botany Bay, where the houses are less grand than those you've been passing recently, but no less attractive. Walk the grassed paths heading east, and you'll start to see the apartment buildings and bungalows of **Margate**; the route runs through the outskirts and passes the Art Deco tower of the lido at Cliftonville before descending to the harbour.

Once in Margate, you can explore the lovely arc of the harbour with its independent cafés and bars, check out the art at the bold **Turner Contemporary** gallery (Tues–Sun 9am–5pm), or just soak up the Thanet skies beloved of J.M.W. Turner – the gallery sits on the site of the boarding house where the painter used to stay. There are plenty to places to whet your whistle: one of the nicest is *The Lifeboat Ale and Cider House* at 1

Market St, which serves Kentish ales, ciders and perries and has sawdust on the floors, a cosy wood stove, a convivial vibe and delicious free cheese and olives to nibble on. More substantial snacks cost from £6.50.

To get to the station, go back to the harbour and turn left along it, passing a couple of remarkable Margate landmarks: first there's the century-old revitalised **Dreamland** amusement park, and next you come to striking Brutalist Arlington Tower, built in 1964 with undulating facades which echo the nearby waves. Take the second left at the roundabout to reach the **station**.

The North Wessex Downs to the New Forest

STONEHENGE

The North Wessex Downs to the New Forest

6

Much of the area covered by this chapter has a strong sense of antiquity, dotted with stone monuments, burial mounds and hillforts which comprise the earliest evidence of the impact of Britons on their natural environment. Nowhere is this more apparent than at Stonehenge, the most famous prehistoric structure in Europe, which sits in the middle of the downs of Salisbury Plain. Just to the north, the North Wessex Downs – a vast tract of chalky downland and ancient woodland, stretching from the edge of the Chilterns in the east to the Vale of the White Horse in the west – are home to a rich assortment of ancient monuments, and to the Ridgeway, thought to be the oldest surviving road in Britain. To the southeast of Salisbury is the New Forest, a swathe of forest, heath and bog that has a striking wilderness feel, belying the fact that it has been systematically managed since the Norman period.

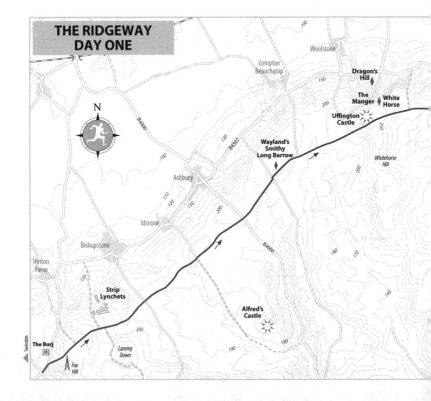

The Ridgeway

Foxhill to Wantage and Goring

Distance and difficulty day one: 17.5km; day two: 25km; strenuous
Minimum duration day one: 4hr 20min; day two: 6hr 15min
Trains London Paddington to Swindon (every 20min; 1hr); return from Goring to London Paddington (every 15min; 1hr); Great Western Railway
Maps OS Landranger 174: *Newbury & Wantage*; OS Explorer 170: *Abingdon, Wantage & Vale of White Horse*

6

The **Ridgeway**, a 136km path starting at Overton Hill in Wiltshire and ending at Ivinghoe Beacon in Buckinghamshire, formed part of an ancient **trading route** between southwest England and mainland Europe, which may have started on the Dorset coast and run up to Norfolk. The route has been used by traders, invaders and drovers for at least five thousand years, the proliferation of Neolithic and Bronze Age burial sites and Iron Age forts along the way attesting to its cultural and strategic importance. The Ridgeway was the scene of skirmishes between the Saxons, under Alfred the Great (see page 162), and the Vikings, who sought to use it to penetrate the kingdom of Wessex. Its primary purpose in the medieval period was as a drove road between Wales and the Home Counties. There probably wasn't one specific road here until the Enclosure Acts of 1750 – the modern Ridgeway is an amalgam of several smaller routes and originally people would have used the easiest and driest section available on the day.

The section of the Ridgeway covered here leads east from **Foxhill** to the **Vale of the White Horse**, passing some of England's most intriguing prehistoric sites including Wayland's Smithy, Uffington Castle and the White Horse itself. You can return to

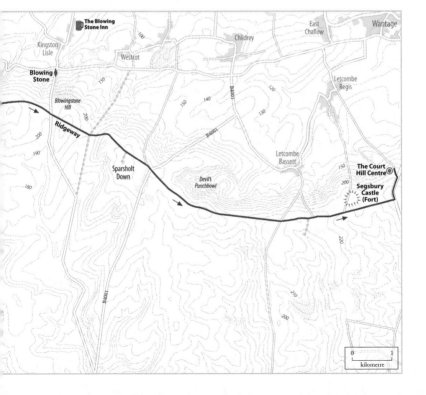

6

ALFRED THE GREAT

The first written mention of the Ridgeway is in the *Anglo-Saxon Chronicle*, which describes Danish raiders sweeping along the route, from Ashdown to Scutchamer Knob. The chronicle was in part a record of the exploits of the scholar-king Alfred the Great, who almost certainly commissioned it. **Alfred's military achievements** are recalled in sites along the route of the Ridgeway, from the battle ground at Ashdown to the Blowing Stone (see page 164). Lying low during a lull between battles, this local lad, born in Wantage in 849, famously allowed himself to be scolded by a peasant woman for leaving her cakes to burn. He was venerated, in his time and even now, more than a thousand years later, both as a brilliant general and as a protector of the poor.

Alfred began his onslaught against the Danes during the reign of his brother Ethelred, culminating in the famous victory at the **Battle of Ashdown** in 871. The following year Ethelred died and Alfred became king of Wessex. Periods of peace alternated with renewed Danish attacks, until Alfred finally defeated the invaders once and for all in 897. One of his innovations as a tactician was the establishment of fortified burghs – grass-covered earthworks that are still a part of the landscape of the Ridgeway.

A thoughtful and inspired peacetime leader, Alfred used the lulls between conflicts to focus on civic reorganization. The monasteries, shattered by the Danes, were re-established as centres of learning, and Alfred founded schools in Oxford, even learning Latin himself in middle age and making translations of books of theology, history and philosophy, which he freely infused with his own thoughts, thus contributing to the earliest English literature.

London via **Wantage** at the end of day one, or stay at the spectacularly sited hostel just off the route and continue for a second day to the village of Goring, which sits in a gentle bend of the River Thames. If you only do one day of this walk, make sure it's the first.

Day one

17.5km The first day of the walk is crammed with interest, from medieval field terraces to the cluster of prehistoric sights at the **Vale of the White Horse**. The pubs to the north of the Ridgeway at Ashbury, Woolstone and Kingston Lisle all make decent **lunch** stops, although as these all involve a 3km round-trip detour from the route, you might prefer to take a picnic lunch. Day one ends near **Wantage** – you can either get a taxi into town for the station if you want to end your walk, or stay at *The Court Hill Centre*, which lies just off the route.

Getting started

Walk straight ahead out of **Swindon station** and up Wellington Street to the **bus station**. From here, take bus #46, #48 or #48a to Foxhill (Mon–Fri hourly, Sat every 40min; 25min; 01793 428428); ask the driver to drop you at *The Burj* restaurant. A **taxi** (01793 536666 or 01793 511199) to Foxhill will cost around £15.

Foxhill and the Strip Lynchets

5km Get off the bus at **Foxhill** (there's a row of terraced cottages on the right) and, with *The Burj* on your left, head straight up the sealed minor road, signposted to the village of Hinton Parva. After 200m, follow a second sign, on the right, which signals the start of this stage of the **Ridgeway**. Head along the route, ignoring the public path that leads off to Charlbury Hill after around 750m. The path ascends quite steeply for 500m, over the brow of a hill, with the tumulus of **Lammy Down** visible to the right.

A worthwhile detour leads left for 200m down a path (marked with a bridleway sign) to the **Strip Lynchets**, a well-preserved example of the medieval system of field terracing. These grassy steps sit in a lovely valley, with glorious views ahead to the green swell of Uffington Castle and down to the village of Bishopstone.

Returning to the Ridgeway, you descend steadily for another 3km, crossing two minor roads, the first to Bishopstone and the second to Idstone. At the Idstone Road, down to the right, is the small Iron Age fort of **Alfred's Castle**, where Alfred fought the Danes in 871. This piece of ground was developed earlier by the Romans, and traces of what may have been a villa or temple have been excavated, along with a cache of ten babies' skeletons. Roman law did not permit burial within towns or forts, but babies under ten days old were exempt from this, as they were not classed as citizens.

Wayland's Smithy

1.5km Returning to the Ridgeway, it's another 1.5km to the atmospheric Neolithic tomb of **Wayland's Smithy**; cross the road to Ashbury and walk through a strip of woodland; the tomb's tall sarsen stones can just be seen to the left in a stately circle of beech trees.

Wayland's Smithy, thought to be 5500 years old, originally comprised a wooden, tent-shaped chamber containing the remains of fourteen people. Around 3300 BC, a longer cruciform tomb was built on top of the old one, which was covered over with a mound of chalk and stone. The three stone chambers of the more recent tomb were excavated in the 1920s and eight bodies were found. The tomb acquired its name when the Saxons stumbled upon it and, ignorant of its real function, appropriated it for their god, Wayland the Smith; it was said that Wayland would shoe travellers' horses if they left a penny on the capstone of the tomb. You may see offerings of flowers, grain, fruit and feathers around the tomb, left by New Agers.

The Vale of the White Horse

1.5km Some 1.5km beyond Wayland's Smithy, the Ridgeway climbs a steepish hill to reach the **Vale of the White Horse**, a unique collection of prehistoric sights; at the brow of the hill turn left through the gate at the National Trust sign.

The landscape opens out to reveal the great circular earthwork of **Uffington Castle**, built between 300 BC and 43 AD and encircled by a bank and ditch, now eroded and grazed by sheep and scattered with field scabious, poppies, pyramidal orchids and cowslips. The "castle" – or, more accurately, fort – is roughly oval in shape and eight acres in extent. It had a single entrance to the northwest and its ramparts would have been faced with sarsen stone. One in a chain of such defensive structures, it's thought that Uffington Castle was built to protect travellers along the Ridgeway from attack from the north.

About 200m beyond the fort, the land tumbles down to the undulating glacial valley called the **Manger**. Obscured by the steepness of the valley wall until you are almost upon it is the **White Horse** (legend is that the horse comes down off its hill at night to graze in the Manger). It was popularly thought that the 114m-long horse was cut into the turf to commemorate Alfred's victory over the Danes, but in fact it's much more ancient, being the oldest chalk figure in the country and dating back three thousand years. One of the many curious things about the horse is that its shape can only properly be seen from a distance because of the curve of the hill. Nearby signs feature a drawing of the horse, which will help you appreciate the figure's abstract beauty which looks as if it was sketched by Matisse in a few deft strokes. The local legend which asserts that "while men sleep the horse climbs up the hill" is not as whimsical as it sounds; the upper edges of the chalk lines are gradually eroding and the lower edges silting up, causing the horse to edge up the hillside.

Fairs at Uffington Castle, the first record of which is in 1677, were held every seven years or so until 1857; thirty thousand people were said to have attended in 1780. These were celebratory occasions when the White Horse was "scoured", or cleaned;

the maintenance of the horse was one of the conditions by which the lord of the manor held his land. Horse and ass races were a feature of the fair, as was the bizarre practice of sliding down the hill on a horse's jawbone, according to one eighteenth-century account.

Just below the horse is a small artificial hillock, **Dragon's Hill**, which, according to local legend, is where St George killed the dragon. Two oval mounds between the horse and the fort were excavated in 1857 and found to contain fifty Roman skeletons. Five of the bodies held coins between their teeth, to pay the ferryman to carry them over the River Styx into the underworld.

The White Horse to the Blowing Stone

2.5km Continue on the Ridgeway for 2.5km to the next minor road which crosses the route – to the left down the Blowingstone Hill is the village of Kingstone Lisle. On the right, towards the bottom of the hill, you can detour off the route for 1.5km to the garden of a cottage that encloses the **Blowing Stone**, a rough block of sarsen that resembles a holey cheese (though it's quite a steep hill, so only make the detour if you're feeling energetic). The legend connected with the stone is that King Alfred blew into it to call the Saxons to fight the Danes. With some determination you can produce a strange booming sound by blowing into one of the holes in the stone; local advice is to blow a raspberry into it, covering the hole completely with your mouth.

If you fancy a pub stop at this point, cross the B4507, which cuts across Blowingstone Hill, and carry straight on for 700m past the idyllic thatched cottages and country gardens of Kingston Lisle, bearing right at the junction for *The Blowing Stone Inn*.

EATING AND DRINKING

The Blowing Stone Inn Kingston Lisle OX12 9QL, 01235 612 707, http://theblowingstone.co.uk. A gentrified but pleasant pub which serves cod and chips, steaks and so on for around £14–28. Daily noon–3pm & 6–11pm.

To Segsbury Castle and The Court Hill Centre

7km Back on the Ridgeway, past long lines of gallops – fenced areas used for exercising racehorses – the route ascends **Sparsholt Down**; you'll see a radio mast on the right-hand side and a farm and paddock where there's a **drinking-water tap**. Turn right onto the sealed road that crosses the **B4001** to Wantage; the Ridgeway resumes opposite the "give way" sign.

The grassy ground to the left of the Ridgeway falls dramatically away to form a smooth valley called the **Devil's Punchbowl**. After 1.5km, you cross a track that runs north to **Letcombe Bassett**, immortalized as Cresscombe in Thomas Hardy's *Jude the Obscure*.

Around 1.5km from here, a broad track to the left opposite some corrugated-iron farm buildings leads for 100m to another Iron Age relic, **Segsbury Castle**. It was, according to an eighteenth-century account, fronted by tall sarsen stones – these have since been removed and all you see now is a steep grassy mound. Nineteenth-century excavations uncovered human bones in a stone chamber, flint scrapers and pottery, plus what is thought to be a boss from a Saxon shield.

If you're doing both days of the walk, you can spend the night at the excellent *Court Hill Centre*: turn left onto the **A338**, past Redhouse Cottage, and go down the hill. It's a very attractive building, constructed from five disused barns and designed to exploit the superb views of the valley below. The dorms resemble wooden ship berths, and there's a sense of space and light throughout. If you want to end your walk here, a **taxi** (01235 762035) from *The Court Hill Centre* to Wantage will cost around £6.

ACCOMMODATION

The Court Hill Centre Court Hill OX12 9NE, 01235 760 253, http://courthill.org.uk. A great independent hostel, with family rooms and large dorms. Aim to arrive by 6pm, so you can order dinner (£8.50), though you can arrange it by phone in advance. Breakfast is also available and there's a shop selling drinks and chocolate as well as packed lunches (order before 10.30pm the night before) – a good option if you don't want to detour away from the Ridgeway on day two. Dorms £22; family rooms from £50

Day two

25km The second day of the walk is less exciting than the first, although the Saxon burial mound at **Scutchamer Knob** provides some atmosphere, and there's a good pub **lunch** detour to East Ilsley. The walk ends at the pretty conjoined villages of **Streatley** and **Goring**.

Getting started

7km To return to the Ridgeway, take the path signed "to the Ridgeway" immediately opposite the hostel drive. After 200m, turn left onto the chalky farm track and then where the track bends left 100m further on, go straight ahead up the narrow grassy path. The path eventually curves left to rejoin the Ridgeway (you'll see the wooden Ridgeway fingerpost on your left). Just over 1km from the road, the route divides into two wide paths – follow the one to the left. Cross the B4494 to Wantage, beyond which you'll come to a tall **monument** to the right of the route, erected by Baroness Wantage in 1901 in memory of her husband.

Scutchamer Knob towards Rodden Downs

6.5km Three kilometres past the monument is the easy-to-miss **Scutchamer Knob** (it lies in a little copse off to the right, behind iron railings). A horseshoe-shaped mound of earth, Scutchamer Knob is thought to be the burial place of the Saxon king **Cwicchelm**, who died

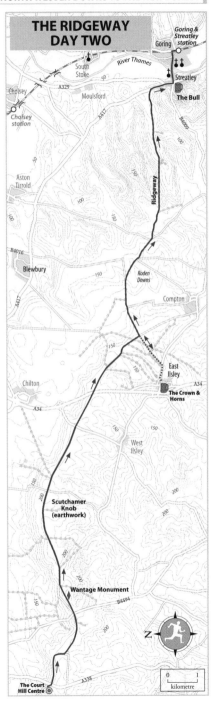

6

6

in 593 AD. Whatever the mound's original function, it's a restful spot, with views over the rolling fields to the south. Just south of here, off the Ridgeway, is one of several "**Starveall Farms**", the name probably an echo of an ancient famine. Other settlements along the route – Woolpack and Woolstone, for example – recall the area's wealth in wool and meat during the Middle Ages, when the Ridgeway was used as a drove road.

Cross the minor road to East Hendred. On the far side, you'll see lines of gallops in the field to the right – many racehorses are trained and stabled around here. The panorama also takes in one of the few signs of industrial England visible on the walk, **Didcot Power station**, almost 10km away. When permission was given to build the power station, it was on condition that it was modified, with six cooling towers grouped in two groups of three rather than the usual eight grouped in two groups of four, supposedly to make it more attractive.

After 500m you cross another minor road, walking through a small car park; 1.5km from here the route dips under the busy **A34**.

Over Rodden Downs

5km For a short stretch beyond the underpass the Ridgeway is paved; 2.5km beyond the underpass you reach a crossroads: bear left to stay on the Ridgeway. If you fancy a diversion for a **pub lunch**, take a right on the path to the village of **East Ilsley**, 1.5km distant – after just over 1km, turn right onto the path into the village that runs parallel to the road. *The Crown & Horns* is next to *The Swan*, which you can see as you approach. Sheep fairs were held at East Ilsley for hundreds of years – in the mid-eighteenth century around eighty thousand sheep were sold at its annual fair, and there were thirteen pubs to sustain the drovers and farmers.

EATING AND DRINKING

The Crown & Horns Compton Rd, East Ilsley RG20 7LH, 01635 281 545, http://crownandhorns.com. The welcoming *Crown & Horns* in East Ilsley serves filling pub food and real ales – there's outdoor seating in the stable yard. Mon–Sat 11am–11pm, Sun noon–10.30pm.

Continuing along the Ridgeway, the route ascends **Rodden Downs**. Bear right at the crossroads 2.5km beyond the East Ilsley turn-off; the left-hand fork runs up to **Lowbury Hill** which is said to be haunted, perhaps by the Roman woman who was found buried here under an earth bank.

To Streatley and Goring

6.5km After a long slow climb, the landscape opens out for the gradual descent towards **Streatley**, with undulating fields to either side. The path drops through a wooded avenue to a thatched cottage and farm, then bears left. From this point the remainder of the walk is on a sealed road.

Continue along the road past a row of red-brick terraced houses and, at the "give way" sign, turn right onto the A417 to Streatley and bear right again at the second "give way" sign. Carry on for another 300m and you'll come to the handsome fifteenth-century *Bull Inn*. Opposite the pub, the turning to the left leads down, past an attractive jumble of brick, flint and thatched houses, towards the Thames. Just before you cross the river, you could detour 50m to the left to **St Mary's**, a pretty thirteenth-century church that was heavily restored by the Victorians.

A double-humped bridge takes you across the river to **Goring**. Off to the right is the handsome Norman church of **St Thomas**. The interior is in an attractive state of decay, with peeling paint and metal braces straining round huge circular columns. To reach **Goring station**, head straight up the hill and turn right after the railway bridge.

The North Wessex Downs

Kintbury to Inkpen and back

Distance and difficulty 16km; moderate–strenuous

Minimum duration 4hr

Trains London Paddington to Kintbury (hourly; 1hr); return from Kintbury to London Paddington (hourly; 1hr); Great Western Railway

Maps OS Landranger 174: *Newbury & Wantage*; OS Explorer 158: *Newbury & Hungerford*

The **North Wessex Downs** reach their highest point at **Inkpen Hill**, between Newbury and Hungerford, which is crowned by the remains of a vast Iron Age fort and a long barrow, still surmounted by a gibbet that was originally erected in the seventeenth century. The walk starts from the village of **Kintbury**, sitting snug in the valley of the Kennet, and goes across farmland to the ramblingly attractive village of **Inkpen**. From Inkpen it's a steep but short scramble up on to the ridge of the downs, where the sweeping views take in five counties. Paths and minor roads bring you in a circle back to Kintbury, where the handsome *Blue Ball* pub, or *The Dundas Arms*, sitting prettily on the river, are great spots to nurse a pint while waiting for your train home.

Kintbury to Inkpen

5km From the station, head left towards *The Dundas Arms*. Cross the canal at **Kintbury Lock**, and then the river, where you'll see a weir up to the right. Go up the road, which curves to the right through the village. Just past the *Blue Ball* pub on the right, follow Wallington's Road to the left, a dead end that leads towards the St Cassian Centre, a Catholic youth retreat.

After 500m, at the gates of **St Cassian's**, take the signposted public footpath to the left, rather than the private road to the centre. After 200m you'll reach some dilapidated farm buildings. Follow the public footpath sign that points across the fields to the right, then cross the road 150m beyond. Carry on up the field, with St Cassian's to the left and beyond that a concrete track. Go through a patch of woodland for 250m to emerge into a field; head straight across the field, and turn right onto a minor road. Head down the drive that leads past **Balsdon Farm** (don't be deterred by the "private" signs – this isn't a bridleway, but it is a public footpath).

Beyond the farm are some signposts; follow the public footpath sign to the left, rather than the bridleway sign. Ahead you can see the ridge of the downs. After 100m, cross the plank bridge over a stream – another 600m further on, you'll see the pretty but dilapidated buildings of Northcroft Farm to the left. Where the path comes out on a minor road, turn right and follow the road for 500m until you get to a small, triangular green and a red phone box. This is the western edge of **Inkpen**, known as **Lower Green**.

Inkpen Hill

5km Head up the road past the phone box and then along the road signed towards Ham. The road curves round to the right; after 250m you'll see thirteenth-century **Inkpen Church** a couple of hundred metres away to the left – continue following the road. Some 200m past the church, follow the public bridleway sign pointing to the left and go along this track, which leads up to the long grassy ridge of the **downs** – the gibbet is visible on top of the hill ahead of you. Go through an avenue of trees for 400m, after which the path begins to climb the steep hill. After 100m, it's joined by a grassy track leading diagonally to the left up the hill. Don't turn left on the first path you reach at the top of the ridge (which leads down the ridge and away from the fort); instead, keep going for 50m or so until you reach a track enclosed by fences; turn left here.

Combe Gibbet long barrow, 600m further on, dates from around 3500 BC, which makes it even older than similar Wayland's Smithy on the nearby Ridgeway (see

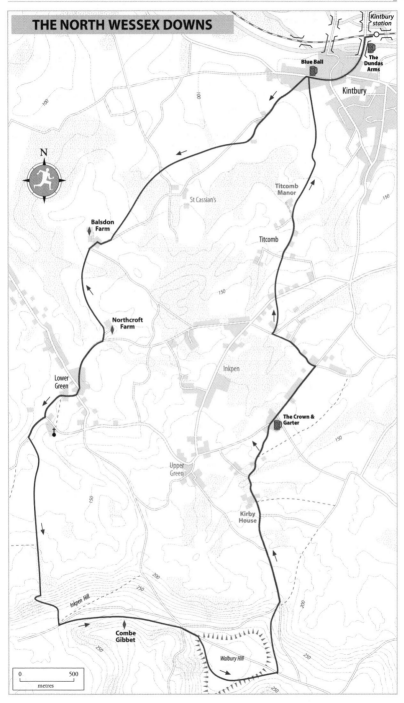

THE NORTH WESSEX DOWNS

Kintbury station

Blue Ball

The Dundas Arms

Kintbury

Titcomb Manor

St Cassian's

Balsdon Farm

Titcomb

Northcroft Farm

Inkpen

Lower Green

The Crown & Garter

Upper Green

Kirby House

Inkpen Hill

Combe Gibbet

Walbury Hill

N

0   500
metres

6

6

page 163). Little is known about the site, which has never been excavated, but as well as being a burial mound, its prominent position suggests it delineated the territory of the people who built it. The **gibbet** was first erected in 1676 to hang locals George Broomham and his mistress Dorothy Newman – the pair murdered George's wife and son, but were seen by the village idiot, "Mad Thomas". They were hanged from either side of the gibbet, which explains its unusual shape – most gibbets have just one arm. This is not the original gibbet: the structure has been replaced several times over the centuries. The first gibbet rotted away, the second was struck by lightning, and the third was blown over in a storm in 1949. The people of Inkpen, however, had by this time become so fond of the sight of a gibbet looming over their village that they clubbed together for a new one, which was made of oak and erected in 1950.

Carry on along the chalky track past the gibbet and the car park onto **Walbury Hill** – take the track to the right of the early Iron Age hillfort. Walk round the fort – the largest in the country, stretching for 700m.

Back to Kintbury

6km A hundred metres beyond the fort, between it and the next car park, follow the signed public footpath to the left, which leads down the hill and to the left – follow it round to cross a stile and go through woodland, descending to a **minor road**. Turn left onto the road and continue to a junction, then go straight ahead, following the signs to Kintbury. Just beyond lies **Kirby House**, an elegantly proportioned Queen Anne country mansion, flanked by avenues of trees and stables.

EATING AND DRINKING

The Crown & Garter Great Common Road, Inkpen Common, RG17 9QR, 01488 668 325, http://crownandgarter.co.uk. Award-winning pub with all your favourite classics such as steak and burgers. They also offer heartier meals such as braised ox cheek served with salt-baked celeriac and heritage carrots. For pudding pick the rhubarb and custard pannacotta. End your meal with a lovely coffee. Mon–Thurs noon–10pm, Fri & Sat noon–11pm, Sun noon–4.30pm.

Just past Kirby House, follow the sign on the right along the road to Kintbury. After 500m you come out at a junction; immediately to the right is *The Crown & Garter* – turn right and go past the pub, and then, after another 200m, past a row of white houses on the left and a silver-birch wood to the right. A hundred metres beyond the houses, take the public bridleway to the left, signed to "PO and Folly roads". This track passes a couple of farms, and then after 250m dips down into woodland and over a little bridge. Head up the hill out of the woods and onto a narrow track. Ignore the public bridleway sign to the left and go straight ahead, following the public footpath sign along a fence and then around the fields, past a handful of houses on the outer edge of Inkpen.

Cross the road here and go straight ahead, after which you soon leave the houses behind, heading downhill through a field. Go through the squeeze gate and down through another field. At the end of the field you emerge at a post with public footpath signs, which point back the way you came and to the left; go straight ahead here, down the road, ignoring the public footpath sign 200m further on to the right. Ahead, you can make out **Titcomb Manor**, but before you reach it go through the squeeze gate on the right and turn left through a field. Halfway across the next field, go through the wooden gate marked with public right of way signs and then follow the enclosed path. Go over the bridge and almost immediately turn left through another gate, then go through a tunnel of trees to emerge onto the High Street in Kintbury, opposite the *Blue Ball*, an excellent spot for a post-walk dinner. Turn right to get back to the **station**.

Stonehenge

Salisbury to Stonehenge via Old Sarum

Distance and difficulty 16.5km; moderate–strenuous

Minimum duration 4hr 20min

Trains London Waterloo to Salisbury (every 30min; 1hr
30min); return from Salisbury to London Waterloo (every
30min; 1hr 30min); Southwestern Railway

Maps OS Landranger 184: *Salisbury & The Plain*; OS Explorer
130: *Salisbury & Stonehenge*

This walk starts in the cathedral city
of **Salisbury**, heading to the circular
ruins of the Norman city of **Old
Sarum**, Salisbury's predecessor, which
was abandoned in the fourteenth
century due to water shortages.
From Old Sarum, the route runs to
the handsome old village of Upper
Woodford where *The Bridge Inn* is
a decent stop for **lunch**. From here,
country lanes and footpaths lead
through the lush Avon Valley and
past increasing numbers of tumuli –
prehistoric burial mounds that dot
the whole area. Long, low **Normanton
Down**, its summit crowned by a line
of tumuli, brings you onto downland
and within sight of **Stonehenge** – a
stunning sight, however familiar it
may be from photographs.

You must **book ahead** if you want
to visit Stonehenge, and bring a
printout of the ticket with you or
show it on your phone. Bear in mind
that the complex closes early in winter
(see page 175). It's best to plan to
start walking by 10am – and check
the times of the **return bus** before
you set out. The Salisbury bus and
Stonehenge entry price make this an
expensive outing: you could content
yourself with looking at the stones
from outside the payment zone and,
with enough time, returning on foot
to Salisbury.

Getting started

4km From **Salisbury station**, bear left,
following the sign to the city centre.
Go right onto Fisherton Street for
500m, crossing the river. At the large
stone market cross head left up Minster
Street and then straight ahead along

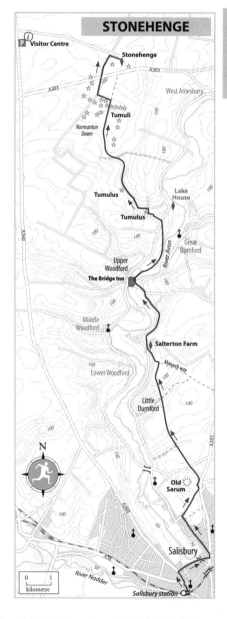

6

Castle Street. Go under the railway bridge on the left-hand side, emerging at the Castle Roundabout; head through the underpass beneath the roundabout – you come out into the centre – then turn left through another underpass and then right up the steps.

Follow the brown Stonehenge and Old Sarum sign and then, some 250m beyond the underpass, take the road signed towards **Stratford Subcastle**. Follow the Stratford Subcastle road for just over 1km, with views of the downs emerging as the houses give way to the countryside. You'll see a footpath sign; ignore this and carry on for another 100m where a track leads off to the right, to the side of a long thatched cottage. Head straight ahead up this track, which soon narrows to become a path. Gaps in the hedgerow give occasional views of the downland and of the outline of Old Sarum. Around 100m before the busy road ahead, turn left and head to the top right-hand corner of the field, then turn left towards Old Sarum, through a wooden gate and up the drive into the site.

Old Sarum

1km Cross a wooden bridge over the deep ditches of an Iron Age hillfort to the remains of **Old Sarum** (daily: April–Sept 10am–6pm; Oct 10am–5pm; Nov–March 10am–4pm; £5.40; EH). The site, within the remains of circular walls, is surprisingly compact, considering it once contained a Norman castle and garrison. There was also a substantial religious community attached to the Romanesque cathedral, the remains of which lie just outside the walls of Old Sarum – the outline of the foundations can be clearly seen in the grass.

This was originally an Iron Age hillfort, resettled by Saxons and then the Normans; the bishopric of Sherbourne was moved to the site in the 1070s and the cathedral was built soon after. Old Sarum suffered water shortages though, and its exposed position on Salisbury Plain must have made it a windswept and inhospitable place in winter. In 1220, the clergy, following conflict with the town's other occupants, appealed to the pope for permission to relocate to New Sarum (which subsequently became known as Salisbury). Sarum Cathedral was destroyed in 1331 to provide building material for the new town, and the old town gradually emptied, although the notorious "rotten borough" of Old Sarum returned two MPs until 1833, William Pitt being one of the incumbents.

You get very little sense of Old Sarum's past from the scant ruins of the buildings: all that remains are low walls and grass-covered mounds. However, there are tremendous views north to **Salisbury Plain** and south to Salisbury itself and the soaring spire of its cathedral.

Across country to Upper Woodford

5km From the entrance to Old Sarum, head back down the drive and follow it round to the left. After 100m the drive curves round to the right, but instead of following it go straight ahead through two wooden gates, following the **bridleway** sign. Follow the path down the hill to cross a minor road.

Continue straight ahead for 1km, past a red-brick house, followed by a patch of woodland on your left. At the crossroads at the thatched cottage go straight ahead through the cornfield. The grassy track peters out at the end of a field, joining a narrower path marked by a blue arrow – follow this through woodland until you come to a post with a bridleway sign. Don't go through the metal gate ahead; instead, turn left and head down through the trees. The path winds round to the right, running along the valley wall; there's a fence on your left, beyond which the land drops down to lush farmland.

The path emerges at **Salterton Farm**. Where you come out at the road and some farm buildings, turn immediately right, onto the bridleway track. At the wooden bench 300m further on, turn left over the stile, and walk along the edge of the field to an old metal gate which leads into woodland. Follow the path for 1km as it gently descends through the woods. Joining the tarred road again, turn right and follow it for another 1km, as it meanders past mansions and cottages. Cross the River Avon to the riverside *Bridge Inn* in **Upper Woodford**, a good stop for **lunch** or a pint.

EATING AND DRINKING

The Bridge Inn Upper Woodford SP4 6NU, 01722 782 203, http://bridgeinnupperwoodfordpub.co.uk. This heavily restored pub serves local ales and good seasonal food (mains from £15). There's a garden with a sweeping view of the River Avon. Mon–Sat 11am–3pm & 6–11pm, Sun noon–10.30pm.

6

Upper Woodford

2km Turn left out of the pub, and after 200m, opposite Boreland House, take the gravel path on the right marked with a green public footpath sign. Follow the path as it curves round to the left; go straight ahead instead of towards the house down to the right and, at the point where the track curves up to the left, take the path directly in front of you. This is a very pretty stretch, lined with ash, beech and poplar trees, with the **River Avon** down to the right and cornfields to the left. After 800m you come to a bridge over the Avon; ignore this and continue along the path.

The Normanton Down Barrows

3km The path emerges at a minor road; cross this and go over the stile ahead of you, where you'll see public footpath signs (the distinct mound of a tumulus can be seen just off the path and down to the right). Carry on straight ahead up the field, keeping its boundary and the wood to your immediate left; down the hill to the right you'll see Lake House, a Jacobean manor house that's home to Sting and his wife, Trudi Styler.

Continue down the path to reach a stile to the right of a metal gate – cross this and head down the path. Once through the woodland, go right down the edge of the field, then turn left on the chalky road. Continue along the valley bottom for 1.3km. At **Springbottom Farm**, turn left past the big barn. The track then splits – take the right-hand fork.

There's a long ascent of the hill ahead, up the wide grassy path, but you should be revived by the extraordinary first sight of **Stonehenge**, the focal point of an epic stretch of downland. One of the strange properties of the stones is the way their proportions appear to change: from this distance they appear elongated, a little nearer and they seem quite squat, and when you're up as close as you're allowed to get they are broodingly large.

The ridge commanding this spectacular view is capped by the **Normanton Down Barrows**, a line of low mounds to your left and right, which lie on private farmland and aren't accessible to the public. The barrows stretch for a kilometre and include the early Bronze Age **Bush Barrow**, where the most significant finds were uncovered – it contained the grave of a tall, stout man who was buried with artefacts to carry to the afterlife, including a bronze axe, three bronze daggers and a lozenge-shaped sheet of gold.

Stonehenge

1.5km Just beyond the Normanton Down Barrows, turn left through a field for 300m, then turn right towards the A303. Cross the thunderingly busy A303 (no easy feat), then follow the track which bears right, to the point where visitors are disgorged from the minibuses that shuttle to and from the **visitor centre** and ticket office where you will need to collect your tickets before entering the site.

The site

The exact function and significance of Stonehenge – and the way in which it was built – have been the source of endless speculation over the centuries; it has been attributed to Romans, Danes, druids and even extraterrestrials.

The site contains the ruins of stone monuments and earth structures dating from between 3000 and 1000 BC. Its earliest features are a circular **bank and ditch** and the **Heel Stone**, an irregular upright megalith that sits just to the northeast of the ditch. Inside the ditch a circle of 56 pits was found, filled with a mixture of earth and human ash.

But it's the central section of the complex, constructed around 2000 BC, which makes Stonehenge unique. This is where the huge trilithons – two uprights linked by a capstone – stand. These sarsen stones were transported from the Marlborough Downs, around 30km away, and were then smoothed and shaped with a swelling in the middle, designed to counter perspectival distortions (a technique later employed by the builders of the Parthenon). A circle of 25 trilithons was formed, with a horseshoe of **trilithons** in the middle of the circle – the capstones were fastened to each other with tongue-and-groove joints and to the upright stones with mortice-and-tenon joints.

There is an earlier, uncompleted circle of smaller stones amongst the trilithons – these are **bluestones** from Preseli in Wales, 300km distant. In 2015, archeologists discovered that these stones were quarried 500 years before Stonehenge was built, in 3400 and 3200 BC – the dates come from carbon dating of hazelnut shells and charcoal from the quarry site in Preseli. These findings suggest either that Stonehenge is even older than previously thought, or that the bluestones were used to create a monument in Wales before being dismantled and transported.

STONEHENGE AND THE DRUIDS

Modern fascination with the **druids**, fuelled by lurid tales of sacrifice and magic rites, can be dated to the Renaissance and the rebirth of interest in the Classical world. Descriptions of the druids come from Classical writers such as Pliny, Tacitus and Julius Caesar – Caesar wrote that the druids "know much about the stars and celestial motions, and about the size of the earth and the universe, and about the essential nature of things, and about the powers and authority of the immortal gods; and these things they teach to their pupils".

There are no physical descriptions of druids, but it is probably because of the connection with Roman writers that, in the popular imagination, they come clad in white, toga-like garments. All that's known for certain is that they formed a class of priests, practised a religion dictated by nature and the seasons, and that they performed animal and human sacrifices.

Seventeenth- and eighteenth-century antiquarians such as **John Aubrey** and **William Stukeley** seized on these Classical descriptions – it was they who made the speculative connection between the druids and the building of Stonehenge, even though Classical descriptions of druidic rites place them in the natural world, amongst groves and springs, suggesting that they would have had little interest in fashioning the enormous megaliths of Stonehenge.

Subsequent events further clouded the real identity of the druids. William Stukeley is thought to have founded the **First Order of Druids** in Primrose Hill in London in 1717, a quasi-mystical order that also took inspiration from freemasonry. This was supplanted by the **Ancient Order of Druids**, which continued through the nineteenth century and into the twentieth – Winston Churchill was a member, hosting a gathering of "druids" at Blenheim Palace in 1908.

Exactly when the first **summer solstice** celebrations were held at Stonehenge is unclear, but by 1900 the then owner of Stonehenge, Sir Edward Antrobus, was so alarmed by the numbers attending the rites that he had the site fenced in and imposed an entry fee, which the druids refused to pay. The annual celebrations continued, though, and eventually took on a less ritualistic and more celebratory character; by the 1970s, the masonic form of druidism had been replaced by hippy-influenced neo-paganism. Clashes between the police and summer-solstice worshippers became an annual occurrence, reaching a climax at the "Battle of the Beanfield" in 1985, when seven hundred people were arrested. The 6km exclusion zone that operated after the riots was relaxed in 1999, and access is now permitted on the solstice.

VISITING STONEHENGE

Stonehenge is open daily (June–Aug 9am–8pm; Sept to mid-Oct 9.30am–7pm; mid-Oct to mid-March 9.30am–5pm; last admission 2hr before closing time; £19; NT & EH). Most people access the site from the **visitor centre** and arrive from there on the (free) minibus. You need to pre-book and bring a printed-out ticket (or the version on your phone) to be sure of accessing the site. With your ticket you can return to the visitor centre on the minibus. The visitor centre is also the departure point for the bus into Salisbury, and there's a café plus the inevitable shop.

6

In any case, the stones were carefully laid out on this site, oriented towards the northeast for the **midsummer** sunrise and the midwinter sunset; if you were to stand at the centre of the horseshoe at dawn on midsummer's day, you'd see the sun rising directly above the Heel Stone. The precise nature of this alignment suggests that Stonehenge may have been used as an observatory or time-measuring device.

Buses leave for Salisbury from the car park near the visitor centre (7–15 daily; 30min; £11 single; 01202 338420, http://thestonehengetour.info). A **taxi** (call 01722 505050 or 01722 423000) to Salisbury station will cost around £23.

The New Forest

Lymington to Brockenhurst

Distance and difficulty 11km; easy

Minimum duration 2hr 45min

Trains London Waterloo to Lymington Town (hourly; 1hr 38min); return from Brockenhurst to London Waterloo (every 30min; 1hr 30min); South Western Railway

Maps OS Landranger 196: *The Solent & Isle of Wight*; OS Explorer 22: *New Forest*

Despite its name, the **New Forest** isn't just made up of woodland – the name describes an area of some 230 square kilometres that was (and to an extent still is) governed by an ancient system of forest law. Along with tracts of medieval woodland, the forest also covers large areas of gorse-covered heath and bogs, all rich in plant and, especially, animal life. Wherever you go you'll see the cute-looking **ponies** for which the area is famous – they're said to be descendants of Spanish ponies from Armada vessels that were wrecked on the coast – while the woods are home to large populations of red, roe, fallow and tiny sika **deer**, as well as badgers and foxes, and otters can be spotted in the Lymington River. The spring **flowers** in the woods are wonderful too: violets, primroses and wood anemones, followed by bluebells.

This walk takes in a variety of New Forest landscapes, from the boggy banks of the **Lymington River**, a haven for migratory birds, to stretches of dense ancient **woodland**. You can also detour from the village of **Pilley** – where a thousand-year-old pub provides posh lunches for which you need to book in advance – onto the open expanses of **Beaulieu Heath** (don't attempt this if conditions are wet).

Getting started

2.5km Leaving **Lymington Town station**, turn right onto Waterloo Road, then go right again at the T-junction at the end of the road to cross the railway line and the estuary of the Lymington River; on the far side of the bridge, turn left onto the road for Beaulieu (pronounced "Bew-Lee"). After 100m, where the Beaulieu road curves round to the right, go straight ahead, up the minor road. Continue along this road for 900m

---

THE LAWS OF THE NEW FOREST

The **New Forest** was named by William the Conqueror in 1079, when he established it as his personal hunting ground. He and his son, William Rufus, ruled over their land with an iron hand, imposing violent penalties on poachers, from mutilation to execution. The locals must have breathed a sigh of relief when Rufus, named for his rosy features, was killed in the forest in 1100 in a "hunting accident" (most probably a political assassination).

The **Charter of the Forest**, drawn up in 1217, modified forest law in favour of the inhabitants, who are still known as **Commoners**. Commoners' rights include "turbary" (the right to cut peat or turf as fuel); "estovers" (the right to collect firewood); and "mast" (the right to turn pigs out during a period known as "pannage"). This creates one of the forest's great sights in the autumn, when pigs roam free, guzzling acorns, beech mast and crab apples; the punky silver rings in their snouts are to prevent damage to root systems.

This forest law system is still maintained by the **Verderers Court**, one of the oldest judicial courts in Britain. The Verderers were originally charged with implementing the harsh Norman laws, but in 1877 the largely defunct court was reinvented, and it now upholds the rights of Commoners and oversees the health and welfare of the forest animals. They meet ten times a year in the seventeenth-century **Verderer's Hall** in Lyndhurst, where the Crown Stirrup is also preserved – in Norman times, any dog too large to fit through the stirrup was lamed so that it couldn't chase deer. The eleven Verderers appoint six **Agisters**, who manage the five thousand ponies and cattle that roam the forest.

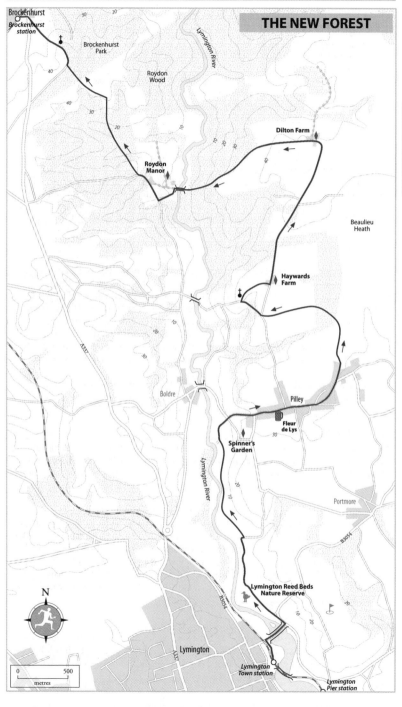

THE NEW FOREST

6

Brockenhurst

Brockenhurst station

Brockenhurst Park

Roydon Wood

Lymington River

Dilton Farm

Roydon Manor

Beaulieu Heath

Haywards Farm

A337

Boldre

Pilley

Fleur de Lys

Spinner's Garden

Lymington River

Portmore

B3054

Lymington Reed Beds Nature Reserve

Lymington

B3054

A337

Lymington Town station

Lymington Pier station

N

0   500
metres

6

BEAULIEU HEATH

Beaulieu Heath is a great open expanse, its 14km circumference framed by woodland. The thin soil supports a meagre covering of heather and gorse, but the boggy areas are rich in rare plant and insect life. Even on a short detour you can get a real sense of isolation, but bear in mind that the paths across it are unmarked and faint, and can easily be confused with tracks made by the pint-sized ponies. The lack of clearly definable tracks makes it impossible to describe a route here – if you do want to venture out onto the heath, arm yourself with OS Explorer 22: *New Forest*.

---

then, where the road bends sharply to the right, follow the bridleway sign into the **Lymington Reed Beds Nature Reserve**.

Once in the reserve, the path leads initially through woodland and then through more open boggy land along the right bank of the Lymington River. You can often see wild ponies splashing through the marsh, but the otters that live in the reserve are more reticent. The entire reserve is also a feeding place for birds such as black-headed gulls, oystercatchers, ringed plovers and Brent geese.

To Pilley

1.5km At the end of the reserve you reach a gate – go through and continue along the path for a longish stretch to a second gate. Go straight ahead on the paved track for 300m to reach a road, then turn right up the hill towards Pilley. After 200m you'll see a sign on the right pointing to **Spinner's Garden** (April–Sept Wed–Sat 10am–5pm, Oct Thurs & Fri 10am–5pm; £5; http://spinnersgarden.co.uk); it's worth a visit if you have an interest in gardening and is only another 200m off the road. Built on a slope overlooking the river valley, this luxuriant and exotic woodland garden is planted with azaleas, rhododendrons and magnolias, interspersed with curly ferns, irises and rare shrubs such as the purple Judas Tree.

The thatched *Fleur de Lys* **pub** is 300m beyond the turn-off to the garden, on the straggling outskirts of **Pilley**. They claim to have been serving up drinks since 1096, and you'll see a list of landlords at the entrance, dating back to 1498.

EATING AND DRINKING

Fleur de Lys Pilley St, Pilley SO41 5QG, 01590 672 158, http://fleurdelys-pilley.co.uk. The *Fleur de Lys* serves restaurant-style food: roasts, steaks and New Forest venison (mains around £20); the restaurant isn't the place for muddy boots, so you might want to have a drink and a snack in the more rugged bar. There's a small garden at the back and a snug interior, complete with big inglenook fireplaces. Tues–Sat 11am–3pm & 6–11pm, Sun noon–3pm.

Coming out of the pub, turn right and head up the road through the village. You pass a harness maker's and the Boldre working men's club on your left, and cross a cattle-grid. Walk for 300m along the main road until it bends sharply right, where you take the little paved path to the left. After 100m turn left, and after a further 50m you'll see a footpath sign on the right. Follow this across the field, along the slightly ridged grassy path, to reach a line of trees on the far side of the field, then turn left immediately as you pass them (unless you want to make a detour onto **Beaulieu Heath**, in which case go straight ahead).

To Roydon Wood

6km You'll see two footpaths ahead – a bridleway on the left and a footpath over a stile to the right. Take the latter and go diagonally through the woods until, after 50m, you emerge at the bottom right-hand side of a clearing. Again, head diagonally to its top

6

left-hand side. After a few metres you should see a metal kissing gate with a yellow arrow, on the left through the trees; go through this, and then straight ahead across the fields for 700m.

You come out onto a crossroads – go down the paved road to the right for 200m to the Norman and medieval **Church of St John the Baptist**. Unusually, the church, which sits on a mound, is in an isolated position away from any village – it's thought to have been built on the site of a prehistoric place of worship. The writer and illustrator **William Gilpin** was rector here in the late eighteenth century and wrote scathingly about the "indolent race" of foresters who marred the serenity of the New Forest by "forest pilfer … deer stealing, poaching or purloining timber".

From the church, follow the footpath sign towards the car park, where you'll see a yellow arrow on the gate post ahead of you, pointing forwards. This path emerges after 200m at **Haywards Farm**; go straight ahead past the farmhouse, then turn left onto the gravel road and continue ahead for another 600m. Approaching Dilton Farm, which you'll see ahead of you, take the track that curves round to the left, marked with a blue bridleway sign, rather than going straight ahead to the farm. Round the back of the farm you join a farm track – turn left onto this rather than following the path straight ahead.

After 650m you enter the signed **Roydon Wood Nature Reserve**, an area of broad-leaved woodland, some of it ancient and undisturbed. Just over 1km into the wood you come to a junction with bridleway signs. Go straight ahead, following the sign to Brockenhurst, heading down the hill to cross the wooden bridge over the Lymington River. On the right is **Roydon Manor**, a seventeenth-century brick mansion, thought to have been a chapel of the Knights Templar.

The path comes out onto a track. Turn right here following the bridleway sign; the track leads after 200m to a red-brick cottage. Turn left up the hill for 100m then follow the wiggly bridleway ahead of you, rather than continuing along the track, which curves to the left. The track continues through the woods for 700m, dipping down and then climbing steeply before coming out of the trees with a field to the right. Continue into Brockenhurst Park and then join the minor road.

Brockenhurst

1km Turn right along the road and walk 200m to reach the **Church of St Nicholas** (daily 2–5pm), the oldest church in the New Forest – Christians have worshipped on this site since the eighth century. Some Saxon herringbone stonework survives in the south wall of the nave, though the building is mainly Norman, with an eighteenth-century brick tower and Victorian additions. The dark shaggy yew tree next to the church is at least a thousand years old. A hundred casualties of World War I are buried in the graveyard, among them 93 New Zealanders, one Australian and three Indians, brought from French battlefields to be treated at Brockenhurst Hospital.

Don't miss the curious marble grave of local snake-catcher **"Brusher" Mills**, depicting a bearded Brusher with the tools of his trade – a forked stick and sack. Brusher lived in a hut in the forest and took up snake-catching in the 1880s; some of his snakes were sent to London Zoo to feed the birds of prey, while others were used to make ointments. Brusher once emptied a bag of snakes onto the floor of his regular, the *Railway Inn* in Brockenhurst (now called *The Snake Catcher*), to help clear a path to the bar.

To reach **Brockenhurst station**, carry on down the road beyond the church for 300m – it's across the busy road.

The Thames Valley

WINDSOR CASTLE

The Thames Valley

The towns and villages of the Thames Valley comprise what is still the most prized part of London's commuter belt, lending parts of the area an exclusive and sometimes snobbish air. More positively, the not-in-my-back-yard mentality has ensured that the region remains largely unblighted by development, despite its proximity to London, and the countryside around Silchester and Hambleden is beautifully unspoilt. The first walk in this chapter leads through expansive Windsor Great Park, dominated by the imposing medieval castle. The second walk takes you along the Thames Path from Henley to the picturesque Chilterns village of Hambleden, and on via wooded hills to Marlow, another prosperous little Thames-side town. The final route lies to the south of the river, running from Stratfield Mortimer to the strikingly evocative remains of the Roman settlement of Calleva, just outside the village of Silchester, and then across country to Bramley.

7

Windsor Great Park

The Long Walk to Savill Garden

Distance and difficulty 16.5km; moderate

Minimum duration 4hr 15min

Trains London Waterloo to Windsor & Eton Riverside (every 30min; 50min) or London Paddington to Windsor & Eton Riverside (every 30min; 40min); return from Windsor & Eton Riverside to London Waterloo (every 30min; 50min) or London Paddington (every 30min; 45min); Great Western Railway and South Western Railway

Maps OS Landranger 175: *Reading & Windsor*; OS Explorer 160: *Windsor and Weybridge*

Windsor Great Park, measuring some 24km in circumference, is too extensive to be a park in the ordinary sense of the word, and while there are some formal gardens and graceful avenues of trees, large sections remain wooded and relatively wild, and parts are given over to farmland. Giant oaks and beeches flourish, some standing solitary and some in thick clusters – several of the oaks date back to the Norman Conquest. Medieval Windsor Castle (parts of which are open to the public), one of the major seats of the royal family, is theatrical if slightly Disneyfied, while the grace-and-favour houses scattered throughout the park certainly give you a sense of how the other half lives – if you enjoy seeing the upper classes at play, the polo ground might provide some amusement. The best **time to visit** is late May and early June, when the rhododendrons and azaleas are in bloom; the park is open daily from dawn till dusk and is free to enter.

   Lunch, snacks and cakes can be bought at the Savill Building in the heart of the park, and you can end the walk with a pint at the atmospheric *Two Brewers* just outside the gates. The terrain would make this a good option for cyclists, but bikes are banned from the Long Walk.

Getting started

0.5km Exit **Windsor & Eton Riverside station** and turn right towards Windsor town centre, then take the first left towards the information office and the **castle**, which you'll see rising up on the left-hand side. Continue up the hill and round the flanks of the castle, then head straight up the High Street, following signs for the **Long Walk**. At the end of the main street, turn slightly to the left up Park Street. You'll see the flower-covered *Two Brewers* pub on the left; go through the gates just beyond and into the park, then turn right for the Long Walk.

The Long Walk

5km The **Long Walk**, laid out in the time of Charles II and William III, runs in a straight sweep, lined with plane and horse chestnut trees and bookended by Windsor Castle and a bombastic copper statue of George III on horseback, known as the **Copper Horse**. The walk crosses Albert Road (the A308), but is otherwise uninterrupted, except for the gate you pass through 400m beyond the road to enter the deer park. At the end of the long paved path, climb up the little mound to the Copper Horse; behind it go straight ahead, crossing the sandy riding track and following the wide grassy path that runs through a metal gate and then between hedgerows, before passing a small patch of oak woodland to the left.

To Savill Garden

2km You emerge onto a paved road. Turn left and almost immediately right, following the signs to handsome **Cumberland Lodge**, built in the time of Oliver Cromwell and named for the Duke of Cumberland (see page 187). It's now a conference centre, set up with royal approval to facilitate discussion about the Commonwealth from a Christian perspective. Immediately before you get to the lodge (marked "private"), take the path that curves round it to the left. At the main gate to the lodge, turn left and, where the drive splits, go straight ahead. Some 150m further on, turn right at the crossroad onto the paved path. You pass some tile-hung cottages before coming to an orange-brick gatehouse, **Cumberland Gate**.

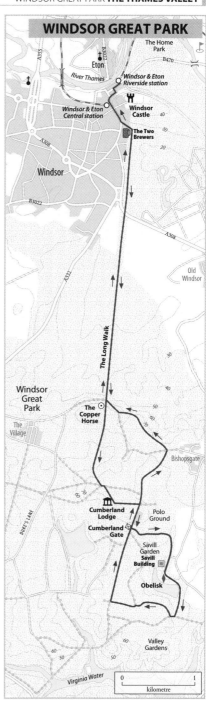

WINDSOR GREAT PARK

WINDSOR: MONARCHS, FIRE AND GHOSTS

Windsor Castle (daily: March–Oct 9.45am–5.15pm; Nov–Feb 9.45am–4.15pm; £23.50; http://royalcollection.org.uk) lies at the northeastern edge of Windsor on a low mound, which gives it a commanding position above the town and park. William the Conqueror acquired the surrounding forest for hunting and established the castle as an important residence of the English sovereigns, which it remains today. The castle's first round tower was built by Henry III around 1272, but Edward III reconstructed it in about 1344 as a meeting place for the newly established Knights of the Garter. Subsequent additions were made over the centuries until the 1820s, when over-the-top restoration by George IV gave it a toy-town look that chimes with the heavily heritage-bound atmosphere of Windsor itself. The Chapel of St George within the castle walls, however, is one of the finest examples of Perpendicular architecture in England, and ranks second only to Westminster Abbey as a royal mausoleum.

Since the time of William the Conqueror, the castle has played an important role in English history. Most dramatically, it was seized in 1642 by the **Parliamentary army** under Colonel Venn, who desecrated the chapel and killed the park's deer. Charles I was imprisoned in the castle in 1648 and later taken from there to Whitehall, where he was executed. His body was returned to Windsor in a coffin and was buried without ceremony.

The most significant event in the castle's recent history was the **fire** during the queen's "annus horribilis" of 1992, which gutted many of the State Apartments; the royals were inadequately insured, so the queen was obliged to fork out for half the £50 million repair bill, the nation having expressed reluctance to shoulder the entire burden.

The **park** itself was enclosed for the hunting of boar and deer in the thirteenth century. In 1580, Lord Burleigh ordered the planting of trees in the park to replenish timber stocks following the war with Spain. His successor Charles II planted the **Long Walk**, which links the castle and the park, in 1680. George III was confined at Windsor during his "madness", diagnosed in the twentieth century as a rare metabolic disorder; he famously jumped from his carriage to address an oak tree as the King of Prussia. The unstable monarch, known as Farmer George, was responsible for introducing agriculture to the park – farming and forestry interests were later developed by Prince Albert, and remain a significant part of the park's profile. More whimsically, the park is said to have been haunted for the last thousand years by **Herne the Hunter**, who wears stag antlers and rides a black stallion with a pack of black hounds at his feet; he appears when there is trouble ahead, then gallops through the park and melts into the air.

Go through the gate and turn immediately left onto the paved path, along the polo ground, passing a beautiful dove-grey Georgian house on the left and going through walkways of rhododendrons and azaleas. Continue to follow the signs along the sinuous path leading towards Savill Garden – you'll see the walled gardens on the right-hand side and a huge greenhouse. The path curves round to the right; follow it for another 250m to the entrance to the **Savill Building**. Constructed using four hundred larch trees and one hundred oaks from the park itself, the 90m-long building is topped by a wonderfully organic wavy roof. Via the building you can access the **Savill Garden** (daily: March–Oct 10am–6pm; Nov–Feb 10am–4.30pm; £9.75), a woodland garden begun in the 1930s, which incorporates herbaceous borders, rose gardens, peat beds and a bog garden, as well as umpteen rhododendrons and azaleas.

EATING AND DRINKING

Savill Building Wick Lane, Englefield Green TW20 0UU, 01784 485 402, http://theroyallandscape.co.uk. Houses the airy canteen-style *Savill Garden Kitchen* restaurant which serves up wood-fired pizzas salads and burgers (mains £10–17, as well as the smaller *Gallery Café*. Daily March–Oct 10am–5.50pm; Nov–Feb 10am–4pm.

Obelisk Pond and the polo ground

2.5km To continue the walk, take a right out of the Savill Building. After 150m you'll see a huge **obelisk** on the right-hand side, raised by George II for his son, William, Duke of Cumberland. This overblown monument recalls the commander who became known as "the butcher" for his cruel treatment of soldiers and civilians following the Battle of Culloden in 1746. Follow the paved path, to the left as you face the obelisk; the **Obelisk Pond** lies on the right, surrounded by sweet chestnuts and rhododendrons and edged by yellow irises.

Around 200m beyond the pond, you come to a junction. Turn right and continue until you emerge at the bottom of the **polo ground**, then carry on for 500m along the field, keeping it to your right and passing the stands and the low wooden Guards Polo Club building. The path splits; take the right-hand fork and ascend the length of the polo field, returning to **Cumberland Gate**. The bronze **equestrian statue** you pass on the left is of Albert, Prince Consort, given to Queen Victoria by the "daughters of her Empire" and unveiled in 1890, nearly thirty years after Albert's death.

To the Long Walk

2km Either return to the Long Walk the way you came or, for a slightly different route, don't turn left for Cumberland Lodge but continue straight ahead on the tarred path for 1km. At the crossroads by the **pink gatehouse** go straight ahead, following the road as it curves left. You return to the foot of the mound surmounted by the Copper Horse.

Back to Windsor

4.5km From here, rejoin the **Long Walk** to head back up to Windsor. Towards evening, the great trees lining the walk throw long shadows, the deer are more in evidence, and the imposing asymmetry of Windsor Castle makes a fine backdrop. You may see huge herds of deer crossing the road ahead of you at dusk – they will be keen to avoid you, but be sure to keep your distance in the rutting season in the autumn, and stay away from does with their young. Just out of the gates of the park, on the right, the welcoming *Two Brewers* is an excellent place to stop for a pint before you head home.

EATING AND DRINKING

The Two Brewers 34 Park St, Windsor SL4 1LB, 01753 855 426, http://twobrewerswindsor.co.uk. *The Two Brewers* began life in 1709 as a coffee house and now has a fabulously snug and cluttered interior plus a good list of old world wines, artisan spirits and real ales. Mon–Thurs 11.30am–11pm, Fri & Sat 11.30am–11.30pm, Sun noon–10.30pm.

The Thames path and the Chiltern Way

Henley to Marlow via Hambleden

Distance and difficulty 14.5km; moderate

Minimum duration 3hr 40min

Trains London Paddington to Henley (hourly; 55min); return from Marlow to Maidenhead (hourly; 20min), Maidenhead to London Paddington (every 20min; 40min); Great Western Railway

Maps OS Landranger 175: *Reading & Windsor*; OS Explorer 171 and 172: *Chiltern Hills West* and *Chiltern Hills East*

This satisfying walk runs between the affluent Thames towns of **Henley** and **Marlow**, passing through the Chilterns village of **Hambleden** en route, which makes a good stop for a pub lunch. The route from Henley goes along the east bank of the **Thames**, past rowing clubs housed in neat pavilions and elegant villas with wooden boathouses. The crowds of dog-walkers and families thin out as you walk further north up the Thames, until the only passers-by are rowing coaches who cycle up and down the path, yelling at rowers in the passing racing boats. At **Hambleden Lock** you cross the Thames over a wide weir to **Mill's End**. From here the route leaves the river and runs across meadows to the unspoilt village of **Hambleden**. Beyond Hambleden, a steep climb takes you into the Chilterns, after which the route – now following the **Chiltern Way** – levels out, taking you across farmland and downs and through dense stretches of **woodland**. From the woods you descend, via minor roads, into **Marlow**.

From Marlow you need to buy a single ticket to Maidenhead, where you connect with the Henley–London service.

Getting started

0.5km Coming out of **Henley station**, turn right and walk for 50m. Turn right and head down to the river, then turn left towards the eighteenth-century *The Angel on the Bridge* pub. At *The Angel on the Bridge*, cross the bridge then turn left, following the Thames Path sign towards Hambleden Lock.

The Thames Path

4km The **Thames Path** runs down the wide and grassy east bank of the river. This is where crowds gather for the **Henley Regatta**, which runs from the last Wednesday in June to the first week in July. The regatta's first incarnation was as the Oxford and Cambridge boat race, which ran between Hambleden Lock and Henley Bridge in 1829, but which was soon moved to London; Henley Regatta itself was established in 1839. It's a major fixture in the British social and sporting calendar, culminating in mass upper-class drunkenness and lots of people falling into the river.

Less than 2km beyond Henley, just off the route to the right, you'll see a church and a cluster of houses that comprise the village of **Remenham** – to the left across the river is red-brick **Fawley Court**, designed by Christopher Wren in 1684; James Wyatt made additions to the house in the 1770s, at which time Capability Brown designed

THE THAMES VALLEY

The most marked characteristic of the **Thames Valley** is – as it has been for centuries – affluence. The stretch of the river immediately to the west of London has long provided an escape from the capital for the wealthy: the Romans built villas along the river's fertile banks, and it later became a rural escape route for the monarchy who, from Henry II onwards, have generally preferred Windsor Castle as their principal place of residence. The area was again favoured during the Victorian era, when wealthy industrialists built Neoclassical villas along the river banks; it was also much visited by day-tripping Londoners – nearly seven thousand people took the train to Henley to enjoy the 1888 regatta.

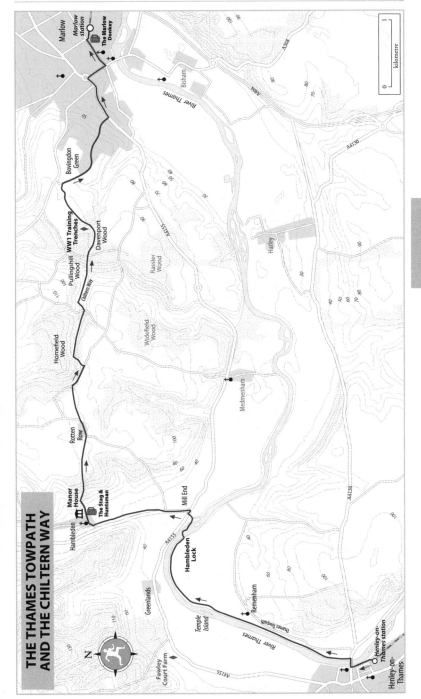

THE THAMES TOWPATH AND THE CHILTERN WAY

7

the gardens. Just over 500m beyond the house, **Temple Island** is home to a little white temple, designed by James Wyatt as the fishing lodge for Fawley Court; it now marks the start of the Henley Regatta course. Some 700m beyond Temple Island, on the opposite bank, stands the village of **Greenlands**, with a gleaming white Neoclassical mansion built by the newsagent W.H. Smith in 1853. Smith is buried in Hambleden churchyard (see below).

Seven hundred metres beyond Greenlands is **Hambleden Lock**: follow the public footpath sign to cross it. The path leads for 300m along and above the weir, through the middle of the river, with the water thundering down to the right.

Mill End to Hambleden

1.5km On the north side of the river is the tiny settlement of **Mill End**. There has been a mill here since at least 1086; the present mill, a substantial clapboard building with a slate roof, only stopped operating in 1952. Go past the mill and the cluster of attractive cottages beyond and on to the road. Turn right here, then left almost immediately after, following the road sign to Hambleden.

After 300m you come to a minor road on the right signed to Rotten Row. At this junction, follow the signed **public footpath**, which runs through the fields parallel to the road you've been on. Ahead are gentle rolling hills, topped by woodland; Hambleden's **Manor House** (see below) can be seen up ahead, as well as the orange-tiled roofs and square grey church tower of the village itself. After 500m the path emerges onto a little track; turn right and continue for a few metres, then take the signed public footpath on the left, which runs for another 500m through meadows to the village.

You come out at a tiny arched bridge over the stream that edges **Hambleden**, with red-brick and flint houses surrounded by cottage gardens. Go straight ahead through the village to the mainly Norman **Church of St Mary the Virgin**. Inside, don't miss the alabaster and marble memorial to Cope and Martha D'Oyley (died 1633 and 1618 respectively) and their five sons and five daughters. Two of the sons wear Royalist outfits; the rest Puritan. The children who predeceased their father hold skulls, a macabre touch intensified by the masterful depiction of each member of the family – it's thought they are actual, rather than idealized, portraits.

Continue along the road through the village to reach the **pub**.

EATING AND DRINKING

The Stag & Huntsman Hambleden RG9 6RP, 01491 571 227, http://thestagandhuntsman.com. The friendly and bustling *Stag & Huntsman* serves excellent food (snacks from £7, mains from £11), real ale on handpump and farm cider. There's a large garden at the back. Mon 11am–3pm & 6–11.30pm, Sun noon–3pm & 7–10.30pm.

The Chiltern Way to Marlow

6km From Hambleden, the route ascends into the Chilterns, picking up the **Chiltern Way**, which you follow for most of the return route to the outskirts of Marlow. Go through the pub car park, then left up the field to emerge near the Manor House. Turn right onto the track here, then left up the skinny path that leads steeply through a field, passing the **Manor House** on the left. The house's plain brick Georgian facade conceals an early seventeenth-century interior; Charles I stayed here in 1646 during his flight from Oxford to St Albans, just before his imprisonment. Continue along the path uphill through the woods for 400m. When you're nearly through the wood, follow the Chiltern Way through a kissing gate into a field.

Four hundred metres beyond the woodland, the path comes out onto a track; go straight ahead towards the flint farm buildings that comprise the hamlet of **Rotten Row**. After 200m you come onto the curve of a road; turn left towards the buildings of Rotten Row, passing the farm on your left and a pond on the right. Go straight ahead, following the Chiltern Way sign into the field, going through a couple of

RED KITES

Keep an eye on the sky on this walk, as you're sure to see **red kites** soaring above you. These marvellous birds, with a mighty wingspan of 1.5m, are identified by their deeply forked tails and russet colour, though the wings also have a patch of white and the jagged wing tips are black. They float on currents of air and make a harsh mewing sound.

The birds died out in Britain in the nineteenth century, with the exception of Wales where a few pairs struggled on. They were poisoned by gamekeepers and farmers, though in fact they pose little threat to lambs and other livestock, as they mainly feed on carrion, as well as worms, young birds and the odd small mammal. The birds were successfully reintroduced to the Chilterns by the RSPB in the 1990s, and there are now thought to be a thousand breeding pairs in the area.

kissing gates and across a second field. At the end of this field cross the stile and, just inside the woods, turn right onto a minor road. Ignore the public footpath sign to the left after 150m and carry on down the road for another 200m to reach a second public footpath sign on the left, with Woodside House to the left.

The path leads down through the beech woods, skirting round the edge of **Homefield Hall**. The path is faint here – just be sure to head downhill till you reach a track. Turn right on the track and continue through **Homefield Wood**, a National Trust nature reserve. After 650m you come out onto a minor road; turn right along the road for a few metres, then go left, following the Chiltern Way signs. Carry on for 500m across the grassy downland and along a fenced path till you reach **Pullingshill Wood**. Go straight ahead, following the Chiltern Way signs and climbing steeply up the hill – the path is rather faint, but bear in mind that 200m into the wood you need to cross the road that runs through it. To the left of the path here, look out for a network of **WW1 training trenches** dug in 1915 by the Grenadier Guards. There are 1400m of trenches in total, around 2m deep and 2m wide.

Once across the road, the path continues straight ahead through **Davenport Wood**, though again it's rather indistinct – the white arrows painted on the trees every 50m or so should keep you on course. Carry on through the woods, following both the Chiltern Way signs and the white arrows. After 600m you emerge from the woods, going through a wooden kissing gate and two squeeze gates, with some orange-brick houses ahead.

Into Marlow

2.5km You come out at the village of **Bovingdon Green** — rather than crossing the green, turn right past the row of red-brick cottages. Walk down the minor road for just over 1km, with villas and cottages lining the road. The road, signed after 600m as **Spinfield Lane**, leads downhill into **Marlow** and joins a main road at the bottom of the hill. Turn left and, 250m past the pub, look out on the left for a white villa where Percy Shelley and his wife Mary lived from 1817 to 1818 – it was here that Mary wrote *Frankenstein*, at the tender age of 21.

Some 650m beyond the point where you turned left along the main road, you reach a roundabout. Turn right here, following the signs to the station, down Marlow's busy High Street, which is lined with Georgian and Victorian buildings. At the end of the street, turn left onto Station Road at the roundabout and carry on for 650m; **Marlow station** is on the road ahead and slightly to the right, just beyond the *Marlow Donkey* pub.

Roman Silchester

Stratfield Mortimer to Bramley via Calleva

Distance and difficulty 14km; moderate

Minimum duration 3hr 30min

Trains London Paddington to Mortimer via Reading (hourly; 40min); return from Bramley to London Paddington via Reading (every 30min; 40min); Great Western Railway

Maps OS Landranger 175: *Reading & Windsor*; OS Explorer 159: *Reading*

This satisfying walk runs along footpaths and country lanes from the hamlet of **Stratfield Mortimer** to the picturesque remains of the Roman town of **Calleva** – a ring of defensive walls and a well-preserved amphitheatre, one of only sixteen built in Roman Britain. There's a convenient **lunch** stop at *The Calleva Arms* in the nearby village of **Silchester**, though you might prefer to have a picnic at Calleva itself, where there are plenty of scenic spots. From the ruins, the route leads across country to the station at **Bramley**.

7

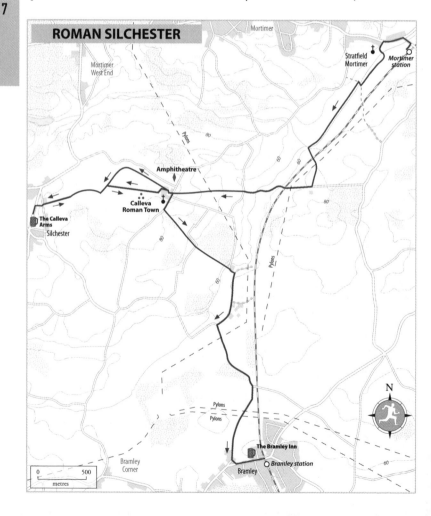

Along Foundry Brook

1.5km From **Mortimer station**, turn left down Station Road; when you come to the junction at the end of the road, turn left again. Continue up this road for 200m, then turn left at the green metal "byway" sign and follow the path past the church.

Beyond the church, at the end of the track, turn right, keeping **Foudry Brook** to your right. After 500m there's a junction – cross over Foundry Brook using the metal bridge and then continue along the path on the other side of the brook. Walk along the brook for 1km, until you see a metal gate on the left. Go across the field to the brook, turn right and continue along the field with the brook to your left. At the end of the field, cross the wooden bridge over the stream. After 200m you come to a wooden gate with yellow signs, marking a public right of way; cross this and go over the bridge over Foundry Brook.

Towards Calleva

5km Ascend the gentle slope away from the brook and cross the metal bridge over the railway line. Head over the field, keeping the line of the hedge to your right. The footpath emerges onto a narrow tarred road, with a red-brick cottage ahead; turn right, over the railway bridge, and follow the road, lined with damson and apple trees, for 800m until it comes to a T-junction. Head straight across the junction and into the field beyond, following the path that leads across the field, rejoining the tarmac opposite a red-brick house. You'll see a red postbox on the right and, beyond that, a wooden gate that leads to the amphitheatre.

7

The amphitheatre

Built in 55–75 AD in earth and timber, and rebuilt in stone in the third century, Calleva's **amphitheatre**, ringed with oak, silver birch, holly and ash, lacks the grandeur of those in mainland Europe, though it's still dramatic with steeply raked concave walls and an arena. Public entertainments took place here on holidays and festivals and are thought to have featured riding displays, animal hunts and wild beast shows rather than gladiatorial contests.

THE LIFE AND DEATH OF CALLEVA

No one knows why **Calleva** was abandoned when the Romans withdrew from Britain at the beginning of the fifth century, unlike similar towns such as Winchester and Canterbury. Whatever the reasons, the fact that the site was never developed means that its layout remains spectacularly intact. The walls form an irregular hexagon and were built in the third century when, like many Western European towns, Calleva must have felt the threat of barbarian invasion. Traces of Roman roads radiate out from the main gates; these would have cut through thick forest to link the town with Winchester, London and other lesser settlements.

At the heart of the town lay the **forum**, a great open square lined with two-storey colonnaded public buildings and shops; it was here that the town's principal roads converged. Along the forum's west side was the **basilica**, an aisled hall, thought to have been 25m high and constructed using marble from Italy – taxes were collected here, and justice was meted out. Just southeast of the forum sat a small fourth-century **church**, built after 313 AD, when Christianity was no longer a proscribed religion. The town's other major buildings included an elaborate bathhouse with an exercise court, three temples and an official guesthouse.

There were only around eighty houses of any significance at Calleva, their scant number and modest though graceful mosaics and frescoes suggesting that the town was not populous or extravagantly wealthy. Calleva served as the market town for the surrounding area, and there was some commercial activity: metal-working, pottery-making, glass- and lead-production, carpentry, milling and brewing.

There is some evidence – such as the apparently deliberate filling up of the town's wells with rubble – to suggest that Calleva was systematically evacuated and then destroyed, perhaps because of the political rise of Dorchester-on-Thames in the post-Roman period.

The Roman Town Trail and Silchester

3.5km From the amphitheatre, go back to the red postbox and take the wooden gate opposite leading up onto the walls. You are now on the **Roman Town Trail** that circles round the walls, which are punctuated by lofty oak and ash trees.

From the top of the walls you can appreciate the scope and symmetry of the site, as well as its tactical significance – it occupies high ground, with sweeping views to the south and east. The **walls** themselves, striped in flint and mortar, stand as high as 4.5m in some places, their expensive materials reflecting Calleva's importance. A number of gateways stud the 2.5km circumference; a pair of human skulls were found outside the north gate, which guarded the route towards Dorchester-on-Thames – it's thought that severed heads on poles stood grisly guard on either side.

You can explore in any direction – but the best way to get to the pub in Silchester is to turn right and follow the high grassy path for 800m. Halfway around the walls you go through a wooden kissing gate and across the track that bisects Calleva. Just beyond this is a gate to the right with a small **Silchester Village** sign. Go through the gate and up the lane, crossing a minor road. At the second road turn left, and walk for 600m to Silchester and *The Calleva Arms*.

EATING AND DRINKING

The Calleva Arms Little London Rd, The Common, Silchester RG7 2PH, 01189 700 305, http://calleva arms.co.uk. This pub is beautifully sited on a green and has an attractive beer garden, but the food is nothing special. Mon–Fri 11am–3pm & 5.30–11pm, Sat & Sun 11am–11pm.

From the pub, retrace your steps to Calleva and the **Roman Town Trail**. Either circle to the right round the walls, or take the track that cuts across Calleva. Both routes lead east to St Mary's Church.

St Mary the Virgin Church

Just outside the walls is **St Mary the Virgin Church**, a twelfth-century building with a low bell tower, partly built using stone from Calleva; a column from one of the Roman temples lies just to the west of the church. Another striking feature is the Tudor rood screen decorated with angels; it was hidden during the Reformation and rediscovered in a barn. (The number of mid-fourteenth-century names in the list of clergy in the church reflects the toll taken by the Black Death.)

Across country to Bramley

4km Opposite the driveway to St Mary's, go up the slope through the hedgerow, and head across the field towards the trees. When you get to the far side, go into the woods and across the next field. Head straight on to where the path dips slightly into a field, curve round the field to the right, and then go straight ahead. The path eventually joins a little track.

Go straight ahead on the track, then go right over a stile, with a copse on the left. Head up the field and keep the fence to the left; go over the gate straight ahead (ignoring the one to the right) and cross a concrete bridge – after 50m you go through a metal gate and join the road, with a red-brick house on the left-hand side.

Follow the road as it curves round to the right – ignore the left-hand footpath sign. After 750m you come to a T-junction: take the left-hand route to Bramley. Some 800m further on, take the turning on the right, just before the red-brick railway bridge. Heading down the road, you'll see tall pylons marching towards an electricity substation to the right of the road. Entering the village of **Bramley**, look out for the quirky barn to the left, resting on stone toadstools that protect its contents from rodents.

Just beyond the barn, turn left towards Bramley train station; adjoining it is the *Bramley Inn* which dishes up pretty good Indian food.

The Chilterns and Blenheim

CHILTERN HILLS

The Chilterns and Blenheim

Flanking London's northwestern edges, the Chiltern Hills are part of a range of chalk uplands that run from Wiltshire in the west all the way to Yorkshire in the north. The Chilterns are the most dramatic part of these hills within easy reach of London, rising to a high, steeply shelving escarpment offering panoramic views west and backed by beech woodlands that thrive in the chalky soil. The first of these walks heads out from the commuter town of Amersham, through the Chilterns via Misbourne Valley, to the village of Chalfont St Giles. The second starts in Wendover and leads west to the Chilterns' highest viewpoint, Coombe Hill, before descending into the Chequers Estate, the prime minister's country retreat. The third walk follows the Ridgeway trail from Tring to Ivinghoe Beacon, the second highest of the Chilterns' viewpoints. Beyond the Chilterns in Oxfordshire, the last of the walks in this chapter makes a circuit of the Blenheim Estate.

8

The Misbourne Valley

Amersham to Chalfont St Giles and back

Distance and difficulty 16km; moderate

Minimum duration 4hr

Trains Marylebone to Amersham, either by Overground train (every 30min; 30min) or tube (Metropolitan Line); return from Amersham to Marylebone (every 30min; 30min); Chiltern Railways

Maps OS Landranger 165 and 175: *Aylesbury & Leighton Buzzard* and *Reading & Windsor*; OS Explorer 172: *Chiltern Hills East*

This easily accessible walk, reached from London by either train or tube, leads from Amersham to Chalfont St Giles and back again, following the **Misbourne Valley** as it cuts through the Chilterns. Starting at the station in **Amersham-on-the-Hill**, the route begins by descending into the pretty medieval country town of **Amersham**. Past Amersham, the walk follows a ridge of the Chilterns above the Misbourne Valley into **Chalfont St Giles**. Centred on an attractive village green, Chalfont boasts the cottage (now a museum) that John Milton lived in while he completed *Paradise Lost*, as well as a choice of pubs for **lunch**. The **return route** back to Amersham again follows the River Misbourne, but this time along the valley floor, offering a fresh perspective on the chalky surrounding hills.

Getting started

1km Turn left out of the train station into **Amersham-on-the-Hill** and head down to the junction. Turn left onto the main road (A416), heading under the railway bridge and downhill towards Amersham Old Town.

Some 200m beyond the bridge and just before Parsonage Place, a short row of houses set back from the main road, take the well-marked public footpath on the right into **Parsonage Wood**. Keeping close to the easterly edges of the wood, the track rises sharply for the first 50m or so, then levels off as it heads through the heart of the wood. At the first fork in the path bear left. From between the beech trees you can catch glimpses across the valley of the farmland and wooded hilltops through which the walk will take you.

Amersham Old Town

0.5km At the far side of the woodland, 20m from the road ahead, bear left and head downhill on a tarred path and over grassland to **Amersham Old Town**, which sits on the banks of the River Misbourne, its centre marked by the tower of St Mary's parish church. At the bottom of the hill, past allotments on the right, the track ends at a T-junction before a high red-brick wall; to your left is the old **cemetery**. Take the footpath that leads to the left, then, a few metres further on, cross the **River Misbourne** – little more than a babbling brook at this point – via the tiny stone bridge to your right. This brings you to **St Mary's Church**. Though the original church dates from the thirteenth century, much of what you see today – including the flint facing, the stair-turret and much of the interior – are part of a heavy-handed late Victorian restoration.

Turn left into the churchyard, 100m from the bridge, and follow the path through to the aptly named **Broadway**, the old town's main drag. Detour to the right to see the timber-framed and brick-fronted seventeenth-century cottages lining the wide street, and the red-brick **Market Hall**, topped by a wooden bell-turret and with a plaque recounting some of the town's history.

Otherwise, turn left and follow the road for 200m, heading out of town to the roundabout by Tesco. Just beyond the roundabout, a few metres along London Road West and just before **Bury Cottage**, turn right into **Bury Farm**. Bear left to head behind Bury Cottage and go through the gate into a field between a sewage works to your left and the A413 to your right.

Amersham to Upper Bottom House Farm

3.5km At the far side of the field, head under the bridge that carries the A413 and up into farmland. In the hedgerow on the right, 50m or so from the bridge, is a gate; go through this and head through two fields, climbing steadily and aiming for the left-hand side of **Rodger's Wood**, which runs along the brow of Gore Hill, overlooking the valley. At the edge of the wood, go through another gate and take the path on the opposite side, which cuts through the woods to reach a second gate after 100m, at the edge of a field. Head diagonally across the field to the end of the hedgerow on your right, over the access road to **Quarrendon Farm**, and on towards Day's Wood, a small copse 300m ahead. There are views from here back across the valley floor to Amersham and further west into the heart of the Chilterns.

Around 75m before **Day's Wood**, cross a gate in the hedgerow to your right and go into the field. Follow the edge of the field, keeping the wood on your left, until you get to another field with a pylon in it. Cross the field diagonally, to the left of the pylon. In the hedgerow opposite is another gate; go straight ahead and continue downhill to the far right-hand corner of this field, and towards **Upper Bottom House Farm**.

At the end of the hedgerow the path drops down into the farm itself. Curve left round the cowshed, then turn right at the small road. Just before the farmhouse itself head left, uphill on a dirt track.

Chalfont St Giles

3km Keeping the hedgerow to your right, head up the track away from Upper Bottom House Farm for 200m, then turn left onto a minor track just before an enclosed area of woodland. Follow this track uphill until you go through a farm gate and reach a white sign with four pointers: head left for **Chalfont St Giles**, past Hill Farm House and through Rushcroft Wood. You emerge on Mill Lane, at the edge of the village.

Cross this and head straight on down Dodds Lane, which becomes Silver Hill and leads, via the decent *Fox & Hounds* **pub**, after 750m to the attractive little High Street and village green, surrounded by seventeenth-century timber- and brick-built cottages. Turn left to the village green, where the heavily restored *Merlin's Cave* (Mon noon–12.30am, Tues–Sun 8am–12.30am; 01494 875101, http://merlins-cave.com) serves upmarket pub food; to the right of *Merlin's Cave* there's a pretty good **deli**.

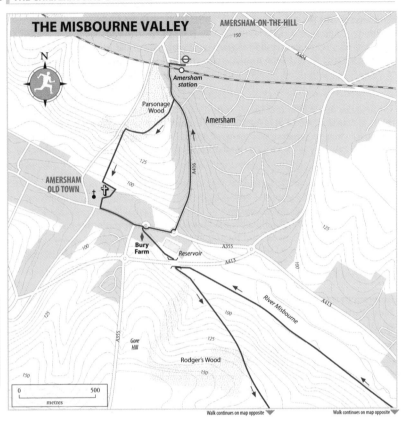

THE MISBOURNE VALLEY

AMERSHAM-ON-THE-HILL

Amersham station

Parsonage Wood

Amersham

AMERSHAM OLD TOWN

Bury Farm

Reservoir

River Misbourne

Gore Hill

Rodger's Wood

0 — 500 metres

Walk continues on map opposite ▼   Walk continues on map opposite ▼

8

Behind High Street, the village's medieval flint **church** rises above the houses – it's well worth a look for the faint fourteenth-century wall paintings which were uncovered after centuries under plaster.

What brings most visitors to Chalfont St Giles is **Milton's Cottage** (March–Oct Tues–Sun 10am–1pm & 2–6pm; £7), in which the poet John Milton sought refuge from plague-stricken London in 1665 as a guest of Thomas Ellwood. Milton completed *Paradise Lost* here, and it was during the same stay that Ellwood suggested to him the idea of *Paradise Regained*. The red-brick and tiled cottage now contains a modest little **museum** devoted to Milton's life and works, including first editions of his poems. The house is a few hundred metres uphill from the village green, to the right as you face *Merlin's Cave*.

Along the Misbourne

2.5km The route back to Amersham is easy to follow. From the village green, take the public footpath, Stratton Chase Drive, just to the right of **Silver Hill**, the road you came down to reach High Street. At the end of this lane, 300m from High Street, the track continues straight on into woodland. Where the route forks, take the narrower right-hand path, along a field and past some cottages to a road. Opposite you is the Old Mill. The road, **Mill Lane**, crosses the River Misbourne a few metres to the right here.

Just to the left of the mill, you rejoin the public footpath at the waymarkers. Again, the track heads through the trees, their branches here arching over the path to make a shady avenue, dappled with light, for the next kilometre or so. The River Misbourne flows some 500m to your right – you'll catch glimpses of it intermittently for the rest of the walk – and there are views across the Misbourne Valley and over to Pollards Wood on the hillside opposite.

Across country to Amersham train station

5.5km The path through the avenue of trees ends at a gate. Go through into a field and from here continue straight ahead, along easily followed paths, crossing fields for a little over 4km.

With the wooded hills east of Amersham rising above you to the right and the hills along which you walked earlier looming up to the left, this is a much more enclosed route than the walk out to Chalfont St Giles. The going is easier too, as the path not only follows the flat valley floor, but also largely crosses pasture rather than arable land.

Several fields later you reach the tunnel under the A413, which leads out to the field before Bury Farm; head back through the farm and down its drive to London Road West. From here, just to the left of **Bury Cottage**, you can retrace your steps back via Amersham Old Town to return to Amersham station.

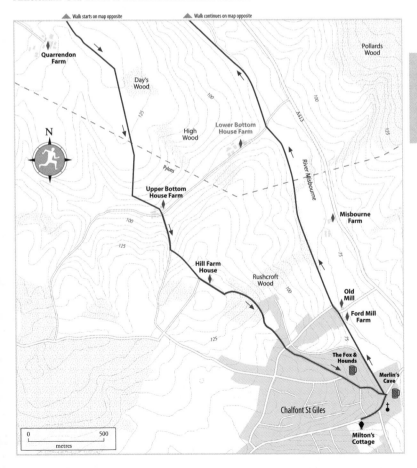

The Northern Chilterns

Wendover to Chequers via Coombe Hill

Distance and difficulty 15km; moderate

Minimum duration 3hr 45min

Trains London Marylebone to Wendover (1–2 hourly; 45min); return from Wendover to London Marylebone (1–2 hourly; 45min)

Maps OS Landranger 165: *Aylesbury & Leighton Buzzard*; OS Explorer 181: *Chiltern Hills North*

This varied and beautiful circular route begins and ends at **Wendover**, a small medieval market town that sits in a gap in the Chilterns. From Wendover, the walk joins the **Ridgeway**, which climbs up onto **Coombe Hill**, the highest viewpoint in the Chilterns, before looping around the **Chequers Estate**, the prime minister's country retreat. Beyond Chequers, the route heads into the village of **Great Kimble**, where *The Swan* makes for a good **lunchtime** break. The return route to Wendover takes you along public footpaths through the rich agricultural land of the **Vale of Aylesbury**.

Getting started

0.5km The walk begins at **Wendover station**, though it's worth making time to look around the town itself before setting off on the walk – the High Street is lined with picturesque timber-framed houses and grander Georgian mansions.

To begin the walk, turn right out of the station and head up to the main road; turn right onto this and head out of Wendover via the road bridge over the busy A413 and on past a row of terraced cottages. After a couple of hundred metres you reach a bend in the road; on the left-hand side of the road there's a large brown sign for Bacombe Hill by two waymarked tracks. Take the right-hand track, waymarked as part of the **Ridgeway** (see page 161; signs show a white acorn on a brown post). A few metres beyond the metal gate, bear left onto a side track, still following the Ridgeway signs, and head uphill along a steep and frequently muddy path.

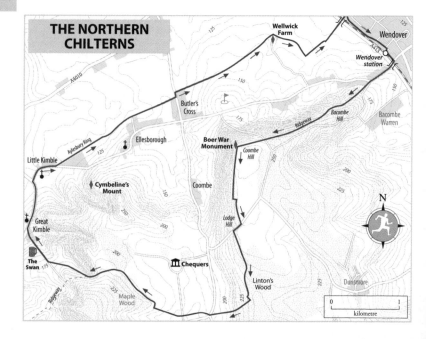

THE NORTHERN CHILTERNS

Bacombe Hill and Coombe Hill

2km The path climbs steeply for 300m, then rises gently along the northern flank of **Bacombe Hill** to reach the summit of **Coombe Hill**, 2km beyond. The track is well signposted, and there are good views north and west over the Vale of Aylesbury and back across Wendover.

Just before the summit of Coombe Hill, beyond a small thicket of trees, you pass through a metal gate and the view opens up to reveal the **Boer War monument**, which tops the hill and dominates the skyline for many kilometres around. Built in 1904 and topped by a gilded sculpture representing an eternal flame, it was erected to honour the dead of the Royal Bucks Hussars. The monument stands in a 106-acre National Trust site that was gifted in 1918 by Arthur Hamilton, who also gave the Chequers Estate to the nation.

Coombe Hill to Chequers

2.5km From **Coombe Hill**, head for the Ridgeway waymarker by the row of trees just to the left of the monument as you approach it from Wendover. Continue for a few hundred metres along the western flank of the hill. The hillside falls away steeply to your right down to the hamlet of **Coombe**; beyond, the Chequers Estate begins to come into view in the lee of angular Beacon Hill, the red-brick chimney tops of its Elizabethan manor house visible above the trees.

The track continues gently downhill for 500m. Eventually you reach a metal gate – go straight ahead into the beech wood, following the Ridgeway sign. The gate marks the southern boundary of the National Trust property and takes you along the Chilterns escarpment, here called **Lodge Hill**, for 250m to reach a quiet lane through the woodland opposite a handsome red-brick and flint cottage. Turn right and follow the lane downhill for around 100m to an access road on the left into **Lodge Hill Farm**, set in a small woodland clearing on the opposite side of the road.

Walk down this track for 10m and regain the Ridgeway through **Linton's Wood**. The path through the woods is faint at points, but just look out for the numerous Ridgeway signs among the trees. The path eventually becomes a wide dirt track; keep going along this to emerge from the woods at a bend in a tarred lane. The gate opposite marks the southeast corner of the Chequers Estate – hence the CCTV cameras that watch over the prime minister's country retreat and grounds.

8

Chequers to Great Kimble

3km Go through the gate and into the estate itself – there are fine views from here up to the mid-sixteenth-century manor house of **Chequers**, which has been the country retreat of British prime ministers since the early twentieth century. Lloyd George was the first prime minister to make use of the house, while Winston Churchill often retreated here during the air raids of World War II, delivering some of his most famous broadcasts from the house. It's regularly used by incumbent prime ministers, both as a retreat from the day-to-day wrangles of political life, and for hosting visiting heads of state.

The house (along with a £100,000 endowment) was given to the nation in 1921 by **Arthur Hamilton** on condition that it be used as the country retreat of the incumbent prime minister. Born in Britain, but half-American, the well-connected and ambitious Hamilton had previously enjoyed a glittering military career, becoming a close friend of Teddy Roosevelt along the way, and later being elected Conservative MP for Fareham and the First Lord of the Admiralty. In recognition of his services – and possibly a little influenced by his generous donations to the state – the British government elevated him to the status of Viscount Lee of Fareham in 1922.

Records show that there has been a settlement on the site since Roman times, though nothing remains of these early buildings. The current house dates from the mid-sixteenth century and, despite the addition of some Gothic features in the nineteenth century, it retains a largely Elizabethan appearance – all red brick, leaded windows and soaring chimneys. Remember, though, that this is a private estate and stick to the public footpath, which heads west, over the main drive and on to a gate. Go through the gate, across the drive just north of the lodge houses, then through two more gates and into a field.

The track climbs gently for 400m through the field towards **Maple Wood**. At the edge of the wood, turn right and follow the track for about 500m to reach another gate. At the next gate, turn left and away from Chequers, heading uphill across a field, over the brow of the hill and down to another gate. Pass through this and head on down the track.

After 100m the track opens up onto a wide field, the boundary of the Chequers Estate, marked to your right by a low fence. Take the right-hand footpath off the **Ridgeway** and head along the fence, towards the woods on the far side of the field. At the end of the field, turn left along the fence for 100m. A metal kissing gate in the corner of the field takes you onto the **North Bucks Way**: turn right here down the hill. The track heads to a tarred lane and leads after a couple of hundred metres to a T-junction with the A4010. Turn right here and head uphill into **Great Kimble** – little more than a church and a row of Victorian cottages.

Great Kimble to Ellesborough: the Aylesbury Ring

2.5km Turn left down Church Lane for 800m to reach *The Swan* pub. Otherwise, continue along the A4010 towards Little Kimble. After 500m, turn right down **Ellesborough Road**, passing **Little Kimble**'s church, **All Saints**, which boasts some of the finest medieval wall paintings in the county; they feature the martyrdom of St Margaret, and you can also make out St James in his wide pilgrim's hat, St Christopher bearing Christ on his shoulder and the elegant figure of St George. Continue past the church straight on towards Ellesborough; ignore the green public footpath sign to the left just beyond the church.

EATING AND DRINKING

The Swan Grove Lane, Great Kimble HP17 9TR, 01844 275 288, http://the-swan-aylesbury.edan.io. A nice traditional two-bar inn, opened as a free house in 1840. They serve a seasonal weekly ale and home-cooked pub food including Sunday roasts. Mon & Tues noon–3pm & 5–10pm, Wed–Sat noon–3.30pm & 5–11pm, Sun noon–8pm.

About 500m beyond the turn-off from the A4010, on the edge of Little Kimble, turn left. Go through the gate next to a modern house, following the black sign (the sign is very lost in the overgrown hedge, so you have to keep your eyes well peeled to spot it) to the **Aylesbury Ring** – this is still a dedicated public footpath, although you might feel as if you're trespassing since the footpath has been incorporated into the house's lawn. After a few metres, the footpath bends round to the right, continuing between the older properties at the edge of Little Kimble.

After 100m, at the end of this short track between the houses, go through the gate and out into farmland, and continue straight on. Almost immediately, Ellesborough's church comes into view, an impressive Victorian flint and brick pile with an imposing stair-turret tower, sitting on a small hill at the roadside a few hundred metres off to your right. To the right of the church rises the man-made mound nicknamed **Cymbeline's Mount** – the motte of a small medieval castle.

Ellesborough to Wellwick Farm

2.5km The track here leads across the rich arable farmland of the **Vale of Aylesbury**; to your right, the Chiltern escarpment rises steeply above the villages – Little Kimble, **Ellesborough** and Butler's Cross – strung out along the Ellesborough Road, itself a good 500m beyond and above the public footpath.

Follow the public footpath, passing below the church, and come out after 800m at the end of a lane by the thatched Springs Cottage. Head straight on along the lane, which marks the southern boundary of Ellesborough; where it bends round to go up to the main road, pick up the trail to the left of the houses and go straight ahead, between two fields. The path passes through fields and paddocks to come out after around 500m at the busy road into **Butler's Cross**.

Turn left, cross the road just beyond Southfield Cottages and pick up the path on the far side at a metal gate. The track continues east, before climbing gently for 500m to the brow of a hill, then heads downhill again towards a small copse another 700m further on. The copse hides the splendid Elizabethan red-brick and flint **Wellwick Farm** from view until you're almost at the house. There are good views of the house as you follow the path, close by its northern facade and on around the easterly side through a gate into a field. From here, follow the waymarkers up into the farmyard.

Wellwick Farm to Wendover station

2km Head out of the farmyard, straight over the access road and into the next field, then follow the waymarkers across the field. Just before the hedgerow begins, turn left, heading straight on towards the bridge – a farmyard track over the A413 – a few hundred metres further on. You come out in a field just before the **bridge**.

On the far side of the bridge, turn right at the public footpath sign and follow the narrow track, which leads behind houses to emerge on a quiet access road after 200m; this leads to a small industrial estate. **Wendover station** is just under 500m along this road from here.

8

Ivinghoe Beacon

Tring to Aldbury

Distance and difficulty 13.5km; moderate

Minimum duration 3hr 20min

Trains London Euston to Tring (Mon–Sat every 30min, Sun hourly; 40min); return from Tring to London Euston (Mon–Sat every 30min, Sun hourly; 40min)

Maps OS Landranger 165: *Aylesbury & Leighton Buzzard*; OS Explorer 181: *Chiltern Hills North*

This superb circular walk leads from **Tring station** in Hertfordshire and up onto the Chiltern escarpment. The first half of the route follows the **Ridgeway Long-Distance Footpath** (see page 161), a 136km hilltop track that begins in Wiltshire and ends at **Ivinghoe Beacon**, one of the highest points in the Chiltern Hills.

Passing through beech woodland and over chalk uplands, the walk gives fine views over the Vale of Aylesbury, a patchwork of farmland dotted with small villages and towns. From Ivinghoe Beacon, the route leads back through the woods of the extensive **Ashridge Estate**, once the seat of the dukes of Bridgewater and now home to a network of public footpaths and a handily placed **tearoom**. Beyond the **Bridgewater Monument**, which dominates the hillside hereabouts, the route drops down into the handsome village of **Aldbury**, with half-timbered cottages and a duck pond. From Aldbury, it's a short walk back to Tring station.

For lunch take a **picnic** – there are lots of good picnic spots, not least Ivinghoe Beacon itself – or eat at the National Trust tearooms by the Bridgewater Monument. There's a good **pub**, *The Greyhound Inn* in Aldbury, located close to the end of the walk.

Getting started

0.5km From **Tring station**, turn right onto Station Road and walk along it for 300m, passing a turning off to your left. At a bend in the road, turn left, following the fingerpost for the Ridgeway up the access road to **Westland Farm**. This short concrete road leads after 100m past the entrance to the farm and via a short stretch of track to the **Ridgeway Long-Distance Footpath**.

Through Aldbury Nowers

1.5km Turn left onto the Ridgeway and follow it gently uphill through an avenue of hawthorns behind Westland Farm. After 600m you come to an intersection with another public footpath; turn right, following the fingerpost signs for the Ridgeway along the steep track up into **Aldbury Nowers**, a mature beech wood on the chalky upland above Tring.

A few metres into the wood, turn left off the main track at the next Ridgeway fingerpost and head up a series of dirt steps. At the top of the steps, the path veers off to the left and briefly heads out of the trees, giving great views across the rich farmland of the **Vale of Aylesbury**. Within a few metres you begin to climb quite steeply into the woods again. At the top of this rise, the track, which is clear and wide at this point, bears right and heads through the heart of the woodland along the edge of the Chiltern escarpment.

From here there are views out across the valley: a patchwork of fields dotted with small settlements and farm buildings. The dominant feature, however, is what looks like a large reservoir a few kilometres to the northwest. This is actually a disused **chalk pit**, beyond which lies the (also disused) Pitstone Cement Works, for which the chalk pit was dug. The gentle walk through Aldbury Nowers ends at a wooden kissing gate after just under 1km; beyond lies open chalk upland, with the summit of Pitstone Hill rising steeply to your right and the Chiltern escarpment dropping steeply down to your left.

8

Pitstone Hill

1.5km Follow the Ridgeway signs straight on along the wide grassy track that follows the edge of the escarpment, just below **Pitstone Hill**, and then winds its way up to the summit, following **Grim's Ditch**, one of many ancient earthworks in the area that may have acted as land boundaries. At the top of the hill (head for the blue and yellow waymarkers in front of the hawthorn bush ahead), the views to the east across the

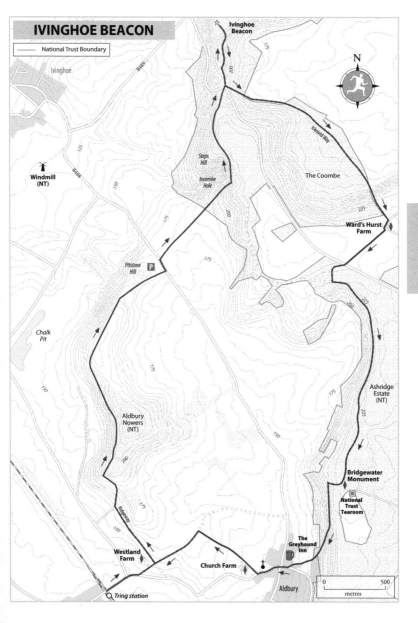

Ashridge Estate and ahead to Ivinghoe Beacon open up, with the Chiltern escarpment rising with dramatic suddenness out of the flat farmland.

A couple of kilometres away in the valley below, in fields between the disused chalk pit and the villages of Pitstone and Ivinghoe, stands **Pitstone Windmill**, a traditional, seventeenth-century post mill which is one of the oldest of its type in Britain. Post mills were built around a central post that could be turned round to allow the sails to catch the wind – an essential feature for a working mill in what could otherwise be a windless spot.

The wide grassy path at the top of the hill leads along the ridge for 800m before dropping down steeply, flanking the edge of some fields on your right; continue straight on, following the fingerpost to your right then a blue waymarker just to the right of the mound, to come out at a wooden kissing gate by a telegraph pole.

Incombe Hole and Steps Hill

1.7km The gate leads through to a picnic area at the edge of a car park. Go through the car park and then turn right to cross the lane which heads left to right towards Pitstone and Ivinghoe villages. Go through a kissing gate opposite the entrance to the car park and continue straight on along the wide track through farmland. The bowl of Incombe Hole (see below) lies straight ahead, rising dramatically in front of you; beyond it, along the rippling folds of the escarpment, are, in turn, **Steps Hill** and **Ivinghoe Beacon**.

This glacial valley is at its most dramatic here: to either side flat farmland stretches out along the valley floor; ahead, the escarpment rises steeply, the Ridgeway heading straight on and up the escarpment by **Incombe Hole**. A dramatic depression in the escarpment, the "hole" is a good example of a so-called "dry valley", formed by ice melt in the frozen limestone of the escarpment at the end of the last ice age. Follow the track up the escarpment and round the edge of Incombe Hole to a gate 700m or so from the valley bottom (ignore the yellow waymarker off to the right at the bend).

Following the waymarkers, continue along a track to the left of the gate and head into the hawthorn thicket ahead; the way through the thicket is clear and well marked, and brings you out after around 100m to the grassy side of **Steps Hill**. Head downhill for a further hundred metres, keeping close to the barbed-wire fence to your right, and go out of the field through the wooden gate. The route leads up to the right and over scrubland for 300m before heading downhill to a bend in a road (Beacon Road) that runs round the base of Ivinghoe Beacon.

Ivinghoe Beacon

1km Cross the road, on the far side of which you'll find the junction of three waymarked public footpaths. Go left here and up the final 500m ascent to the top of **Ivinghoe Beacon**. The last few metres are a steep scramble, but worth it for the panoramic views: south and west across the Chilterns and the Vale of Aylesbury respectively, north towards Buckingham and the Midlands, and east along Gallows Hill towards Whipsnade and the Dunstable Downs.

Ivinghoe Beacon marks the northern end of the Ridgeway Long-Distance Footpath, though the ancient trail is thought to have once continued down off the escarpment and on towards East Anglia. Standing 223m high, the hill takes its name from the beacons that were periodically lit here, part of an early warning system against potential invasion, from Roman times through the Spanish Armada to World War II. Ivinghoe Beacon was also the site of one of Britain's earliest **hillforts**; metalwork and pottery finds from its summit indicate that it was occupied from as early as the eighth or seventh century BC, and you can still make out parts of the enclosure and fortifications – including the ditches and mounds that bounded the fort – at the summit.

BOER WAR MONUMENT ON TOP OF COOMBE HILL

Through The Coombe

2.3km From the Beacon, retrace your steps back down to the three waymarked public footpaths by Beacon Road and go right. After a few metres this path leads to a gate at the edge of sheep-farming land. You're now on the **Icknield Way**, another famous long-distance footpath, which you follow for the next couple of kilometres. Head down across the field to a gate 150m further on; go through the gate and continue straight on.

After 400m you reach another gate, leading into the field to your right. Take the lower of two paths that lead around the side of the hill before you – a few metres on you'll spot a yellow waymarker in the distance pointing towards a beech wood. This is **The Coombe**, an outlying part of the Ashridge Estate.

The track through it is easy to follow for the first 600m, after which you come to the edge of a well-established fir plantation, with rows of giant firs stretching on ahead of you. The track, marked by a yellow waymarker at this point, is just to the left of the row of firs directly in front of you. Follow the path as it zigzags between the rows of trees to emerge after 300m at the edge of the woodland.

Follow the yellow waymarker, heading straight on along the edge of the woods and then up the steep, wooded bank that rises a few metres ahead of you. The initial sharp climb is followed by a steady ascent to a gate at the far (southerly) end of The Coombe, just before **Ward's Hurst Farm**. Go through the gate and continue along the edge of the field beyond it for 30m, to come out into the farmyard. The route leaves the Icknield Way at this point; turn right, following the public footpath signs, and go through the farmyard and down the long drive back to **Beacon Road**.

The Bridgewater Monument

2km Cross Beacon Road and head into the beech woods at the public footpath sign opposite. The path heads into the heart of the National Trust-managed **Ashridge Estate**, the former estate of the dukes of Bridgewater. A few metres on from Beacon Road, turn right onto a wide dirt track and follow this round for 300m in a long, gradual curve as it heads down through the woodland to a crossroads. Turn left here (ignoring the yellow waymarkers straight on down a minor track), following the main track along the chalky ridge through the heart of the estate; you'll soon start to see official waymarkers for the **Ashridge Estate Boundary Trail** every few hundred metres.

The trail follows a ridge of the Chilterns for 1.5km, giving good views out across the valley towards Aldbury Nowers, passing a bijou log cabin and crossing a wooden bridge over a dry ditch (part of an ancient earthworks) before coming out at the **Bridgewater Monument**. It's owned by the National Trust, which also has a **tearoom** here; you can climb to the top of the monument (April–Oct Sat & Sun noon–5pm; £2.50) for great views out across the surrounding countryside. The monument – a Doric column topped by a square plinth and copper bowl – was erected in 1837 in honour of Francis, third duke of Bridgewater, the "father of inland navigation". The duke, inspired by the navigational waterways he'd seen in France, commissioned the building of a canal at his coal mine in Worsley, northwest of Manchester, in the late 1760s. Though not the country's first canal (the Sankey Brook Navigation Canal in St Helen's claims that title), the **Bridgewater Canal** was the prototype for the man-made waterways that crisscrossed the country by the early nineteenth century.

Aldbury to Tring station

3km Head straight across the clearing and follow the bridleway beyond the disabled car park outside the tearooms, waymarked as part of the **Hertfordshire Way**, a 265km, circular long-distance footpath round the county. The path leads downhill, ever more steeply, through a cutting in the chalky hillside to come out after just under 1km in the village of **Aldbury**. Turn right along the lane and head down to the handsome village green, complete with a reed-lined duck pond and village stocks, and surrounded by half-timbered Tudor cottages, a tiny village post office, a medieval church and the welcoming *Greyhound Inn*.

To return to Tring station, head straight along Station Road past the church. Just beyond the churchyard, and before a bend in the road, turn right and head through a kissing gate. The path leads through a gate and across a paddock behind the farm buildings of **Church Farm**. A few metres ahead you come to another kissing gate by the line of buildings to your left. Go through this and turn right, exiting the paddock onto a dirt track that runs behind the farmyard buildings and beside a hedgerow to reach two metal gates, either side of a farm track; go through these and carry straight on between fields to a wooden kissing gate, some 750m beyond the farm. Here, the path meets a bridleway, just before a golf course; turn left onto the bridleway and follow it downhill for 600m to a metal gate and down some steps to return to the **Ridgeway**, just by Westland Farm.

From here, retrace your steps: go straight on at the signposts and down the concrete road, past the gate into **Westland Farm**, to the lane (Station Road). Turn right and follow this lane back to **Tring station**, 300m further on.

EATING AND DRINKING

The Greyhound Inn Stocks Rd, Aldbury HP23 5RT, 01442 851 228, http://greyhoundaldbury.co.uk. A sweet village pub with plenty and nooks and crannies to settle into. Giant roasts are available (from £13.50) along with a set menu from Mondays to Thursdays for just £15. Plenty of gin on offer, too. Mon–Thurs 11am–9pm, Fri & Sat 11am–9pm, Sun 11am–9pm.

8

Around Blenheim Palace

Long Hanborough to Blenheim Palace and North Leigh Roman Villa

Distance and difficulty 11.5km, plus 7km detour; moderate

Minimum duration 2hr 45min plus 1hr 45min for detour

Trains London Paddington to Hanborough (Mon–Sat hourly, Sun every 2hr; 1hr 15min); return from Hanborough to London Paddington (Mon–Sat hourly, Sun every 2hr; 1hr 15min)

Maps OS Landranger 164: *Oxford*; OS Explorer 180: *Oxford*

This walk runs from the Oxfordshire village of **Bladon**, where Winston Churchill is buried, to his birthplace, the Baroque masterpiece **Blenheim Palace**. The start of this walk is regrettably pretty dull as the pavement of a busy road is the only option. But things then pick up: the route initially skirts the park and runs to the genteel and fantastically pretty small town of **Woodstock**. There are plenty of pubs here, but the nicest option for **lunch** is to buy a picnic at the excellent deli in Woodstock and head into the grounds.

The palace is well worth visiting, but you can see the outside and the grounds on a free **public access route**. Beyond the palace, the route curves through open parkland designed by Capability Brown. Having left the palace grounds, you can either return via country lanes to the station at Long Hanborough, or make a circular **detour** across glorious country to the modest Romano-British remains of **North Leigh Roman Villa** (you're unlikely to have time to make the detour if you do the Blenheim Palace tour, unless you get an early start).

8

To Woodstock

4km From Hanborough **station**, turn right onto the busy A4095. Though you'll see entrances to the park on your left, these are either restricted to local residents or private, so you need to stick to the main road at this point. After 1.5km you come to the village of **Bladon**; the churchyard where **Winston Churchill** is buried is to the right, up a steep narrow path. The surprisingly simple grave lies just beyond the entrance to the church.

Some 750m beyond Bladon you come to a small, triangular green on the left with a road leading up to a gatehouse. To the right of this road, under a big horse chestnut tree, is a **footpath** sign; follow this through a gate, then go up the faint grassy path – the park wall lies to the left. Continue across the field until you come to some farm buildings on the left, then cross the stile ahead to reach the A44. Turn left along the A44 and continue for 750m into Woodstock. To access the palace grounds from here, go past Hampers deli and take the first left onto Market Street. Head past the *Macdonald Bear Hotel* and, at the road's end, you reach the **Triumphal Arch**, the dramatic entry point for the park.

If you are not visiting the palace, then take the free **public right of way** through the grounds, which allows for great views of the exterior. Head straight out of town for 350m until you cross the bridge approaching *The Black Prince* pub. At a green gate marked number 95, head into the park grounds. Take the right-hand route with the lake to your left, and when you reach the far point of the lake bear left towards the palace. You pick up the walk described on page 214 at the near side of the bridge leading to the palace.

EATING AND DRINKING

Hampers 31–33 Oxford St, Woodstock OX20 1TH, 01993 811 535, http://hampersfoodandwine.co.uk. A great place to buy a picnic, with organic bread, local cheeses, meats and good bottled beer for sale. Mon–Fri 8.30am–5.30pm, Sat 8.30am–6pm, Sun 10am–5pm.

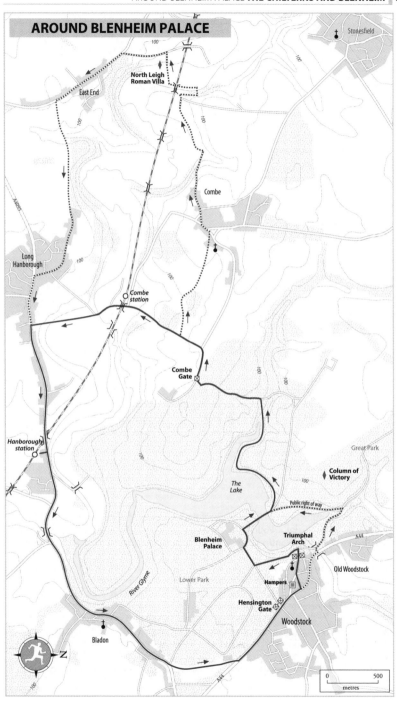

AROUND BLENHEIM PALACE

Stonesfield

East End

North Leigh
Roman Villa

Combe

Long
Hanborough

Combe
station

Combe
Gate

Hanborough
station

Great Park

Column of
Victory

The
Lake

Public right of way

Blenheim
Palace

Triumphal
Arch

Old Woodstock

Hampers

River Glyme

Lower Park

Hensington
Gate

Woodstock

Bladon

8

0   500
metres

BLENHEIM PALACE

When John Churchill, first Duke of Marlborough, defeated the French at the Battle of Blenheim on the Danube in 1704, his reward from a grateful nation was the royal estate at Woodstock, and a staggering £240,000 (worth £25 million today) with which to build a suitable home. The result was the remarkable **Blenheim Palace** (mid-Feb to Oct daily 10.30am–5.30pm; Nov to mid-Dec Wed–Sun 10.30am–5.30pm; £28.50 palace, park and gardens, £18.50 park and gardens; http://blenheimpalace.com), built by John Vanbrugh assisted by Nicholas Hawskmoor. The palace was conceived in a spirit of celebration and triumph, and the humiliation of the French and their king is trumpeted by many subtle and not-so-subtle devices. The gateways to the stable courtyards feature carvings depicting the Lion of England attacking the Cock of France; a bust of Louis XIV was stuck on the south front of Blenheim, "like a head on a stake", as the duke described it; while in the palace rooms a portrait of the French king is flanked by tapestries depicting the battle, with English soldiers charging towards their victim from either side.

The triumphalism is tempered by a strong theatrical element, seen in the arcaded lines of the building and in the stage-like central courtyard, a strangely blank space that seems to be awaiting some drama – this quality may stem from the fact that Vanbrugh was also a playwright. Certain features of the building are whimsical and high-spirited, notably the pinnacles and turrets that run along the rooftop and lighten the symmetry of the palace.

Vanbrugh's genius went unappreciated in his time. The Duchess of Marlborough would have preferred Christopher Wren, but the duke – who had been impressed by Vanbrugh's designs for Castle Howard – overruled her. The duchess was openly hostile to Vanbrugh and it was left to Hawksmoor to act as diplomat. Money ran short, the duchess accused Vanburgh of mismanagement, and he finally left, deeply offended, taking Hawksmoor with him. The building was then completed under the direction of the duchess, who watered down many of the original designs, by general consensus considered overly flamboyant and even vulgar. When Vanbrugh tried to visit the palace in 1725, a year before his death, he was refused entry.

If you tour the palace, you may feel just a little sympathy for the duchess, who had wanted "a clean sweet house and garden be it ever so small". The scale of the interior is totally undomestic; the palace is built entirely on one floor, with hugely high ceilings (three of them sculpted in stucco and gold leaf by Hawksmoor). The rooms were originally conceived to run into each other, providing sweeping vistas that, however visually dramatic, must have been overwhelming to live with. Subsequent restructuring – some carried out during World War II when the palace was the home of MI5 – has closed off several corridors.

Blenheim Palace grounds

4.5km The Triumphal Arch leads into the **palace grounds** (daily 9am–dusk; £18.50, or free with palace ticket). Follow the curving path to the left to reach the palace itself (see above), then cross **Vanbrugh's bridge** – which was conceived to resemble a Roman aqueduct – over the vast artificial lake designed by Capability Brown. In an echo of the victorious note sounded by the palace itself, Brown planted the park's trees so that they represented the formation of the battalions of soldiers at the Battle of Blenheim. The view is dominated by a **statue** of the first Duke of Marlborough, who poses in a toga atop the tall Column of Victory.

Some 100m beyond the bridge, go through the wooden gate to the left and follow the path, which now runs through woodland, skirting the lake, for 1.5km, until you come out at a T-junction under a stand of tall beeches – this is at the point where the lake peters out. Turn left along the track and soon after go left through the gate or over the stile and then follow the grassy path which runs right and gently uphill, curving

past some fir trees. You then join a tarred path; turn left onto that and carry on up the hill. Finally, on the right, there's a turning to **Combe Gate**; you'll see the gatehouse through the trees.

Blenheim to Long Hanborough

3km Turn right out of Combe Gate onto the narrow country lane and then left at the next junction, following the sign to Long Hanborough. If you want to take the **detour** to North Leigh Roman Villa (see below), turn right into the meadow after 250m, following the green footpath sign to Combe.

Missing out the detour, carry on down the road towards **Combe station**. You may be able to get a train from here back to London, but the service is limited. To get to Hanborough station, follow the road under the railway line and continue for 200m, crossing the bridge across the River Evenlode. Just over the bridge, follow the footpath sign that points directly ahead of you (rather than left onto the track here). The path leads across and up a field for 500m, eventually emerging at the A4095. Turn left and follow the road for 1.5km to **Hanborough station**.

Detour to North Leigh Roman Villa

7km The detour to **North Leigh Roman Villa** makes a moderately strenuous but enjoyable cross-country circuit. Though the remains of the villa aren't exactly breathtaking, it's fun to discover them as you cross the field, and the church at **Combe** with its medieval wall paintings is well worth a look.

Across country to Combe

1km The **public footpath** leading off the road to Combe station runs for 250m to a clump of woodland – skirt the woodland, keeping it to your right, then turn right into the field: follow the yellow arrow, and take the path across the field. This is a gorgeous part of the walk, with a thatched cottage to the right and the tower of Combe's church ahead.

The path leads straight across two fields towards the church and comes out at the village playing field, just opposite **St Laurence's Church**. This is a handsome fourteenth-century parish church whose unusually wide nave is decorated with fifteenth-century **wall paintings**. These were painted over following the Reformation and only uncovered in 1892. Though the figures are painted rather crudely, with heavy outlines, the scenes are lively and inventive and the scheme as a whole must have been strikingly colourful. The most substantial tableau is over the chancel arch and would have sent an unequivocal message to the medieval congregation. It depicts the Last Judgement, with Christ seated on a rainbow, the blessed floating up serenely from their graves to his right and, to his left, the damned being poked down into the open mouth of hell by red demons. Other paintings show the Crucifixion, set in a border of stylized clouds, to the left of the chancel arch; a much damaged St Christopher, on the south wall, with a shark, an otter, fish and a mermaid frolicking in the river around him; and, to the right of the chancel arch, the touching fragments of an Annunciation scene, with just the eyes and wing tip of the Angel remaining, and the hand of God floating above. Apart from the paintings, look out for the medieval **stained glass** and the **pulpit**, decorated with blind tracery.

Combe to North Leigh Roman Villa

2km Coming out of the church, turn left into **Combe** to reach the village green and pub, then turn left along the green and follow the road signposted to Long Hanborough. Turn right immediately after the renovated chapel and carry on up the road called West End, continuing straight ahead, past Chatterpie Lane.

From here, continue straight on for 750m, past Higher Westfield Farm and downhill, past the sewage works, to **Lower Westfield Farm**. Go over the stile just beyond the farm buildings; the track leads across and down the field – turn right along the stream through the gate, and then take a left over the bridge. Turn left immediately after the bridge, with the stream on your left, and carry on till you pass under the railway bridge. Just beyond the bridge, head across the field to the right; you can see the buildings of North Leigh Roman Villa from here. Cross a stile to go along the field, with the villa to your left; go through the gap in the hedge to reach the villa ruins.

North Leigh Roman Villa

North Leigh Roman Villa is one of many such remains that dot the area, its extent marked by low foundation walls. A modern structure has been built to protect the partially intact **mosaic floor**; the door is generally locked, but you can see the floor through a large viewing window.

The term "Roman villa" is rather misleading; by the fourth century, when this villa's buildings reached their most developed form, such houses would have been built and lived in by Britons. Although these villas featured Roman-style courtyards and bathhouses, they were otherwise so adapted to a colder climate that they resembled later manor houses rather than continental Roman villas. Like a manor house, this villa was essentially a farm, but it did feature luxury items such as the mosaic floor itself. This, rather prosaically, would have been ordered from one of seven factories in Cirencester – buyers chose a design from plans issued by the factory, and the floor would have been constructed there, rather than *in situ* at the villa. Slabs of mosaic floor were wrapped in straw and transported to the site by bullock cart, and the slabs were then laid, the skill being to disguise the joins between them. The interlocking geometric decoration that edges the floor was for good luck, a charm protecting anyone who stood within it.

To Long Hanborough via East End

4km From the villa, take the main track up the hill and turn left, heading up to a minor road, where you turn left again. The road leads through the pretty, straggling village of **East End**. Walk right through the village, ignoring the first footpath sign on the left-hand side, then turn left at the second path, 100m further on, marked with a blue bridleway sign. The path runs for around 750m, dipping down the field and then up past woodland before joining the minor road into Long Hanborough; carry on straight ahead for 750m. At the junction, go straight ahead till the road joins the A4095. Here, turn left and follow the road for 1.5km – **Hanborough station** is on the right.

8

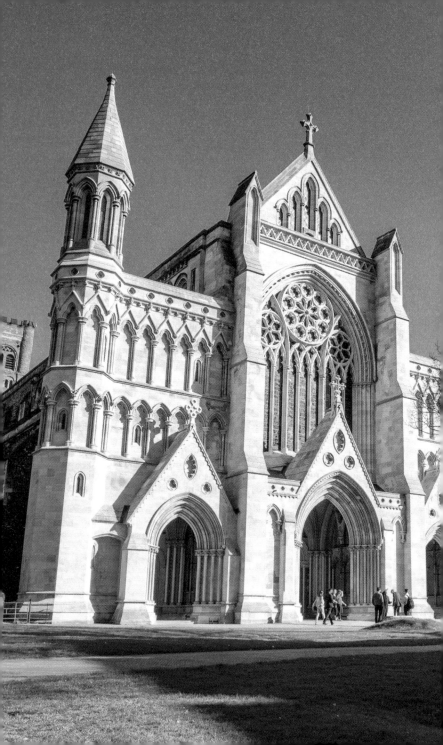

St Albans to Bedford-shire

ST ALBANS CATHEDRAL

9 | St Albans to Bedfordshire

The affluent and densely populated county of Hertfordshire provides the setting for the first two walks in this chapter, both set on or near the course of Watling Street, the great Roman Road that once ran from Londinium (London) to Deva (Chester), and both dotted with the remains of previous eras, from Roman villas to Belgic earthworks. The first walk begins and ends in Harpenden, a stop north of St Albans on the railway line from London, following the Lea Valley Walk to nearby Wheathampstead, on whose eastern limits are the massive earthworks of Oppidum. The second leads from Harpenden, along the River Ver and through Roman Verulamium to the medieval market town of St Albans. Further north is Bedfordshire's chief attraction, the Woburn Estate, with an impressive stately home and England's largest safari park.

The Lea Valley Walk

Harpenden via Wheathampstead to Oppidum

Distance and difficulty 15.5km; moderate
Minimum duration 3hr 50min
Trains London St Pancras to Harpenden (every 5–10min; 30–45min); return from Harpenden to London St Pancras (every 5–10min; 30–45min); Thameslink
Maps OS Landranger 166: *Luton & Hertford*; OS Explorer 182: *St Albans & Hatfield*

This varied walk starts from the commuter town of **Harpenden** and heads along the **Lea Valley Walk** – an 80km route that follows the **River Lea** (sometimes spelt Lee) from its source north of Luton to the River Thames. The route passes through the handsome medieval village of **Wheathampstead**, named for the wheat that was harvested and milled there for over a millennium. Beyond Wheathampstead the walk heads through the massive earthworks, known as the **Devil's Dyke**, that once protected the Celtic settlement of **Oppidum**, then continues southwest into **Nomansland Common** and on to nearby **Amwell**, where *The Elephant & Castle* pub makes a decent stop for **lunch**; an alternative is the closer *Wicked Lady*, just outside Wheathampstead. From Amwell, the route continues north to rejoin the Lea Valley Walk and head back into Harpenden.

Getting started

2km Turn right out of Harpenden **train station** and head down the station drive to the main road; turn right here, go through the tunnel under the railway and uphill along Station Road (the B652). Continue along this busy road for just over 1km to reach the **River Lea** at a bend in the road; with grassy slopes running down to the river at a series of weirs, it's a popular spot with the feel of a village green. Take the path from Marquis Lane signalled by the Batford Springs sign, which leads to the river, then turn right, following the near side of the river, passing the weirs by a children's playground.

After 300m you come out at a lane. Turn right here and continue 100m to reach a left-hand turn into a lane in front of the *Marquis of Granby* pub. Houses line the right-hand side of the lane; to the left, fields lead down to the river. After just over 200m you pass under a bridge at the entrance to a small sewage works (don't worry:

things will improve shortly). Take the steps immediately on your left up onto the track, then turn right, following the **Lea Valley Walk** signs, which lead you out of town and onto a country lane.

Into Wheathampstead
3km The well-maintained track continues east out of Harpenden, with views across the shallow **Lea Valley**, the river meandering below you along the valley floor. To your right, Piggotshill Wood stands on the hillside, while below it the greens of a golf course run down to the public footpath. A kilometre or so from Harpenden, you reach the hamlet of **Leasey Bridge**. Turn right on Leasey Bridge Lane and walk 50m along the lane to **Little Croft**, a modern bungalow; the public footpath, clearly

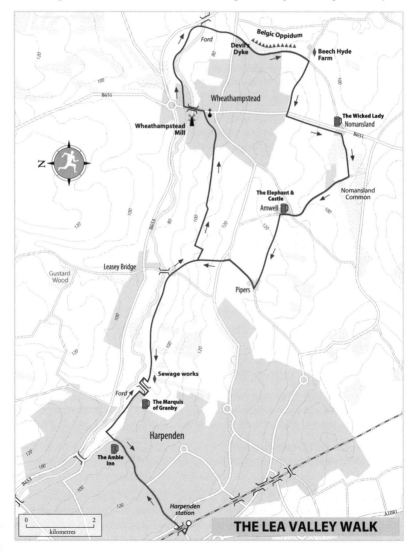

THE LEA VALLEY WALK

9

waymarked from the verge, leads up the bungalow's driveway to a metal kissing gate in the hedgerow to the right. Head diagonally across the paddock to reach a kissing gate in the far corner. Keeping the hedgerow close to your right, continue uphill to reach a third kissing gate 100m further on, just to the right of a large barn. (You'll return here towards the end of the walk.)

Go through the gate and turn left onto the track in front of the barn, following the Lea Valley Walk signs along the track, at first following the boundaries of the neighbouring paddocks for 250m, then heading right along a hawthorn hedge out into farmland. The path is 20m above the valley floor at this point, giving good views over the surrounding countryside and scattered farm buildings, and over to Gustard Wood, which stands on the hillside on the far side of the valley. Some 600m further on, go through the wooden gate in the hedgerow ahead and then straight on across the field and through the metal kissing gate, towards the modern development at the western edge of Wheathampstead.

Wheathampstead

0.5km The attractive medieval village of **Wheathampstead** was developed – and named – as a result of local wheat production, for which this part of Hertfordshire was well known prior to the Industrial Revolution; there was a working mill on the river here as early as 1086. It's now a commuter town, though the old high street has an attractive cluster of half-timbered and brick cottages.

The public footpath along the Lea Valley leads into town via a short alley through a housing estate. At the end of the alley, turn left and head down to a T-junction (there are faded yellow waymarkers on the lampposts), then turn right for 100m to Church Street. Turn left to reach a T-junction with Wheathampstead's High Street. Just to your left is the village church, **St Helen's**, on Bury Green. Built in the late fourteenth century but with Saxon foundations, the flint church is topped by an unusual lead-clad spire, which begins like a pyramidal roof and culminates in an octagonal spire – a Victorian addition, built in imitation of an earlier medieval version.

Turn left onto the High Street, a particularly attractive spot, lined with whitewashed medieval cottages, and head downhill for 200m to return to the banks of the River Lea. The Loafing bakery (Mon–Sat 7am–5pm) serves good filled rolls and pastries to take away. Straddling the river is **Wheathampstead Mill**, a rambling brick structure dating from the sixteenth century which was in operation until the early twentieth century; it's now home to craft and food shops.

Towards Devil's Dyke

1.5km Cross the river and take the first turning right into a modern housing estate at the edge of the village. Follow the waymarkers, which take you out of the estate after 100m, and straight ahead along the wooden fences. For the next 750m the track runs a few metres above the river bank before ending at a wooden kissing gate by Wheathampstead's bypass.

Go through the gate, turn right and head down the track that runs parallel to the road. After 150m you reach a wider track. Turn right and follow this down to the river and over the ford just before **Marford Farm**. Follow the lane for 300m up to a main road, then cross the road and carry straight on, up Dyke Lane, following waymarkers for the **Hertfordshire Way**, a long-distance footpath that makes a 265km circuit of the county.

Devil's Dyke to Amwell

3km Just 200m from the main road, a wrought-iron gate to your left flanked by red-brick gateposts marks the northern end of **Devil's Dyke**. This is the western defensive ditch of **Oppidum**, the earliest capital of the Belgic Catuvellauni tribe. The 100-acre site, now farmland, was first excavated in the 1930s, and again in the

CATUVELLAUNIAN BRITAIN

A hundred years before the arrival of the Romans, Britain was invaded by the **Catuvellauni** (meaning "expert warriors"), an aggressive warrior tribe from Belgium who, by the first century BC, had gained control of much of southern Britain, making **Oppidum** (and later Verlamion, outside St Albans) their capital. The Catuvellauni also had a hand in events on the continent, making raids back across the English Channel and assisting their kinsfolk, the Gauls, who were holding back the Roman armies in northern Europe.

Julius Caesar considered the Catuvellauni's influence in Gaul to be so significant that he launched an expedition across the English Channel and reputedly killed their king, Cassivallaunus, at Oppidum in 54 BC. With the Belgic tribe weakened, the Romans were able to seize Gaul and prepare their plans for an invasion of Britain – though in the event this was not to occur for a further century. The Catuvellauni were still a significant threat to the invading Roman army, however, so much so that one of the earliest fortifications in the area was within sight of the then Catuvellaunian capital, Verlamion, just outside present-day St Albans (see page 230).

1970s; all the finds are now on display at the Verulamium Museum in St Albans. Go through the gate and walk through the dyke itself, whose massive fortifications are still an impressive sight: a tree-filled dell up to 12m deep, 40m wide and half a kilometre long. The dyke is one of two remaining earthworks bounding the site; the second, **The Slad**, lies 600m to the east – it's just as impressive, but unfortunately is on private land.

Near the far end of Devil's Dyke, take the wooden steps to rejoin Dyke Lane. Turn left along the lane and continue for 200m to the public footpath signs opposite the entrance to Beech Hyde Farm. Turn right here, taking the track across open fields back towards Wheathampstead. Some 300m from the lane, the track runs behind houses to come out after 200m at the main road into the village from the south.

Go straight across this and turn left, following the public footpath signs downhill towards **Nomansland Common**, which you reach after 800m, emerging opposite *The Wicked Lady* pub/restaurant, which is over-gentrified but provides an alternative to *The Elephant & Castle* (see page 224) for **lunch**. The unusual name of the common derives from an ecclesiastical squabble in the fifteenth century, when the monasteries of St Albans and Westminster both claimed it as part of their territory. After twenty years of wrangling, a jury ordered that both parishes should share it as grazing land – hence the moniker of No Man's Land, retained to this day. The common's other claim to fame is that Irish heavyweight champ Simon Byrne – The Emerald Gem – died here after a 99-round bareknuckle fight in 1833.

Opposite *The Wicked Lady*, a small access road leads off to your right to some cricket huts. Cross straight over this and onto the edge of the cricket pitch, following the line of benches. At the third bench, bear right and head towards the trees bordering the northwest corner of the cricket pitch. Here, a gap in the trees marks the start of a track – the gap is clear enough, though the track itself is a little hard to spot at the very edge of the wood; you should soon pick it up, though: look out for the information board about the woodland and go straight ahead from here.

The track runs west for 300m before emerging at a lane. Turn right here and head uphill through **Nomansland village** – little more than a hamlet of half-timbered houses at the edge of the common – and on uphill towards **Amwell** village. At the southern limits of Amwell, 500m on from the common in a fork in the road, stands *The Elephant & Castle* **pub**.

EATING AND DRINKING

The Elephant & Castle Amwell Lane, Wheathampstead AL4 8EA, 01582 832 175, http://theelephantandcastle. co.uk. A nice old pub, with a large inglenook fireplace and tiled floors. Mains such as burgers and fish'n'chips cost around £10. Food is served Mon–Fri noon–2pm & 6–9pm, Sat noon–9pm, Sun noon–3pm.

Amwell to the Lea Valley Walk

2km Take the left fork at *The Elephant & Castle*, following the signs for Down Green, and continue 150m up this lane, then turn left at the public footpath sign opposite Weaver's Cottage, up the wooden steps to a track that runs straight on, along the edge of a golf course. The views across the Hertfordshire countryside open up here, with the hamlet of Ayres End, 1km to the south on a wooded hillside, the only settlement that interrupts the folds of the valley. At the end of the golf course, head straight on through a gap in the hedge, and continue through the middle of fields and towards the buildings of **Pipers Stud Farm**, which flank the track to the left, for 150m until you reach Pipers Lane. Turn right onto the lane, past a clutch of large Arts & Crafts houses – the first and smallest of the houses, the half-timbered and red-tiled **Pipers Croft**, is a typical example.

After 400m the lane ends at a T-junction with the main Harpenden Road. Cross straight over the road and carry on into a field beyond the hedgerow, following the public footpath sign. Go diagonally across the field, heading down to the left to the large barn. Go past the barn to the metal kissing gate and a fingerpost sign, to rejoin the path you were on earlier in the walk.

Back to Harpenden station

3.5km Retrace your steps from here, going back through the metal kissing gate you passed through on the way to Wheathampstead down to Leasey Bridge, then along the track that flanks the southern bank of the River Lea into Harpenden. Turn right by the *Marquis of Granby* pub, then left, following the riverside track to come out at the weirs by the children's playground. Go along the pavement by the hawthorn hedge and up Station Road, from the bend by *The Amble Inn* pub, to return to **Harpenden station**.

9 Along the Ver to St Albans

St Albans via Verulamium to Gorhambury

Distance and difficulty 15.5km plus 5km detour; easy

Minimum duration 4hr

Trains St Pancras to Harpenden (every 15–20min; 30min); return from St Albans City to St Pancras (every 15–20min; 30min); Thameslink

Maps OS Landranger 166: *Luton & Hertford*; OS Explorer 182: *St Albans & Hatfield*

Starting in **Harpenden**, this gentle walk is crammed with historical and architectural interest. The route cuts across an intriguing section of farmland and woodland and

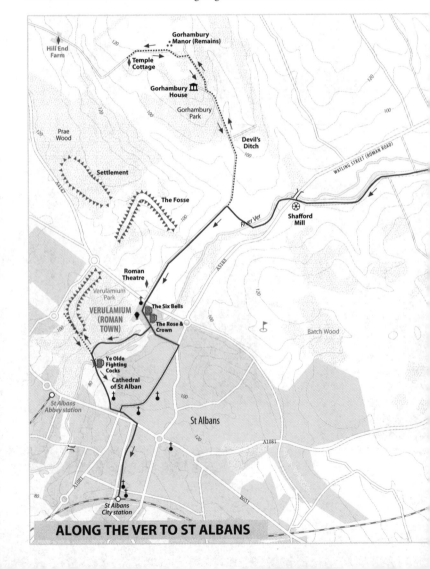

ALONG THE VER TO ST ALBANS

then leads along the **River Ver**, a much diminished but still attractive chalk stream, with a handy stop at striking **Redbournbury Mill** (weekends only) where you can snack on their excellent baked goods. There's a possible detour to **Gorhambury**, whose fine Georgian country house stands next to the picturesque Tudor ruins of an earlier manor. Otherwise, visit the Roman theatre en route to the beautiful cathedral city of **St Albans**; a couple of great **pubs** on the way offer good grub, or explore Roman remains of Verulamium Park and have a pint at the ancient *Ye Olde Fighting Cocks* in St Albans, said to be the oldest pub in Britain.

You can time your walk to coincide with evensong in St Albans Cathedral, which is usually at 5pm every day except Sunday, when it's held at 6.30pm.

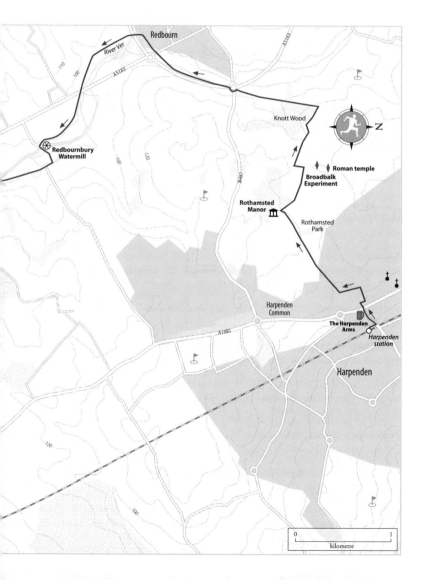

9

Getting started
300m Coming out of Harpenden Station, take the main street that curves down the hill. At *The Harpenden Arms* you come to Harpenden Common – cross at the zebra crossing.

Harpenden Common to Rothamsted Research Station
3.2km Skirt round the public loos and head across the road to **Amenbury Lane**. Go up the lane past a pub and up the gentle hill, passing handsome villas. Just past the tennis courts on the left, there's a gap in the foliage – follow the public footpath sign into the field. Curve to the left past the pavilion, and head down the field and back up again to where there's a large oak tree on the left and a stone trough to the right. Follow the track ahead towards some signs under the trees. There's a three-way footpath sign – turn right and almost immediately the path forks. Take the narrow right-hand fork.

Head down the bridleway along the beech hedge. You'll see a line of conifers ahead, and open fields to either side. Some 700m from the turn-off you emerge with a long brick wall ahead. It's well worth detouring left at the wall to have a peek at the gabled frontage and clock tower of **Rothamsted Manor**, now a private wedding venue and events space. Constructed in the 1620s, the manor was requisitioned during the war and became a listening post, sending information to Bletchley Park for decoding.

Head back to the junction to continue on the paved lane. Under an oak tree, a signpost introduces the **Broadbalk Experiment**, an agricultural trial which was founded way back in 1843. Then follow the bridleway sign which zigzgs and runs along the edge of Knott Wood, eventually meeting a wide path.

Along the Nickey Line
1km Turn left at the crossroads down the wide cycle track known as the **Nickey Line**, lined by coppiced hornbeam, which follows the course of the former Harpenden to Hemel Hempstead Railway. You emerge at a busy road – cross it and then head right on the path towards the roundabout – cross another road, then follow the blue signs along the wooden fence to rejoin the path. The route is crossed by a paved path which leads to a traveller's site, and then the Nickey Line, elevated at this point, crosses over a second roundabout. Soon after the roundabout, you will see the 'River Ver below. Around 200m beyond the river crossing turn left, following the 'river trail' sign.

Along the Ver to Redbournbury Watermill
3km Cross the road to a metal gate – go round the gate and along the paved path, following the blue **River Ver** trail signs. You come out at a wooden gate, continuing to follow the river trail signs. At this point you may be wondering where the Ver actually is. Sadly, this rare chalk stream – which once flowed profusely and powered eleven watermills – has suffered greatly from water extraction and canalisation. As a result of protests by the Ver Valley Society, the Environment Agency, St Albans District Council and Affinity Water are attempting to restore the flow of this precious water course, which will help protect its fragile population of otters, water voles and water shrews.

Cross the road, and carry on along the path through the fields. Eventually you'll see a bakery building on the right, and the **Redbournbury Watermill** (Sat 9am–1pm, Sun 1.30–5pm) on the left – the origins of the watermill go way back to the eleventh century. Watermill is actually misnomer – due to the drying up of the Ver the mill is powered by a diesel engine. Despite this, and the fact that it suffered a severe fire in 1987, the charismatic building is very well worth a visit, especially when milling is underway and the oak timbers shake as the grain is stoneground to produce organic flour. The bakery is only open on Saturday mornings, but you can buy delicious breads, Eccles cakes and oats at the mill itself.

9

The Ver Valley

3km From the mill, turn left to go along the river, crossing plank bridges over the ponds formed by the river, and skirting the farm buildings. Follow the footpath signs to St Albans, which lead through light woodland and along the fields. The reedy Ver is more evident at this point, the path meandering to an attractive cluster of buildings which includes renovated Shafford Mill. Beyond the mill you come to some timbered and pebble-dash cottages – cross the road here and go through the wooden gate. Follow the meanders of the Ver along the tree-lined path. You emerge at a little tiled brick building on the river – turn right here and head up the track, where you come to a T-junction. Ahead you'll see grand Gorhambury House through the trees.

Detour through Gorhambury Park

5km If you're intrigued by the sight of **Gorhambury House** (http://gorhamburyestate. co.uk) and want to see more, turn right at the T-junction and continue up the track, which makes a wide arc round the front of the building. Created in the late eighteenth century, the house's creamy white facade is made from Portland stone, fronted by a Corinthian portico. The house takes its name from Geoffrey de Gorham, the Abbot of St Albans from 1119 to 1146, who had the first manor house built here on what was then abbey land. Gorhambury House is open one day a week in summer; exhibits include a lively 1618 portrait of Sir Francis Bacon, and Chippendale furniture.

Beyond the house, the path turns a corner, giving you your first view of the romantic ruins of old **Gorhambury Manor**. The estate was sold off following the dissolution of the monasteries, and a generation later fell into the hands of Sir Nicholas Bacon, father of philosopher Francis and Lord Keeper of the Great Seal to Elizabeth I. In 1563–68 Bacon senior constructed the house whose ruins you now see, reusing remains from Verulamium and the abbey buildings at St Albans. Sir Francis Bacon inherited the estate when his father died, but with no heir of his own to pass the property on to, he gave Gorhambury to his secretary, who later sold it to the Grimston family. The Grimstons commissioned the new Gorhambury House after the family outgrew the Tudor manor, abandoning it in 1784 and pulling down the old house to create a romantic ruin. The remains – the crumbling porch and part of the red-brick and flint hall – are today managed by English Heritage (free access).

To Verulanium

2km To head directly to Verulanium, take a right at the T-junction and carry on down the country lane for 2km. The remains of a Roman theatre (daily 10am–4/5pm; £3) sit in the field to the right of the track; tickets are sold at the small booth 50m from the main road. The theatre stood on **Watling Street**, the main axis of the Roman town, and several tiers of the original building are clearly visible, though the columns on the stage are modern replicas, added to give a sense of scale to the ruins. You can also take a look at some Roman workshops, just south of the theatre. Exit via the lodge house.

Cross the main road and head down St Michael's Street, and you come to the excellent **Verulamium Museum** (Mon–Sat 10am–5.30pm, Sun 2–5.30pm; £6; http://stalbansmuseums.org.uk/verulamium). This well-put-together museum offers a fascinating insight into life in Roman Britain. The highlight is the collection of five remarkably complete floor mosaics; these were a status symbol in middle-class Roman society. The mosaics were all unearthed locally and date from around 200 AD.

9

ROMAN VERULAMIUM AND ST ALBAN

Following the fall of southern Britain to the advancing Roman armies in 43 AD, the invaders quickly established a fort on the banks of the River Ver, in the present-day suburb of St Michael's. The Romans were attracted not only by the site's strategic location, but also by its symbolic significance, since it stood just northeast of the former Belgic town **Verlamion**, capital of the Catuvellauni, a tribe which Julius Caesar had quashed a century earlier (see page 223). Within five years, the original fort had begun to expand into a prosperous Roman town, and **Verulamium**, as the new settlement became known, quickly developed into an important trading post on the London–Chester and Colchester–Silchester Roman roads. Despite being sacked by **Boudicca** in 79 AD and razed by fire in 155 AD, Verulamium remained an important Roman town until the fourth century, when it was finally abandoned by the retreating Roman armies. Some Roman civilians stayed on, however, and the remains of a middle-class villa dating from this time stand to the north of the city walls in the grounds of Gorhambury.

During the Roman period, the new religion of **Christianity** began to grow in popularity, despite being outlawed by Rome; in 209 AD, **Alban**, a Roman convert from Verulamium, became the first Christian martyr in England. The site of Alban's execution, on the hillside overlooking the town to the northeast, developed into a shrine during Roman times, then later a church and an abbey after the Romans had left. The religious buildings were made from materials pilfered from the abandoned town at the foot of the hill. The abbey was massively extended by the Norman abbot, **Paul of Caen**, in 1077, and the present-day cathedral has changed little since that time.

By 948 AD, records show that market traders were allowed to set up stalls just outside the abbey precinct, marking the beginning of the market town that grew up on the hill around the shrine to St Alban, from which it took its name. Like the abbey, the town buildings were largely made from reclaimed bricks from the Roman site, something that is particularly noticeable in the heart of the medieval city, where flint and brick houses predominate.

From here you can carry on to explore **Verulamium Park**, which is complete with two ornamental lakes and a host of ducks and geese. It occupies the southern half of the site of the walled Roman town of Verulamium (see above) – the River Ver marked the city's eastern boundary. You'll see the extensive remains of various other parts of the city as well as *Ye Olde Fighting Cocks* (Mon–Thurs & Sun noon–10.30pm, Fri & Sat noon–midnight, Sun noon–4pm; 01727 869 152, http://yeoldefightingcocks.co.uk), which claims to be the oldest pub in Britain. It's thought to be an eleventh-century structure on an eighth-century site, but the octagonal oak building has been repaired and re-erected over the centuries, so precise dating is impossible. What is documented is that the handsome, higgledy-piggledy inn once hosted Oliver Cromwell, and that cock-fighting took place in the bar area in the seventeenth and eighteenth centuries. In summer you can sit out on benches by the river.

Fishpool Street to the Cathedral

2km You can carry on to the cathedral across the park from *Ye Olde Fighting Cocks*, or reach it via some wonderfully intriguing back streets from the museum. To do so, carry on down the high street of **St Michael's**, a small eighteenth-century village that has now been absorbed into the city's outlying suburbs. The ancient timbered *Rose & Crown* and *The Six Bells* pubs both serve **food** and have small beer gardens. Where the street forks, bear right and follow Fishpool Street, lined with a wonderful mix of cottages and townhouses, for 700m.

EATING AND DRINKING

Rose & Crown 24 High Street, AL4 9DA, 01727 859 739, http://roseandcrownpubsandridge.co.uk. There are plenty of options for a Sunday roast here, along with a range of burgers. There are a few vegan choices, too, and there is a kids' menu. You'll find a variety of gins to quench your thirst. Mon 5–11pm, Tues–Sat noon–11pm, Sun noon–10.30pm.

Overlooking grassy lawns sloping down to the River Ver, the **Cathedral of St Alban** (daily 8am–5.45pm) is named for the first Christian martyr in Britain, a Roman convert who was executed here in 209 AD. The vast flint and brick building is largely Norman, though there has been an abbey on this site since Saxon times. Materials from the Saxon abbey were reused to build the Norman cathedral but, like much of the city, the flint and brick were taken from the town's Roman remains and recycled here.

Inside, it's the sheer size of the building that impresses: the cathedral has the longest medieval nave in the country. The rounded Norman arches and pillars are, again, clearly built from Roman brick (though those to the south are later additions, elaborate structures that replace the earlier Norman ones, which collapsed in a storm in 1323). Behind the high altar lies the **tomb of St Alban** – its pedestal is a nineteenth-century reconstruction, since the shrine was all but destroyed during the Dissolution. Overlooking the tomb, the intricate 1400 oak **watching loft** is the only one of its type in the country, decorated with images of bear-baiting, wrestling and the saint's martyrdom.

To St Albans Station

1km To get to the station, follow the continuation of Fishpool Street – Romeland Hill which becomes George Street and then High Street. Turn left to follow Chequer Street for 150m, then bear right onto Victoria Street for the 800m walk to the station.

9 Woburn Estate

Aspley Guise to Woburn village

Distance and difficulty 15km; moderate

Minimum duration 3hr 15min

Trains London Euston to Bletchley (every 30min; 50min–1hr), then Bletchley to Aspley Guise (Mon–Sat 1 hourly; 15min); alternatively, London St Pancras to Bedford (every 15min; 30min), then Bedford to Aspley Guise (Mon–Sat 1 hourly; 30min). Return from Aspley Guise to Bletchley (Mon–Sat hourly; 15min), then Bletchley to Euston (every 50min; 50min–1hr); alternatively, Aspley Guise to Bedford (Mon–Sat hourly; 30min), then Bedford to St Pancras (every 15min; 30min); London Midland/Thameslink. Note that services to and from Aspley Guise on Sundays are very limited

Maps OS Landranger 153 and 165: *Bedford & Huntington* and *Aylesbury & Leighton Buzzard*; OS Explorer 192: *Buckingham & Milton Keynes*

Starting in the village of **Aspley Guise**, this circular walk takes you through the **Woburn Estate**, seat of the dukes of Bedford since the seventeenth century and now home to **Woburn Safari Park** – the country's largest – as well as the stately family home, **Woburn Abbey**, named for the monastery that once stood here. The walk loops round the safari park before heading to the estate's **deer park** and past the abbey itself. From the abbey, it's a short walk out to the attractive, largely Georgian village of **Woburn**, which has several **pubs** – the whitewashed and thatched *Royal Oak* is the best located, but the best food in the village is at *Woburn Thai*. The walk back to Aspley Guise takes you through farmland and along lanes to the medieval heart of the village.

Getting started

1km From **Aspley Guise station**, head up the lane (across the level crossing if you're coming from Bletchley; or turn left straight off the platform if you're coming from Bedford) into Aspley Guise. The heart of the village itself lies 1km ahead, beyond the wooded hill. A hundred metres from the station, the road begins to ascend the hill, passing bungalows and whitewashed Victorian workers' cottages and heading up to the village's heavily restored medieval church, whose tower peeps up above the trees on the brow of the hill.

Around 75m beyond the church, at a bend in the road just before a high red-brick wall, turn left, following the public footpath signs onto a path that leads gently downhill to Bedford Road. The path flanks the northern wall of eighteenth-century **Aspley House**, giving views across formal gardens of the red-brick exterior. To your left is a small meadow, a swathe of snowdrops and daffodils in spring.

Aspley Guise to the Woburn Estate

2km The path ends at a kissing gate at the Bedford Road. Turn left here, cross the road at the central reservation a few metres on, then continue along the far side of the road, passing the Tudor halftimbered and thatched **Park** and **Valentine cottages**. Just beyond the cottages, turn right onto **Mount Pleasant**, a quiet lane that leads up past rows of terraced brick cottages and larger Georgian houses to the village limits, where Mount Pleasant becomes **Horsepool Lane**. This runs gently downhill between fields and past a small copse before reaching a cluster of gabled red-brick houses at a T-junction on the A4012.

Woburn Safari Park

2.5km Around 50m to the right, on the opposite side of the road, is one of the entrances to **Woburn Safari Park** (daily 9am–5pm; http://woburnsafari.co.uk). Go through the metal gates at the entrance to the park. The road through the park splits after 150m – take the right-hand fork.

The road runs below wooded **Dean Hills**, which rise to your left. Some 700m along the access road, at a bend, turn left along a grassy waymarked track that follows the bottom of the hills; the track runs parallel to the road, 50m or so to the left of the **leisure area** (you'll see an adventure playground through the trees to your right and a zip wire runs over head). You'll often see rabbits on the wooded hillside, as well as some of the thousands of deer that live on the estate.

Follow the grassy track for 600m. Just before the access road opposite some maintenance buildings turn left, following the waymarked track uphill through the woods of Dean Hills. At the top of the hill, a wooden gate leads out of the trees and onto the pseudo African plain. Below to your right you'll get your first view of the **safari park** itself.

The path continues for 700m, giving uninterrupted views into the park. You're pretty much guaranteed to see elephants, zebras, tigers, lions or rhinos, all of which live in

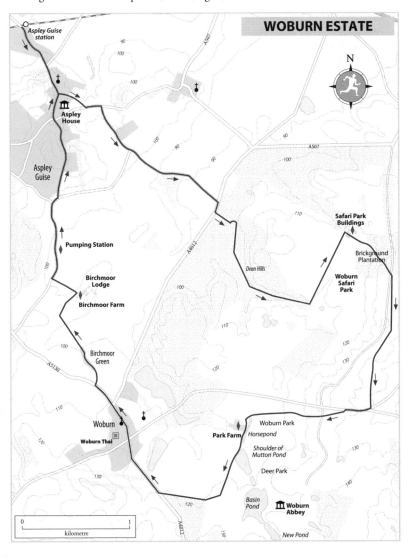

9

WOBURN'S DEER

Home to ten species of **deer** – including the Père David, a species from China that the estate saved from extinction – Woburn is the largest deer sanctuary in the country in terms of number and types of species, although to the lay person they all look pretty much alike. If you're interested, distinguishing features include: a white throat (Axis or Chital deer); an absence of antlers (Chinese water deer); unusual colouring (fallow deer, which can be anything from white to black); tusks as well as antlers (Muntjac); a black stripe down the spine plus an unusually long tail (Père David); a winter mane (Rusa stags); a large white patch on the rump (Manchurian sika); or bat-shaped ears (swamp deer). The park is also home to the red deer, the only one of the ten that is native to Britain.

the enclosures here: it's an unforgettably surreal sight to see Asian elephants ambling through the Bedfordshire countryside. This section of track ends at a large wooden kissing gate by Crawleyheath Farm, right by the **main entrance** to the park. Turn right and go through the farm, past a red telephone box and past (but not through) the main approach to the park, flanked by two lion sculptures, then head for the metal gates in the fence opposite at the boundary of Brickground Plantation, a wooded hill that rises above the entrance to the Safari Park.

On to Woburn Abbey

4km Through the gates of **Brickground Plantation** go straight ahead, up the wide dirt track into the trees. At the top of the hill you come to a road, just to the right of a large whitewashed cottage and a gated entrance at the edge of Woburn's deer park. Head over the double stiles to the left of the cattle grid and then go straight on, following the footpath that runs along the left side of the road. The path heads straight along the high ground for 500m or so. You can see across to Dean Hills here, beyond the safari park, but next to nothing of the park itself.

Just beyond a pond by a small white "No Pedestrian Access" sign, the waymarkers begin to lead you left, away from the access road and downhill towards the red-brick wall of the estate. At the access gate stay inside the park, turning right and heading uphill, following the waymarkers on the far side of the road. Some 200m from the gate, at the end of the first steep rise, the waymarkers begin to lead you away from the road, over an access road to the farm buildings on your left, and uphill to the right of **Whitnoe Orchard Pond**.

You soon come to another access road; cross straight over this and on down the grassy path through a dip in the verge opposite to the heart of the estate's **deer park**.

Head straight across the deer park towards the mock-Tudor pavilion, complete with moat, just to the right of Horse Pond. On the far side of Horse Pond, turn left to head along the access road to Woburn Abbey itself, with Horse Pond on your left and the stable blocks to your right, and continue past **Cowmans Cottage**. You'll see Woburn Abbey away to your left.

Woburn Abbey

The grandiose Georgian pile of **Woburn Abbey** (mid-March to Oct daily 11am–5pm, last entry 4pm; £15; 01525 290333, http://woburnabbey.co.uk, closed for restoration until 2022) is home to the dukes of Bedford and takes its name from the twelfth-century Cistercian abbey that originally stood here. Overlooking a series of ornamental lakes, the west range (which is the one you first see) is its most impressive aspect: two and a half storeys high, with giant Ionic columns and faced with creamy white stone.

The estate was given to Sir John Russell, Earl of Bedford, in 1547 in recognition of his diplomatic missions for Henry VIII, though it didn't become the family home until 1619 or achieve its current form until 1747, when Henry Flitcroft was commissioned by the fourth duke to build the west range. Inside, Flitcroft's lavish staterooms are lined with paintings by artists including Gainsborough, Van Dyck and Reynolds. The **grounds** were landscaped in 1802 by Henry Repton, who introduced the series of ornamental ponds that now stand before the house.

Woburn village

1km The track leads beneath **Shoulder of Mutton Pond**. Carry straight on, passing a small brick maintenance hut on your right, to reach the edge of a wooded area and a large metal kissing gate. Go through the kissing gate and head down the dirt track between fields to your right and woods to your left, both bounded by high wire fencing. After 200m you reach another kissing gate to the right of the red-sandstone **Ivy Lodge**.

Beyond this second kissing gate, turn right and follow the footpath alongside the A4012 for a few hundred metres into **Woburn village**. This beautiful, well-to-do place is mainly Georgian (much of the village was destroyed by fire in 1720 and rebuilt in the style of the day), with tiny cottages lining the wide streets through which drovers once took their sheep to the market.

As well as boutiques and restaurants there are several **pubs**, though none of them are outstanding. Your best option for food is *Woburn Thai* at 2 Leighton Street, which serves soups, curries and rice dishes (from around £7).

EATING AND DRINKING

Woburn Thai 2 Leighton Street, MK17 9PJ, 01525 290 033, http://woburnthai.co.uk. Friendly staff serve up classic Thai dishes in a relaxed setting. Choose from spicy tom yum to milder panang curry. To finish off your meal opt for the banana and coconut milk. Set menus go from £20.95 per person. Features an extensive wine menu, too. Daily noon–2pm & 5–10pm.

Back to Aspley Guise station

4.5km To walk back to Aspley Guise station, head straight through the village along the A4012, passing tiny **Market Place**, just beyond a crossroads. Ignore the first (main) right-hand turn just outside the village and take the second (minor) road 200m further on. Follow this road straight on through the tiny hamlet of **Birchmoor Green**, 100m beyond the turn-off, and then along the dirt track where the road ends, just beyond the village up towards a red-brick farmhouse to **Birchmoor Farm**.

At the hedgerow parallel with the farm buildings, turn right onto another waymarked path that takes you up to the entrance to the farmhouse, then make a sharp left down its drive towards Birchmoor Lodge. Here, you come out onto narrow Aspley Lane: turn right and follow the lane for 800m, passing a Victorian pumping station. From this point on there are white fingerposts directing you uphill into Aspley Guise, which you'll reach after 1km. Cross the main road and head up the road leading off to the right of the tiny village square; after 500m you'll reach St Botolph's church; continue straight on to **Aspley Guise station**.

Essex, Cambridge and the Fens

A DOG LOOKS OUT TO RIVER STORT

Essex, Cambridge and the Fens

Despite its brash reputation, Essex remains one of the least built-up of the Home Counties, while the enticing university town of Cambridge is a well-established day-trip from London – the place retains an archaic, unhurried charm. To the north are the fenlands, with vast, perfectly flat fields of peat-black soil framed by immense skies. The first of these walks goes from Bishop's Stortford to Sawbridgeworth along the River Stort. Further north, the second walk heads out to Saffron Walden, a Saxon market town that made its name from the saffron crocus that once grew in abundance here, and the nearby stately home of Audley End. From Cambridge, the third walk makes the short trip south to Grantchester along the River Cam. North of Cambridge, the Fen Rivers Way runs from Waterbeach, just north of Cambridge, to Ely, whose cathedral dominates the skyline.

Along the River Stort

Bishop's Stortford to Sawbridgeworth

Distance and difficulty 8.5km; moderate

Minimum duration 2hr 10min

Trains London Liverpool Street to Bishop's Stortford (every 30min; 35–55min); return from Sawbridgeworth to London Liverpool Street (1–2 hourly; 40–50min); Abellio Greater Anglia

Maps OS Landranger 167: *Chelmsford*; OS Explorer 195 and 194: *Braintree & Saffron Walden* and *Hertford & Bishop's Stortford*

Starting at the handsome market town of **Bishop's Stortford**, midway between London and Cambridge, this gentle walk follows the **River Stort** as it meanders its way south via picturesque lock houses and through lush pastureland and reed-filled floodplains to the impressive eighteenth-century maltings at **Sawbridgeworth**. The scenery is not dramatic, but the iris- and willow-lined banks of the river, punctuated by colourful canal boats, make for a quietly bucolic landscape (unfortunately the quiet is periodically shattered by planes from nearby Stansted Airport). Now a wealthy commuter town, Sawbridgeworth maintained a steady prosperity on the back of the brewing industry right up until the late nineteenth century. Fittingly, given its history, the town claims to have more pubs per capita than anywhere else in the country, meaning that there are plenty of choices for **lunch or a drink**.

Now plied by pleasure boats, the river was an important waterway during the Industrial Revolution, used chiefly to transport barley from local farms to malt houses along the river banks; Bishop's Stortford was once a major centre for brewing.

Getting started

0.75km Take the main exit out of **Bishop's Stortford station** and follow the slip road up to a T-junction. Turn right here and cross the bridge over the railway, and then turn right again onto the busy A1060, following the rail tracks for a few hundred metres up to a roundabout. Bear right here along the minor road that crosses back over the railway and loops down the hill and towards the **River Stort**.

A low-arched bridge crosses the Stort – take the riverside path that leads off to the left, just beyond the bridge. Around 500m beyond the railway bridge you come to a wooden footbridge over a **weir** – the first of many weirs along the navigable river, which help control the levels of water in it, siphoning excess volume into backwaters, reed beds, marshes or floodplains.

South Mill Lock to Twyford Lock

1.75km Around 100m beyond the weir is the first of the five locks that dot the walk: **South Mill Lock**. Cross the lock gates to the left bank of the river (which you continue to follow for the remainder of the walk). About 500m beyond here, a sign to the left of the path marks the first of two entrances to the **Rushy Mead Nature Reserve**, an 11.5-acre conservation area which protects part of the Stort floodplain. The reserve covers three different wetland habitats – open water, reed and sedge beds – and has a host of aquatic wildlife, including reed warblers, snipes and willow tits. It's possible to make a complete circuit of Rushy Mead – little more than 500m – and pick up the walk a few hundred metres further along the river.

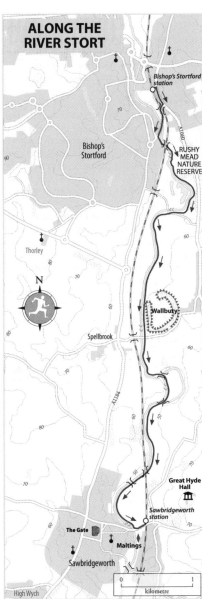

Though it's hard to believe it from the pastoral scenery in the near distance, the bulk of Bishop's Stortford lies less than 500m off to the right of the river. It's not until the next lock – **Twyford** – a few hundred metres further on, that the town is truly left behind.

At Twyford Lock, cross the minor road to rejoin the towpath, through a kissing gate a little to your left on the far side of the road. Passing by pastureland, the path soon rejoins the left river bank.

Past Wallbury to Tednambury Lock

3km Beyond Twyford Lock, the river runs through open countryside, where horses are paddocked and cattle graze. A little under 2km further on it passes a white bridge, from where a path leads up towards the northern flank of **Wallbury**, a Celtic hillfort that rises above the east bank of the river. Little is known about the original inhabitants of Wallbury, though Iron Age pottery has been recovered from the thirty-acre site. The oval-shaped fort was defended by double ramparts and ditches; the original entrance can still be seen on the east side; today, the defences are heavily wooded and it's difficult to make out much of the original earthworks apart from the moat-like ditches that lie immediately below the towpath to your left. Some 500m after the white bridge is a third lock: **Spellbrook**. Cross the little road here, and continue down the riverside path.

Around 500m beyond Spellbrook there's a long, sweeping bend in the river and an even deeper sweep of river which runs behind it in a wooded copse. The towpath follows the navigable stretch, crossing either end of the deeper river bend by way of two small bridges, 400m apart. Between the two is **Tednambury Lock**.

10

Beyond the second of these bridges, the river sweeps round, running close by the railway, with marshy fields and reed beds to the left, fed by two small weirs that siphon water from the river. The path is quite narrow in places and you'll probably spend more time watching your feet than admiring the views, but look out for the abundant plant life, including blackberries and roseships which line the way in late summer.

Sawbridgeworth

3km Just under 2km beyond Tednambury Lock the river passes under a low railway bridge and comes out on the northern outskirts of **Sawbridgeworth**. At the last of the five locks – **Sawbridgeworth Lock** – cross over the access road (which leads off to the right to the lock houses) and continue straight on, along the left bank of the river, passing the backs of large houses, whose gardens run down to the far river bank. After a few hundred metres you come out on the road by some old malt houses; Sawbridgeworth's tiny **train station** lies a few hundred metres beyond them, to your left.

You can return to London from here, but it's worth having a look round the **antiques** shops in the old malt houses, where there's also a tiny **café**. Alternatively, walk up into the town centre, a few hundred metres up the hill to your right, to visit one of the many **pubs**. Head straight up The Forebury, the road at the bend to your right, which leads past a tiny green. Beyond the green, cross the road and take the leafy tarred path to the left past the flint-faced thirteenth-century church, Great St Mary's. Exit the churchyard through the gates and go straight up the lane. You emerge opposite the *Market House Hotel*; go straight ahead and turn right on London Road to reach the friendly real-ale *Gate* pub.

EATING AND DRINKING

The Gate 81 London Rd, Sawbridgeworth CM21 9JJ, 01279 722 313, http://thegatepub.com. A friendly, family-run pub with a great range of beer – they brew their own beer and cider. Mon–Thurs 11.30am–2.30pm & 3.30–11pm, Fri & Sat 11.30am–11pm, Sun noon–11.30pm.

Uttlesford

Newport to Saffron Walden via Audley End

Distance and difficulty 13km; moderate

Minimum duration 3hr 20min

Trains London Liverpool Street to Newport (hourly; 1hr); return from Audley End to London Liverpool Street (every 30min; 1hr); Abellio Greater Anglia

Maps OS Landranger 167 and 154: *Chelmsford* and *Cambridge & Newmarket*; OS Explorer 195: *Braintree & Saffron Walden*

10

This walk takes you through the gently rolling countryside of northwest Essex, or **Uttlesford** as this well-to-do area prefers to be known. Starting at **Newport**, with its wonderful half-timbered medieval cottages, the route heads north for 8km to the wealthy medieval market town of **Saffron Walden**, then loops round the **Audley End Estate**, centred on the sprawling Jacobean mansion of **Audley End**, before heading to Audley End station in the village of **Wendens Ambo**. There's a good **pub** in Saffron Walden, as well as a tearoom and restaurant in the Audley End Estate. Both Newport and Audley End stations are on the London to Cambridge railway line.

Getting started

1km The walk begins at **Newport station**, at the eastern edge of Newport village, though it's well worth making the short detour into the village centre to have a look at its mix of medieval cottages and elegant Georgian houses. To start the walk, cross the footbridge from the northbound platform and exit the station via the path at the foot of the bridge, which leads into a small lane. Turn left here and, after a few metres, ascend the wooden steps onto the field to the right, following the public footpath sign. Climb to the brow of the hill and, at the top, head through the gap in the hedgerow. Keeping the hedgerow to your left, walk round the edge of the farmland, past a new house and on towards a **large barn**.

Debden Water to Rosy Grove

1.5km Before you reach the barn, the path veers left; head downhill, along the thick hedge to meet the Debden Road. Cross this and follow the waymarked path opposite and just to the right, downhill between hedgerows. This leads through a small copse, across a field and down to **Debden Water**, at the foot of a wooded hillside.

Cross the wooden footbridge over Debden Water and turn right on the path through the woodland to reach a gate 50m ahead, which leads out into a field. Turn left and head up the hill, continuing straight on up the edge of the next field; a row of trees here marks the boundary of the field to your left. Keep heading up towards **Rosy Grove**, a clump of trees at the brow of the hill. Immediately before Rosy Grove, turn left, go over a drainage ditch in the hedge to your left and continue uphill, keeping the grove and ditch to your right.

Brakey Ley Wood and Thieves' Corner

1.5km A hundred metres from Rosy Grove you come to a T-junction with a farm track; go straight ahead over the track and along the path, keeping the ditch to your left, to reach the next thicket of trees. Go into the thicket and cross another small footbridge over a deep brook. Continue straight on, keeping the drainage ditch to your left, and head on along the edge of farmland past **Brakey Ley Wood**. At the end of this field, cross a third bridge, this one over tiny **Fulfen Slade**, and bear right, keeping the trees to your left. At the end of the next field you come to a T-junction with another track.

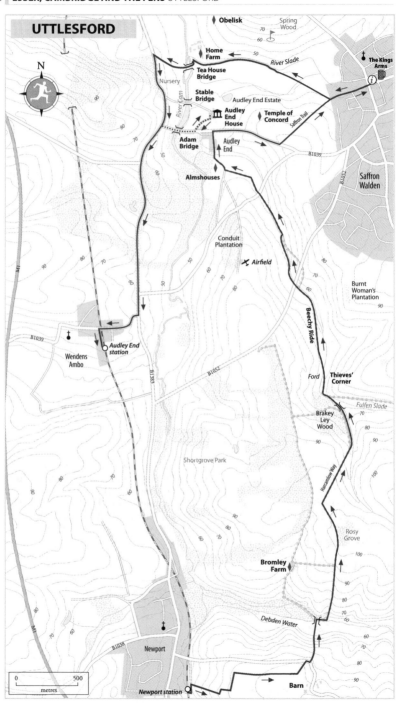

UTTLESFORD

10

N

Obelisk

Spring Wood

Home Farm

River Slade

The Kings Arms

Tea House Bridge

Nursery

Stable Bridge

Audley End Estate

Audley End House

Temple of Concord

Saffron Trail

Adam Bridge

Audley End

River Cam

B1039

Saffron Walden

Almshouses

Conduit Plantation

Airfield

Burnt Woman's Plantation

Beechy Ride

B1039

Audley End station

Wendens Ambo

B1383

B1052

Ford

Thieves' Corner

Fulfen Slade

Brakey Ley Wood

Hacamlow Way

Shortgrove Park

Rosy Grove

Bromley Farm

Debden Water

B1038

Newport

Newport station

Barn

0   500
metres

This unremarkable spot is known by the romantic appellation **Thieves' Corner**, one of many evocative place names hereabouts – at **Burnt Woman's Plantation**, the attractive wooded hillside to the north, women were once executed for charges of witchcraft.

Thieves' Corner to Audley End

2.5km From the T-junction at Thieves' Corner carry on until you reach the Newport Road (B1052).

Cross to the opposite side of the Newport Road, heading gently downhill and along the brook past a small private **airfield**. At a bend in the foot of the track, 500m from the road, Beechy Ride recrosses Fulfen Slade and merges with a lane, running right to left from the main road, above. From here, carry on for 750m to reach quiet **Wenden Road**. Cross this and continue down the track to Abbey Farm opposite (the private road signs apply only to cars).

The track leads past Abbey Farm and some red-brick Jacobean almshouses, now used as a conference centre, before bearing right and heading up between the whitewashed Georgian cottages of **Audley End** village. This one-street settlement was a planned community, part of the Audley End Estate, and has changed little since it was built in the eighteenth century. After 200m the street reaches a T-junction with **Audley End Road**. Here, the chimney tops of **Audley End House** peep above the red-brick wall that flanks the road, marking the boundary of the estate. The main entrance, **Lion Gate**, is 100m to your left down Audley End Road. From here, the walk heads up to Saffron Walden, which lies 1km to your right, before making a circuit of the estate and returning to the main entrance of the house and grounds.

Saffron Walden

1.5km Cross Audley End Road and turn right, following the pavement that runs alongside the estate's red-brick boundary wall to the brow of the hill. Some 600m from the junction with Audley End village, and just before the junction with Wenden Road, turn left through a gate into **Audley End Estate** (this is a public right of way and open at all times, irrespective of whether the house and grounds are open or shut).

Follow the track downhill through an avenue of trees towards the crenellated gatehouse at the bottom of the slope. You can't see anything of the stately house at this point, though if you look over to your left you can see two components of Capability Brown's grand design for the estate grounds (see page 246): the obelisk above Audley Park and, further west, the circular temple nestling on a wooded hillside. At the bottom of the track, 600m beyond Audley End Road, head out of the gate and into **Saffron Walden** via Abbey Lane, passing red-brick Victorian almshouses to your left before coming to a crossroads after 400m. From here, head straight on up George Street and then left onto Market Street, which takes you to the market place at the centre of this historic medieval town.

Set at the heart of rich farmland, there has been a wealthy market town here since Saxon times, when the area became a major supplier of wheat and barley, as well as the country's only producer of the **saffron crocus**, the tiny autumn flower used to dye wool that gave the town its name. There was a thriving weaving industry here, the sheep from the nearby Walden Abbey providing the wool, as well as a maltings industry (thanks to all that home-grown barley), until well into the nineteenth century. The main income, however, came from the locally produced saffron dye and traders came from all over the country to purchase it. Maybe because Saffron Walden never had to rely on one industry, the Industrial Revolution seemed to pass it by, allowing the town to retain its medieval character, with elegant Georgian and Victorian additions.

The medieval **Market Place** is still the commercial heart of Saffron Walden. The **town hall** is the square's most distinctive building, though the original eighteenth-century building is lost behind an overblown mock-Tudor gabled porch that was added in the late nineteenth century. The narrow lanes that radiate out from here are lined with half-timbered houses, filled with antique shops and secondhand bookshops. Just to the north of the square, up Market Hill, is the welcoming *Kings Arms*.

EATING AND DRINKING

The Kings Arms 10 Market Hill, Saffron Walden CB10 1HQ, 01799 522 768, http://thekingsarmssaffron walden.co.uk. A historic town-centre pub, with real fires and real ale, as well as good-quality pub grub such as bangers and mash. Mon–Sat 11am–midnight, Sun noon–midnight.

Audley End Estate

3km From Saffron Walden, the walk heads back into the **Audley End Estate**; go back down George Street and Abbey Lane to return to the crenellated gatehouse at the edge of the estate. Take the path to the right of the one you came down earlier – not the one that leads through an avenue of trees, but the lesser track just to its right that runs straight through a field. At the far side of the field, cross over a small brook and head along the edge of a wood to arrive at the southern edge of Audley End's grounds, the boundary of which is marked by the tiny **River Slade** to your right, beyond which lies a golf course. To your left, the marshy edges of Audley End Park run across to a gentle rise, on top of which is the Corinthian **Temple of Concord**, built in 1791 to celebrate George III's recovery from madness – prematurely, as it turned out. The massive north facade of the house, topped by turrets and copper domes, stands majestically to its right.

Follow the course of the River Slade for 500m to reach a bridge over the river by **Home Farm**. By the bridge, take the path that leads through a small gap in the fence and follows the left bank of the river by the estate wall. In a few minutes, you come out on the main road into Home Farm; turn left and almost immediately you'll cross the River Cam (into which the Slade runs) at the curve in the road. Have a peek over the estate wall at the bend here: you're standing just behind Robert Adam's Palladian **Tea House Bridge**, with views along the landscaped water gardens to a picturesque weir.

When you reach London Road, 500m from the Cam, turn left and head downhill; there are glimpses to your left of the estate **nursery** and, at the original main entrance, the splendid **Jacobean stables**. Here, a ha-ha separates the estate from the roadside, and there are superb views of the crenellated main facade of the house. This western range remains pretty much as it would have been when the house was first built – an expanse of mullioned windows, gables, turrets and chimneys, faced with Ketton stone.

If you want to visit the house, turn left just to the south of it onto Audley End Road, crossing the elegant three-arched **Adam Bridge** over the Cam to reach the main visitors' entrance, just south of Audley End village. Inside, highlights include the massive, wood-panelled Great Hall and Adam's elegant Neoclassical drawing rooms.

Audley End

The estate is home to the country's largest Jacobean mansion, **Audley End** (Easter–Sept Wed–Fri & Sun 11am–5pm, Sat 11am–3.30pm; Oct Sat & Sun 11am–4pm; £18.50; EH), built on the site of the twelfth-century Walden Abbey. Following the Dissolution, the estate passed into the hands of Lord Chancellor Audley, later Baron Audley of Walden. It was his grandson, Thomas Howard, later the Earl of Suffolk, who commissioned the rebuilding of the mansion in 1603, which he named in honour of his grandfather.

The present-day house is actually only a fraction of its original size – modernizing architect **Vanbrugh** was also responsible for demolishing the eastern range and large parts of the south and north ranges in the late eighteenth century to save the then owners money on the upkeep of the vast building. At the same time that Vanbrugh was revamping the house, the grounds were extensively landscaped by **Capability Brown,** with several strategically placed **Robert Adam** structures used to create vistas in Brown's trademark style. Adam's designs here include the Circular Temple, on the hillside to the west of the house, the three-arched Adam Bridge over the Cam and the Palladian Tea House Bridge.

10

To the station
2km From the house, continue down London Road for 2km, turning right at the road sign for **Wendens Ambo** village and **Audley End train station**. Take the first turning left in Wendens Ambo to get to the station itself.

Along the Cam

Cambridge to Grantchester

Distance and difficulty 12.5km; easy

Minimum duration 3hr 10min

Trains London King's Cross or Liverpool Street to Cambridge (every 30min from each station; 45min–1hr); return from Cambridge to London King's Cross or Liverpool Street (every 30min to both stations; 45min–1hr); Great Northern

Maps OS Landranger 154: *Cambridge & Newmarket*; OS Explorer 209: *Cambridge*

10

This walk heads south from **Cambridge** along the bank of the **River Cam** to the picture-postcard village of **Grantchester**, little more than a high street with a church and green and thatched cottages. Grantchester has long been a popular day-trip from the city, and lots of students still pack a picnic, rent a punt and spend a lazy summer's day on the river here. *The Orchard Tea Garden*, right on the river and with its own moorings, is an idyllic spot for **lunch** or afternoon tea. There are also several good **pubs** in the village, all offering bar meals. The return leg of the walk heads north into Cambridge via **The Backs**, the lawns behind the city's colleges from where there are superlative views of the colleges. Past the Backs, the route returns via leafy backstreets to the city's train station.

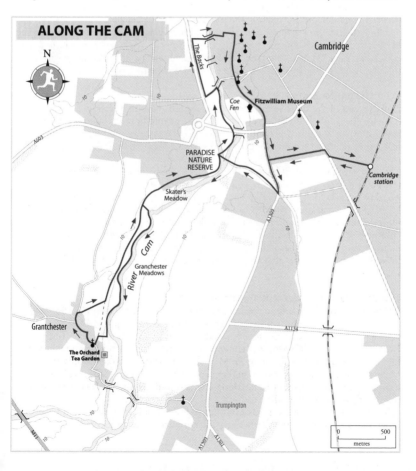

Getting started

1km From **Cambridge station**, head straight up Station Road, turn right at the T-junction onto Hills Road, cross over to the far side at the pedestrian crossing and take the first turning left onto leafy Bateman Street. At the far end of Bateman Street, cross Trumpington Road at the pedestrian crossing and then head left down it for 100m to reach the edge of a meadow. Turn right here at the sign to Newnham and follow a tarred path off to the right.

10

Coe Fen and Paradise Nature Reserve

1.5km Follow the path round the back of Belvoir Terrace. After a few hundred metres you'll reach a pair of metal footbridges marking the southern reaches of **Coe Fen**, a marshy area on the banks of the River Cam. Too soft to be of use for building, the land was historically used as free grazing land, and cows, sheep and horses are still left here to keep the grass trim and to encourage wild flowers to grow.

Cross both footbridges and bear immediately left down the far side of the river bank (by a small car park) and through a kissing gate into the **Paradise Nature Reserve**. Like Coe Fen, this area is managed according to traditional methods; native wild flowers include the rare butterbur, a broad-leafed plant with pale-pink conical spikes that flowers in early spring; the leaves were once used for wrapping butter (hence the name) and for treating the plague.

Follow the riverside path for several hundred metres as it skirts the southern reaches of the city, with meadowland stretching away on the far bank, to emerge onto a quiet cul-de-sac. Bear left into **Grantchester Meadows**, a quiet, well-to-do suburban street that heads off left to the meadows after which it's named.

Grantchester Meadows

2km The end of the street marks the edge of the city, beyond which grass meadows open up. To your left is **Skater's Meadow**, a mass of wild flowers in the spring, while ahead stretches the tarred path you take to Grantchester. After 250m, pass through a metal gate and head left down a grassy track, over a small boardwalk and down to the river bank.

You now follow the west bank of the river as it winds through **Grantchester Meadows**. Like Skater's Meadow, this is still managed grazing land and visitors are asked to keep to the grassy path along the river bank or the tarred path on the rise. You'll cross several small wooden bridges before reaching the edge of Grantchester itself. Here the path widens to a small meadow, with a kissing gate ahead and the chimneys of a house visible to the right; instead of going through the gate, turn to the right and head up the slope until you regain the tarred path, then go left and head through the narrow alley to come out at the southern end of Grantchester's High Street.

The Orchard Tea Garden and Grantchester village

0.5km Just to your left here, on the edge of the village, is *The Orchard Tea Garden*, the essential riverside stop for college undergraduates since they opened in 1897. Like Grantchester itself, the tearooms were made famous a generation later by Rupert Brooke's poem, *The Old Vicarage, Grantchester*, which the Cambridge graduate wrote in a fit of nostalgia while in Berlin in May 1912. Brooke had taken rooms at *The Orchard House*, and his friends – among them E.M. Forster and Virginia Woolf – used to punt upriver to visit him, taking tea there and helping establish a tradition that is still going strong today.

To reach the tearooms, turn left from the end of the public footpath and head downhill to the bend 100m further on. The entrance is clearly marked here.

EATING AND DRINKING

The Orchard Tea Garden 47 Mill Way, Grantchester CB3 9ND, 01223 840 230, http://theorchardteagarden. co.uk. Delightful tearooms serving morning coffee, lunches and afternoon teas, which you can take either alfresco in the orchard itself, scattered with deckchairs, or inside in the original Victorian wooden pavilion. Daily March–May & Sept–Nov 9.30am–5.30pm; June–Aug 9.30am–7pm; Dec–Feb 9.30am–4.30pm.

To get into **Grantchester** village, turn right and head up past the Church of St Andrew and St Mary, parts of which date back to 1100. Rupert Brooke is remembered on the war memorial in the graveyard. Pass the modern vicarage (the Old Vicarage is tucked away down a private lane further up the road) to reach the small village green, edged by a couple of pubs.

Back to Cambridge
3.5km Around 200m beyond the green is *The Rupert Brooke* pub – filled with Brooke memorabilia and its clock set permanently at ten to three. A few metres beyond the pub, a public footpath sign marks the start of the **return route** to Cambridge. Follow the path diagonally downhill until it joins a tarred path heading north towards Cambridge, with the city's skyline visible through the trees ahead. Continue left along this path as it follows the high ground above **Grantchester Meadows**, offering quite different views to those from the grassy path along the Cam that you followed previously, even though it's only a little higher up. The horizon opens out and the river itself can barely be seen between the trees and hedgerows below.

After 1.5km you arrive back at **Skater's Meadow**. Retrace your steps along Grantchester Meadows Road and through Paradise Nature Reserve, past the car park and over the first metal bridge. Here, take the second path on the left (the one that heads diagonally over to the banks of the Cam), then turn left and follow the bank, concreted at this point, along the eastern edge of **Coe Fen** and up to a busy road, the Fen Causeway. Take the underpass under the road, a few metres to the left, and turn left on the tarred path on the opposite side, where you'll soon see the back of the Fitzwilliam Museum and, beyond it, Peterhouse College, through the trees to your right; Coe Fen spreads out to the left.

After a few hundred metres, the city streets begin to close in on the right. Cross the footbridge opposite *The Mill* pub onto **Mill Lane** then turn left along the alley – Laundress Lane – behind *The Anchor* pub. At the end of the alley, turn left onto Silver Street, cross back to the west bank of the river via **Silver Street Bridge** and go over the road at the pedestrian crossing just beyond. The wooden bridge just north of Silver Street Bridge is the so-called **Mathematical Bridge**, a copy of the eighteenth-century original and so called because, it is claimed, it would remain standing even if all its nuts and bolts were removed.

From The Backs to the station
4km Just beyond the pedestrian crossing, the grassy stretch of land that marks the start of the path to **The Backs** begins. The Backs comprise a stretch of grazed lands, carpeted with daffodils and crocuses in spring, which run down to the Cam behind the oldest and most spectacular of the city's colleges, providing unforgettable views of the diverse college buildings. Most of the colleges are open to visitors at limited times (£3.50–8).

Turn right and follow the gravel path, and the sublime sight of **King's College Chapel** comes into view. Founded by Henry VI in the fifteenth century, the chapel is one of the country's finest examples of the Perpendicular style, the ornate late Gothic buttressing and intricate tracery of its exterior offering a taste of the delicate fan vaulting and exquisite stained glass inside. Next up is **Clare College**, founded in 1325 and thus the city's second oldest college. Beyond Clare College lies **Trinity**

10

College, the city's largest, which was founded by Henry VIII in 1546. Trinity has more famous alumni than any other college – from poets and writers such as Byron and Dryden, to the spies Anthony Blunt and Guy Burgess, and scientists and philosophers such as Isaac Newton and Bertrand Russell.

Beyond the gates to Clare College, turn right along pedestrianized Garret Hostel Lane, over the Cam and onto Trinity Lane. Here, bear left then right and, at Trinity Street, right again to head down **King's Parade**, the narrow medieval street that runs past the front of these colleges. Originally the city's high street, King's Parade was half cleared to make way for (and renamed in honour of) its most famous college, King's. The screen that flanks the road is neo-Gothic, masking much of the older buildings from view.

Continue past King's and St Catherine's colleges and onto **Trumpington Street**, a continuation of King's Parade, which runs past Art Deco bakery/café *Fitzbillies* (http://fitzbillies.com), the front of Peterhouse and the grandiose **Fitzwilliam Museum** (Tues–Sat 10am–5pm, Sun 2–5pm; free; http://fitzmuseum.cam.ac.uk), a superbly overblown Neoclassical edifice. The museum was opened in the late nineteenth century to house the private collection of Viscount Fitzwilliam, but has also ended up exhibiting a wonderfully eclectic range of other donations – everything from Egyptian sarcophagi to pieces by David Hockney and Henry Moore.

Continue along the same road for 1.5km to reach the pedestrian crossing that leads across to **Bateman Street**. Retrace your steps along Bateman Street, across Hill Road via the pedestrian crossing and left onto Station Road for the **train station**.

The Fens

Waterbeach to Ely

Distance and difficulty 21km; strenuous

Minimum duration 5hr 15min

Trains London King's Cross to Waterbeach (hourly; 55min); return from Ely to London King's Cross (hourly; 1hr); Great Northern

Maps OS Landranger 154 and 143: *Cambridge & Newmarket and Ely & Wisbech*; OS Explorer 226 and 228: *Cambridge* and *March & Ely*

Heading north from **Waterbeach** along the **Fen Rivers Way**, this walk is easy to follow and strenuous only in so much as it is long. There's a unique appeal to the route, with huge skies and vast flat landscapes stretching out to the horizon. On a clear day you can see for many kilometres, with the odd tractor tracing a line on the vast acreages of farmland, bereft of hedgerows and planted with rapeseed and corn. The walk ends at **Ely**, whose cathedral dominates the flat surrounding farmland from a modest hilltop perch. There's a pub on the route but it's not atmospheric, so it's best to pack a **picnic** and end up with tea and scones in Ely's award-winning **tearoom**.

Getting started

0.5km From platform 1 of **Waterbeach station**, take the path from the station car park that runs parallel to the right-hand side of the road for 500m, before reaching the river. Turn left up onto the road and cross the bridge, turning left and following signs for the **Fen Rivers Way** to Ely. Almost immediately, the wide skies and flat fenlands open up before you. Bottisham Fen lies to the east, Swaffham Fen and North Fen stretch ahead.

To Upware

8km Follow the track along the river bank, passing the clipped lawns of the **Cambridge Sailing Club**, with its pleasure boats and wooden summerhouses. Continue past a lock (Bottisham Sluice) and the bridge over **Bottisham Lode**, one of many man-made tributaries of the Cam that

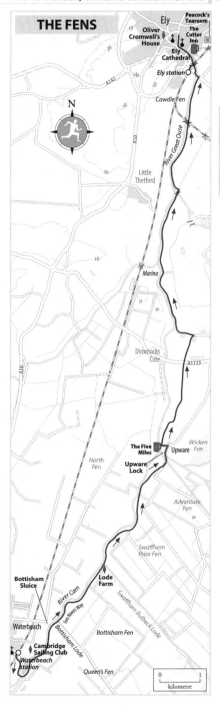

10

lead across to villages on firmer ground further east. Beyond the bridge, go along the grassy track that follows the meandering river for 1.5km before heading up to a track by some private moorings.

Turn left, go through the gate by the entrance to the moorings and continue along the Fen Rivers Way past Lode Farm. Unusually for the Fens – whose rich, peaty soil is used almost exclusively for crop-growing – this farm has cattle, which graze on the embankments here. You may have to negotiate your way past cows on the river bank, as well as towards the end of the route; for advice, see page 9. Carry straight on past the farmhouse and yard, and over the bridge at the sign to **Swaffham Bulbeck**. Don't turn right along the straight lode, but instead veer left to continue along the banks of the Cam. The next 3km or so are dotted with farm buildings, lost in acres of tilled land, and 1km beyond the moorings of Tip Tree Marina is the tiny hamlet of **River Bank**.

The path eventually begins to veer away from the river bank, skirting the edge of **wetlands** – flooded meadows studded with willow trees. Just south of Upware village, you come out on a lane where there are information boards that tell you what to look out for here: the area is home to a rich variety of wetland birds, including redshank and wigeon. Turn left along the lane and across the bridge by **Upware Lock** over Reach Lode.

To continue along the Fen Rivers Way, head down the lane through **Upware** village (ignoring public footpath signs to your left and right) to a junction where you turn left down Old School Lane; a few metres further on head over the wooden footbridge to your right. You'll see a modern pub to the left of the footbridge – *The Five Miles From Anywhere No Hurry Inn* – handy for a drink, but nothing special.

Upware to Ely

11km Follow the track north past a marina and along the left-hand side of a couple of fields. You come to a T-junction with a track – turn right for 200m and then left up the long unsigned drove road. This leads in a little under 1km to the busy A1123 (Dimmock's Cote Road). Carry straight on along the track on the opposite side, eventually following the left-hand bend of the road. Approaching some farm buildings with a "private road" sign, turn left on the grassy track to the left of a dense hedge.

This path eventually emerges beneath the steep embankment of the River Cam, by an impressive stand of geometrically planted trees. Look out for the sign on one of the trees to a willow hide, designed for birdwatchers to spot greenshanks, green sandpipers and other visitors. Just beyond this point the path leads up onto the bank, and along a track above the river. From here, the impressive sight of Ely Cathedral dominates the skyline, making it easy to see how the cathedral – set (like the town around it) on a small island of clay a few metres above the marshy Fens – has been dubbed "the Ship of the Fens".

Continue along the grassy top of the river bank and past a marina on the far side some 500m further on, just beyond which the Cam and Great Ouse rivers merge. Follow the river, now called the **River Great Ouse**. It's a further 2km north along the riverside track from Lode End Bridge to the A142 (Soham Road) into Ely. To head home from here, turn left and follow Soham Road down and under the railway bridge and take the first left for the **station**.

Ely

1.5km Set on a low hill in the midst of pancake-flat fenland, the medieval town of **Ely** still feels like an island in a sea of marsh – its name is a contraction of "Island of the Eels", referring to the eels that once lived in the waters around it. The town

10

TAMING THE FENS

Originally a reed-filled, boggy wilderness, **the Fens** have been ever-more aggressively dyked and drained over the centuries in an attempt to use their land and waters. The Romans were the first to try to tame the Fens, digging out Car Dyke just west of Waterbeach, both to drain the land for farming and to serve as a canal to carry grain from here to their garrison in Lincoln, 112km away. In medieval times, the wealthy monasteries diverted the course of the Ouse to Ely to make use of the river and waterways for transport. Around the same time, a series of "lodes" was dug – these served both as drainage ditches and as canals linking the Cam, the main waterway in the southern Fens, to villages east of the river.

The most significant change to the landscape, however, came when Dutch engineer **Cornelius Vermuyden** was hired by a group of wealthy speculators in the seventeenth century to drain the marshy landscape so that its rich soil could be used for farming.

Vermuyden's plan was to bypass the Great Ouse, creating a new channel to carry the area's floodwaters straight out to the Wash. The project was introduced in two phases: the first cutting, confusingly called the Old Bedford River, was made in 1637; a few years later, the New Bedford River (or Hundred Foot Drain) was cut, just under 1km to the right of the first cutting. Between the two, Vermuyden created a plain, which absorbed the river's floodwaters in winter and could then be used as grazing land when the waters drained away in spring. Although it was successful in taming the fenlands and allowing the area to be farmed, Vermuyden's engineering had one unforeseen side effect: as the drains dried the land, the spongy peat began to shrink back until the entire area fell below sea level. To this day, hundreds of pumps are needed to keep the Fens drained.

---

stands above the left bank of the River Great Ouse, with an attractive willow-fringed marina on the river bank itself.

Follow the Fen Rivers Way from the opposite side of the A142, down the path towards **Ely Marina**, a few hundred metres further on. Pleasure boats trawl the river here, with the odd narrow boat adding a splash of colour. Beyond the marina, Ely waterfront opens up before you. Ahead is *The Cutter Inn*, superbly located and serving good food. Carry on by the river a little further to reach *Peacocks Tearoom* by the pedestrian bridge, with tables in the garden of a handsome old house.

EATING AND DRINKING

The Cutter Inn 42 Annesdale, Ely CB7 4BN, 01353 662 713, http://thecutterinn.co.uk. The waterfront *Cutter Inn* dishes up delicious fishcakes, pies, burgers and so on (from £12). Mon–Sat 11am–11pm, Sun noon–10.30pm.
Peacocks Tearoom 65 Waterside, Ely CB7 4AU, 01353 661 100, http://peacockstearoom.co.uk. Serves light lunches and sandwiches as well as home-made cakes and set afternoon teas (from £8); they have a huge tea selection, including some rarities, and are highly rated by the Tea Guild. Wed–Sun 10.30am–5pm, plus Tues June–Sept.

Before the pub, at the point where the river bends round to the right, turn off and head up **Victoria Street**, a quiet side street lined with tiny cottages. At the top of the street, turn right onto Broad Street. A hundred metres or so along, take a left by a black tourist board signpost up through **Cherry Hill Park** towards the cathedral.

Ely Cathedral

Almost immediately after you enter the park, the view opens up to your right across meadows to **Ely Cathedral** (April–Oct daily 7am–6.30pm, Nov–March Mon–Sat 7am–6.30pm, Sun 7.30am–5.30pm; £8, with Octagonal Tower £16.50; http://elycathedral.org). To your left, the apparent landscaping is actually the remains of a Norman motte and bailey castle. Continue up the path and exit the cathedral close through the medieval Walpole Gate. Turn right and head up **The Gallery**, the medieval heart of the city, which leads after 250m to the main (west) door of the cathedral. Best viewed from the green opposite, the western front owes its lopsided appearance to the lack of one of its transepts, which collapsed in the eighteenth century.

This wasn't the only piece of the cathedral to have fallen down. The original Norman crossing tower collapsed in the fourteenth century, taking part of the chancel out with it, which is how the cathedral came to have its unusual **Octagon**. Outside, the delicate tracery of the eight-sided stone structure – topped at each corner by crocketed pinnacles – is surmounted by a smaller, octagonal timber lantern. Inside, a kaleidoscopic effect is created, with the magnificent fan-vaulted ceiling arching up towards the lantern, decorated in gold, green and red floral patterns.

10

To get to the **station**, retrace your steps through Cherry Hill Park and along the edge of the marina to the A142. Turn right along the road and go below the underpass, turning left into the station.

Small print and index

A ROUGH GUIDE TO ROUGH GUIDES

Published in 1982, the first Rough Guide – to Greece – was a student scheme that became a publishing phenomenon. Mark Ellingham, a recent graduate in English from Bristol University, had been travelling in Greece the previous summer and couldn't find the right guidebook. With a small group of friends he wrote his own guide, combining a contemporary, journalistic style with a thoroughly practical approach to travellers' needs.

The immediate success of the book spawned a series that rapidly covered dozens of destinations. And, in addition to impecunious backpackers, Rough Guides soon acquired a much broader readership that relished the guides' wit and inquisitiveness as much as their enthusiastic, critical approach and value-for-money ethos. These days, Rough Guides include recommendations from budget to luxury and cover more than 120 destinations around the globe, from Amsterdam to Zanzibar, all regularly updated by our team of roaming writers.

Browse all our latest guides, read inspirational features and book your trip at **roughguides.com**.

Rough Guide credits

Editor: Zara Sekhavati
Cartography: Katie Bennett
Picture editor: Tom Smyth

Head of DTP and Pre-Press: Rebeka Davies
Head of Publishing: Sarah Clark

Publishing information

Fourth edition 2021

Distribution

UK, Ireland and Europe
Apa Publications (UK) Ltd; sales@roughguides.com
United States and Canada
Ingram Publisher Services; ips@ingramcontent.com
Australia and New Zealand
Booktopia; retailer@booktopia.com.au
Worldwide
Apa Publications (UK) Ltd; sales@roughguides.com

Special Sales, Content Licensing and CoPublishing
Rough Guides can be purchased in bulk quantities
at discounted prices. We can create special editions,
personalised jackets and corporate imprints tailored to
your needs. sales@roughguides.com.
roughguides.com

Printed in Poland

Help us update

We've gone to a lot of effort to ensure that this edition
of **The Rough Guide to Walks in and around London**
is accurate and up-to-date. However, things change –
places get "discovered", opening hours are notoriously
fickle, restaurants and rooms raise prices or lower
standards. If you feel we've got it wrong or left something
out, we'd like to know, and if you can remember the
address, the price, the hours, the phone number, so
much the better.

Please send your comments with the subject line
"Rough Guide Walks in and around London Update" to
mail@uk.roughguides.com. We'll credit all contributions
and send a copy of the next edition (or any other Rough
Guide if you prefer) for the very best emails.

Acknowledgements

A big thank you to Sarah Clark, Helen Fanthorpe, Luca Hargraves, Rachel Lawrence, Steve Smyth and Aimée White who
helped with the research of this book. And thank you to Buster the dog for helping, too.

ABOUT THE AUTHOR

Helena Smith grew up near the Trossach Mountains in Scotland and under Zomba Plateau in
Malawi, two beautiful places which inspired her love of the outdoors. She is a writer, photographer
and co-founder of Wilder, a social enterprise doing wildlife planting in urban spaces.

Photo credits

Alamy 35, 110/111, 125, 167
Dreamstime 182/183
Helena Smith/Rough Guides 215
Lydia Evans/Apa Publications 9, 158/159

Shutterstock 1, 2, 4, 5, 10, 11, 14/15, 27, 45, 59, 63, 68/69,
77, 85, 94/95, 107, 115, 136/137, 145, 179, 195, 196/197,
209, 218/219, 225, 236/237, 245, 253

Cover: Deer in Richmond Park **Shutterstock**

Index

Map symbols

The symbols below are used on maps throughout the book

	Motorway		Windmill		Castle
	Major road		Mill		Fort
	Minor road		Lighthouse		Stately house
	Very minor road		Observatory		Museum
	Track		Radio mast		Ruins
	Footpath	P	Car park		Orchard
	Route	(i)	Tourist office		Battle site
	Detour route	O	Train station		Tumulus
	Railway		Underground station		Golf course
	Wall		Overground station		Pub
	Earthworks		DLR station		Accommodation
	Cliffs/rocks		Peak		Eating place
	Gate		Locks		Park/forest
	Place of interest		Church/cathedral		Cemetery
	Statue		Mosque		Beach